Gender Archaeology

For

Kim Michael, Megan and Chris

Gender Archaeology

Marie Louise Stig Sørensen

Polity Press

Copyright © Marie Louise Stig Sørensen 2000

The right of Marie Louise Stig Sørensen to be identified as author of this work has been asserted in accordance with the Copyright, Designs and Patents Act 1988.

First published in 2000 by Polity Press
in association with Blackwell Publishers Ltd

Reprinted 2004, 2005

Polity Press
65 Bridge Street
Cambridge CB2 1UR, UK

Polity Press
350 Main Street
Maldon, MA 02148, USA

Library of Congress Cataloging-in-Publication Data

Sørensen, Marie Louise Stig.
    Gender archaeology / Marie Louise Stig Sørensen.
        p.   cm.
    Includes bibliographical references and index.
    ISBN 0-7456-2014-0 — ISBN 0-7456-2015-9 (pbk.)
    1. Social archaeology.   2. Sex role—History.   3. Material culture.   4. Feminist archaeology.   5. Women, Prehistoric.

    CC72.4.S67 2000
    930.1'082—dc21
                                                                00-028542

A catalogue record for this book is available from the British Library and has been applied for from the Library of Congress.

Typeset in 10.5 on 12 pt Sabon
by Ace Filmsetting Ltd, Frome, Somerset

Printed and bound in Great Britain by
Marston Book Services Limited, Oxford

For further information on Polity, visit our website: www.polity.co.uk

This book is printed on acid-free paper.

Contents

List of Illustrations   viii
Acknowledgements   x

Part I

1   Gender into the Past   3

Gender and archaeology: an introduction   3
Arguing for gender archaeology   7
The need for theorizing   10
Outline of an argument   12

2   Gender and Archaeology: a History   16

The development of feminist critique and gender
  archaeology   16
The relatively late inclusion of gender in archaeology?   20
The presentation of women in archaeology and
  prehistory   24
Epistemology, gender and archaeology   34
The nature of gender archaeology: contextualization   37

3   Theorizing Gender: Sex and Gender   41

The sex–gender discussion   42
What is sex? – current discussions within archaeology   45
What is gender? – current discussions and archaeological
  practice   52
On the relationship between sex and gender   54

4   Theorizing Gender: Negotiation and Practice   60

    Gender negotiation   60
    Agency and gender in archaeology   63
    The agent, the individual and archaeology   65
    Woman or women: the question of cross-cultural
        generalizations   67
    Gender (and) archaeology   70

5   The Materiality of Gender: the Gendered Object   74

    Gender and the object   74
    The nature of objects   76
    The materiality of gender: communication and practice 82
    Constructing gender through things, making objects
        gendered   89

Part II

6   Food: the Performance of Feeding and Eating   99

    Nutritious and symbolic: the culture of food   99
    Food and embodiment   102
    Discourse through food   106
    Drinking as social performance   117
    Archaeology, food and gender   122

7   Dressing Gender: Identity through Appearance   124

    The point of clothes   124
    Dress and archaeology: a brief outline   127
    Methodology and analysis   131
    Dress and identity in prehistory   136
    A fabric for discourse   142

8   The Engendering of Space   144

    Gendered space   144
    Archaeology and space   146
    Phenomenology and the landscape's space   152
    House and home   156
    Archaeology, gender and space   166

9   Contact: the Short-lived Triangle   168

    Adultery – changing partner   168

Contact and innovation   169
The archaeology of contact   171
Technology and the danger of the new   177
Gender and contact, gender as contact   180

10 The Beginning: on Becoming Gendered   182

A gendered world, or looking back to the beginning   182
Gender research and the origin of humans   187
Gendered cultural expression and practice during the
    Upper Palaeolithic   190
Gender and the Palaeolithic: self-reflection and artifice 200

11 Reflections   203

References   209
Index   226

Illustrations

Figure 5.1 Gendered lucky dip at the Midsummer Fair, Cambridge, UK, June 1999.   80

Figure 5.2 Example of nineteenth-century interior design that aims to embody ideals of femininity (from the showrooms of the Glasgow furnishing firm Wylie & Lochhead c.1900). (Reproduced from Kinchin 1996, fig. 2)   84

Figure 5.3 Girl's dress on a stall at the Midsummer Fair, Cambridge, UK.   90

Figure 6.1 Ethno-historical account of the annual cycle of activities within a seventeenth-century farming community in Jämtland, Sweden. (Based on Wichman 1968 and information supplied by L. Rathje, Umeå University)   110–11

Figure 6.2 Examples of Central European Hallstatt B plates with interior decoration. (Redrawn after Brun and Mordant 1988)   113

Figure 6.3a Middle Neolithic pedestal bowls and clay spoons from the Tustrup 'temple', Denmark. (Courtesy P. Kjærum and Forhistorisk Museum, Moesgård, Århus) b The location of Middle Neolithic pedestal bowls, clay spoons and other vessels within the Tustrup 'temple', Denmark. (Redrawn after Kjærum 1955)   114

Figure 6.4 More than fifty cups and vessels from two pit deposits at Raddusch, Germany. (After Hänsel, A. and B. 1997: 176–7)   120

Figure 7.1 Florence Nightingale nurses in uniform. (Reproduced courtesy of the Florence Nightingale Museum Trust, London)   125

Figure 7.2 Formal photograph of the farm workers from a middle-sized farm in northern Denmark, late nineteenth

century. (Reproduced courtesy of Vendsyssel Historiske
Museum, Denmark)   126
Figure 7.3   The Palaeolithic figurine from Willendorf,
Austria. (Reproduced courtesy of Naturhistorisches
Museum Wien)   137
Figure 8.1   Structuralist-inspired gender interpretation of
a Romano-British aisled hall at Warnborough, Hants., UK.
(Redrawn after Hingley 1990; reproduced with permission
of the author and Edinburgh University Press)   148
Figure 8.2   Examples of Late Bronze Age house urns from
northern Germany. (Redrawn after Oelmann 1959)   157
Figure 8.3   The rich burial chamber of Hochdorf, southern
Germany. (After Biel 1985)   158
Figure 8.4a Reconstruction of Iron Age house with
oven/hearth structure at Bohuslän, Sweden. b Plan of the
Early Iron Age settlement at Biskupin, Poland. (Redrawn
after Rajewski 1959 and Scarre 1998)   c One of the
houses from the settlement of Biskupin, Poland.
(Redrawn after Rajewski 1959)   162–3
Figure 8.5   Reconstruction of a Late Iron Age long house
from Rogaland, Norway. (Reproduced courtesy of
Stavanger Museum, Norway)   164
Figure 9.1   Example of cremated bones 'dressed' in cloth
and buried as an inhumation grave in a stone cist.
(Brøndsted 1966 based on Herbst)   180
Figure 10.1   Reconstruction of one of the costumes from
the Sungir graves. (Redrawn after Ladier and Welté 1995)   191
Figure 10.2   The human head from Grotte du Pape,
France. (Reproduced courtesy of Musée des antiquités
nationales, Saint-Germain-en-Laye, France)   194

Every effort has been made to trace the copyright holders of the illustrations, but if any have been inadvertently overlooked, the publishers
will be pleased to make the necessary arrangements at the first opportunity.

Acknowledgements

I cannot attempt to mention all the people who over the years have helped me to understand better the question of gender within archaeology. They are all generally but anonymously thanked. The following (in alphabetical order) must, however, be especially acknowledged for their generosity in sharing their thoughts and work: A. Alexandri, E. Arwill-Nordbladh, R. Boast, C. Damm, M. Díaz-Andreu, M. Edmonds, E. Engelstad, C. Evans, C. Hastorf, J. D. Hill, L. Janik, S. Lucy, B. Olsen, M. Rowlands, S. J. Shennan, B. Varenius and T. Whitelaw.

The book has benefited greatly from the references and comments provided by others. I should in particular like to thank C. Damm for discussion of the first outline of the volume in her snow-bound flat in Tromsø while we waited for the storm to break. I would like to acknowledge my colleagues at the Department of Archaeology, Cambridge, for their positive support. I am grateful to E. and T. Vestergård for allowing me access to their anthropological expertise. I should also like to thank John Thompson for believing in this book from before its beginning and for waiting so patiently for me to produce it. The following have read all or large parts of the manuscript and I am grateful for their critical and helpful comments: M. Arroyo-Kalin, E. Bjerregård, C. Damm, E. DeMarrais, J. D. Hill, L. Nordenborg Myhrr and B. Varenius. I am also indebted to P. Mellars, P. Miracle and M. White for reading and commenting upon chapter 10. Thanks also to the staff at Polity Press for being so very accommodating.

A teacher's relationship to her supervisees is complex. It is properly one of the most giving and free-flowing intellectual exchanges that one engages with. To be of use it has to be open and sharing; but it also means that the 'property' right over or even the allocation of 'ownership' to particular ideas becomes confused. I should therefore like particularly to acknowledge Joanna Brück, Joanna Sofaer-Derevenski

and Susan Thomas; I am sure their thoughts on archaeology have influenced mine, even though I cannot distil this influence. In particular,
the exchange of ideas with Joanna Sofaer-Derevenski has had a direct
bearing on my developing the ideas expressed here. I have tried to
reference her work where obvious, but I should like in addition to
acknowledge the more general influence and inspiration gained from
our exchanges.

Chris Evans has followed the book – chapter and verse – we have
discussed, argued and shared many of the issues I have tried to raise.
As always, his comments have been constructive, critical and challenging. I know that the topic was not close to his heart and I am
therefore especially grateful (and impressed) that he made himself my
intellectual companion even on this journey.

The sharing of my thoughts and the discussion of archaeology and
gender with so many impressive individuals has been an exciting experience. Their positive support and intellectual challenges have been
very rewarding intellectually and personally. Needless to say, they do
not necessarily agree with my arguments and for the final version none
but myself is responsible.

I have dedicated the volume to Kim Michael, Megan and Chris.
They are my daily life. Each in their way engenders my world, and
they have taught and shown me many wonderful things about gendered
lives. Following the first steps and stages in the processes of my children becoming gendered persons has been fascinating, challenging and
at a certain level beautiful. For me it provides a subtext of real life. I
cannot, nor do I want to, generalize my children's lives into a theoretical argument, but the tension between my academic struggle with understanding how gender is constructed and the awareness of it
happening just around me has been both exciting and enlightening.

Part I

1

Gender into the Past

I was sixteen when, for the first time, it was pointed out to me how gender becomes associated with other categories. It was my chemistry teacher who told me that the sign for copper was also the astronomical sign for the planet Venus, who was also the goddess of love. And this was also the sign for Woman. The sign for Man was also the sign for iron, for the planet Mars and for Mars the god of war. The links intrigued me, they were neat and obvious, of no apparent relevance to life, but I nonetheless never forgot them.

Gender and archaeology: an introduction

Gender archaeology has finally become a well-established part of the discipline, but still a sense of marginality lingers. This affects our understanding and attitudes to gender as an aspect of both our profession and interpretations of past societies. It is, therefore, timely to acknowledge that the problems encountered within this field are not primarily political; nor can its potentials be explored from a presentist standpoint alone. The problems that we face are rather about the maturing of this research area; it is about learning to think with gender when investigating the past and appreciating how it also affects us. So far our attempts at engendering prehistoric communities have been curiously constrained both in insight and implication, or alternatively little rooted in any of the evidence from these societies. The problem consistently encountered is how to translate theoretical and political convictions about the importance of gender into practical application when investigating strange and unfamiliar societies. In addition, the intellectual and political reasons for studying gender have become set rather than themselves critically involved in the research process. Gender archaeology is therefore now at an interesting juncture where revision and reflection upon its reasons and potentials are needed and could have major impact on its next stage.

The problems suggested by these constraints are further confirmed by the content of the few regular publications on gender archaeology, such as the Norwegian journal *K.A.N.*, and the many conference proceedings and edited volumes (e.g. Casey et al. 1998, Claassen 1992a, Du Cros and Smith 1993, Gero and Conkey 1991, Kent 1998, Moore and Scott 1997, Wadley 1997, Walde and Willows 1991, Wright 1996a). They clearly demonstrate the no more than partial success of our efforts to develop gender archaeology, as certain issues and topics are much better covered than others. This is of concern as it produces a limiting notion of what gender archaeology is and affects our perceived abilities to engage analytically with this dimension of prehistoric societies. The recurrent issues debated in the literature have typically focused on contemporary concerns such as work conditions and membership of the profession – the so-called equity issues – or they concentrate upon the role of women in early historic periods and other societies for which text-aided archaeology is possible. Although of great importance, such work has been either basically sociological (i.e. the study of contemporary social relations) or an archaeology strongly guided by textual information. Substantial understanding of gender relations as part of a past that represents other, unfamiliar cultures is rarely obtained. (See also Claassen (1992b: 5) for a similar comment upon the situation in America.)

It does not follow from this observation that gender archaeology cannot be undertaken. Its progress and the debates it has generated within archaeology have clearly demonstrated its potential. Therefore, rather than a brake upon further involvement with the project of engendering archaeology, the previous limitations are a challenge to our understanding of gender generally and the further development of gender archaeology specifically. At the same time the limitations in our practice so far demonstrate something about how immensely complex the task is. There are, of course, other aspects of past societies, such as age, kin or ethnicity, which are also socially complex and difficult to access through material objects or physical actions. We are, however, used to recognizing the complexity of such variables and we accept them as a routine part of our engagement with the past, not letting the problems of identifying, for example, ethnicity prevent us from including it in analysis. The discovery of gender as a necessary but difficult aspect of our understanding of past societies is, however, new, and with it has followed a degree of critique, scepticism and antagonism that has made the discipline differently aware of what is involved when interpreting this social structure in past societies.

These constraints can be contextualized within the history of gender archaeology itself, and in particular its embedded assumption that it should produce a radical and distinctly different feminist past. This view has been necessary for gender archaeology to find a voice, but it has also been burdensome and it should now be replaced by more complex agendas. The interest in gender arose within archaeology, as will be discussed in chapter 2, primarily in response to contemporary social changes during the 1960s. The call was for women to become visible: in the profession, in the museums and in the past. But such visibility was easier to comprehend and obtain by stressing women as being different, as separate. The aim, furthermore, was explicitly to demonstrate and demand the presence of women, as half of the world, underlined and distinct, but neither as partners to social complexity nor as individual beings. The collective presence of women was not to be circumvented or silenced again, and the compromises suggested by emphasis upon negotiation, analysis of details or attention towards variance and nuances were not desired. This basically political manifesto was effective, but due to its political overtones and associations it also caused established structures to view the claims with suspicion, and gender archaeology was marginalized. The birth of gender archaeology was thus politically and socially revolutionary, but theoretically and analytically it tended to be passive and merely reactionary in terms of existing interpretations. The basic premises used for thinking about men and women in the past were not changing during this phase; role-assignment was merely challenged. 'Merely' may, however, have been much at the time, and the importance of this phase for changing attitudes cannot be overestimated. The foundation was laid, but building upon it so as to reassess and demonstrate more fully its potentials and aims is now needed.

Gender archaeology has increasingly come to see its aim as being to explore variations in prehistoric gender relations as well as the analysis of their generation and maintenance. The second part of this volume explores what this means for archaeology, and how it may be accomplished. It does this by arguing that gender relations are not reproduced but continuously made. This making of gender relations happens in part through the negotiations of rights and obligations which involve and utilize material resources as a medium through which the gender contract can be both expressed and experienced. I have suggested elsewhere that the development of an explorative gender archaeology may result in gender studies becoming less distinct as a sub-discipline of archaeology as it becomes interwoven with all aspects of the discipline and integrated with its social theories (Sørensen 1992: 31). At the same time we also now, for the first time, see gender archaeology being differently and somewhat contrastingly interpreted, as varied interests, different theoretical approaches, political views and the potential split between academic and practical archaeology affect its declared reasons and objectives (see also Wylie 1997). As an illustration of such tension one may look at museums as an example of how institutional context affects the objectives of our practice. The current tendency to contextualize and deconstruct gender roles has made it extremely hard for museum designers to present gender and related issues in an educational and visually powerful way without being subjected to severe critique of simplification. The engendering of museum exhibitions has therefore become difficult. In particular, the designers have not been able to take discussions within archaeology as a guide for their activities, and it has proved necessary for museums to develop their own separate field of debate (e.g. Devonshire and Wood 1996, Porter 1996, Sandahl 1995). This, however, is a meaningful and challenging conflict. It should not be seen as negating the importance of gender archaeology in any of its many expressions. It is rather a sign of 'coming of age' and in that sense part of a positive and necessary growth. It should, however, also be recognized that embedded in this change of status, where gender is accepted as a central issue within any field and relevant to the full range of our practices, is an appropriation and legitimization by the establishment. This will necessarily change the challenge of gender archaeology; it blunts its edge. It is, however, only in this capacity that gender concerns can become a disciplinary challenge permeating more than obvious feminist issues.

The conflict arising from recognizing the complexity and the slipperiness of gender as a basic structure of society is at the same time a tremendous challenge. It shows us the limitations of our knowledge and understanding. This, to me, was graphically illustrated by a display case in Schloß Gottorp, the regional museum of north Germany. It was part of the display of the extraordinary Iron Age deposits of boats and weapons from Nydam, southern Denmark, now housed and exhibited at the museum (see also Sørensen 1999). In addition to one of the large wooden boats the exhibition shows, in several glass cases along the walls and standing in rows on the floor, a large amount of beautifully crafted and often exquisitely decorated items of war. Through their associative relations to men and warriors the objects provide an overwhelming impression of masculinity. A number of cases were used to show the appearance of men: their different uniforms, the attachments to their clothing, personal equipment, the position and combination of weapons and suggestions of regional and status differences in their dress. And then there was a big glass case showing the appearance of the contemporary women. It was left empty! There was just a small notice stating that the archaeological material did not provide sufficient data to show how the women would have been dressed. The impact was striking: it made one aware of the partial nature of the exhibition; and it expressed an explicit challenge to archaeology. This book aims to take up part of this challenge by engaging explicitly with the question of how we can think about gender in the past and engage with it as materiality.

Arguing for gender archaeology

Gender is now recognized as a necessary part of any theory of social relations, and the negotiation of gender relations is seen as one of the dynamics reproducing and maintaining social systems. Gender is therefore deeply ingrained in the particular form societies take and it provides an essential structure of meaning. Appreciating gender as a construction (Conkey and Spector 1984: 1) means understanding that it must be continuously confirmed and constructed by society and that individuals have to obtain and maintain it. 'Gender is not just women and men – it is a result of the ways we live together and construct a universe around us. Gender is an inconsistent but permanent part of history and life' (Sørensen 1988: 17). Gender, while a basic structure of society, is not stable. Any study of society and, in particular, studies of societal change must therefore incorporate gender. It is the realization of these qualities, rather than the emphasis upon 'making women visible', which constitutes the most essential departure of recent gender archaeology from earlier views. It radically rejects the naturalized gender roles established over the last centuries, opening a whole new understanding of culture and history.

The important difference introduced with gender archaeology lies in the way women – and the relationship between women and men – are conceptualized: their recognition as subjects of study and the range of issues associated with this. The appreciation of the active dynamic nature of gender and its role in the historical process has meant that gender construction and relations have become issues of archaeological concern. Gender, furthermore, is becoming recognized as an intimate part of the process of social *reproduction*, rather than just being an element in the *formation* of society. Our understanding of gender is, however, still limited, and we have only just begun to appreciate the spatial and temporal variations and some of the mechanisms behind such variability. Meanwhile, as the organization of gender increasingly has been shown to relate and be integral to most other aspects of past cultural systems, archaeologists should examine

> factors that seem to influence the nature of relations between men and women, the circumstances in which women and men exert power and influence, and the ways that gender arrangements affect or structure group responses to various conditions in their social or natural environments. (Conkey and Spector 1984: 19)

Gender, furthermore, is a situated difference, and its investigation is essential for both the understanding of particular contexts and historical trajectories. Moreover, engendered individuals are social agents and their actions form society. Their activities are, however, influenced both by self-identity and by their socially constructed identities (i.e. the difference between 'I am a woman, and I should do this but not that' and 'women are like this and behave in certain ways'). Such distinctions between gender identity and gender ideology are important for understanding the continuous interaction between self and society which lies behind normative behaviour.

Thus, gender relations of past societies constitute particular problems or areas of concern which not only merit but necessitate specific theories and methodologies. We must construct, therefore, an archaeological framework for investigating gender and the effect of gender. For this it is not sufficient to question previous assumptions like 'man the hunter', or to replace one absolute and static interpretation with another (so-called his- and her-stories). Such assumptions and universal generalizations can be debated, but beyond such exchanges the factors structuring relationships between differently gendered people and groups must be analysed and the mediation and transformation of those relationships investigated. One of the unique tasks of archaeology is then to encourage questioning and clarification of whether gender is always relevant, at what levels and in which form. The feminist debate takes gender as existing; but the time span of archaeology includes societies in which the conceptualization of difference may for the first time have been constructed as gender. It also routinely investigates communities whose construction of gender varied considerably and who apparently assigned it different kinds of importance and certainly gave it particular forms. Out of this, however, does not come a gender archaeology that aims at 'origins stories'; rather archaeology can be seen as a discipline that aims to trace and analyse some of the diverse social and cultural reaction to difference and how this is resolved in a variety of gender arrangements. Archaeology should also use its vast data to investigate in what situations gender relations become particularly expressive, i.e. situations where gender relations are made explicit through material culture. Can such situations be detected and characterized? At present we have neither the theoretical nor methodological means to study such obvious questions systematically. A few distinct activities are, however, easily isolated as commonly involved in communicating gender categories. These include burial activities, individual appearance through costumes, iconography and some types of art. It is, however, equally obvious that gender is also played out in other spheres of action and in different media, and some of these will be explored in the second part of this volume.

Finally, one of the most important potential contributions from archaeology to gender studies generally is its insights into the manner in which material culture becomes partner in the structuring of social relations. In order to understand gender organization and ideology as part of society and its historical transformation it is essential to look at social norms, institutions and relations, and to trace how they are reproduced over time. Material culture plays a special role in such social reproduction, since objects link generations and are fundamental for mediating tradition. Members of society inhabit historic structures coded with meaning, and links are made both from objects to symbols and from symbols to values. In this chain material culture comes to carry socially negotiated meaning; it transforms modes of expression and serves as a bridge between generations and events. Through these linkages material culture participates in assigning gender to individuals and in presenting and preserving gender ideologies, which means that long-term structures develop rather than each generation inventing the world anew.

These characteristics – unique data and the analysis of material culture as partner in social life – are the special aspects of archaeology from which its distinct contribution to gender studies and its analysis of gender in prehistory must develop. Meanwhile, the theoretical framework of gender archaeology does not as yet clearly reflect these strengths. In the urge to create a gender archaeology and strongly influenced by feminism (and probably also by a political desire for solidarity amongst those involved in this 'struggle'), this field has until recently been allowed to develop without explicit and constructive self-reflection. Its critical responses have therefore mainly taken the form of self-defence or arguing for its relevance rather than focusing upon clarification and discussion of subject matter. Certain concepts have therefore become embedded in our expectation of gender archaeology without critical discussion. In particular, concepts have not been adapted to the field in which they are employed, leaving archaeologists with the apparent dilemma of not being able to observe the issues they talk about. Methodology has accordingly gained a prominent position which is neither deserved nor – given its theoretical isolation – particularly productive (e.g. Gibbs 1987). I have previously pointed out that gender archaeology therefore makes basic statements, such as 'gender is a social construct', that have not been properly 'translated' into some correspondence to the discipline's conceptual and analytical language; but nonetheless they still dictate what gender archaeology looks for and how it is being looked at (Sørensen 1992: 32). In response to this lack of theoretical development one can now begin to discern the emergence of approaches that are explicitly concerned with making gender archaeology *archaeological* in its thinking and practice (e.g. Arwill-Nordbladh 1998, Lesick 1997, Sofaer-Derevenski 1997, 1998). Archaeology can and must frame its own gender problems, not detached and isolated from questions asked by other subjects, but nonetheless dictated by its own concerns and potentials. A further limitation to overcome is the way in which gender archaeology has tended to be partial – both in terms of its interpretative interests and its approach to data. Again, there are various political and theoretical reasons for this; but the overall results have often been detrimental, as gender archaeology appears unable to engage with the totality of the archaeological record and inadvertently appears to isolate only selected bits as relevant – and relevant only – to women's experiences and roles.

The need for theorizing

In the literature, certain general statements which encapsulate the rationale for a gender archaeology can be found. Many of these statements originally arose from empirical studies by various disciplines within the social sciences but by now they often appear in the form of a theoretical stratagem or even as 'truth'. It is commonly stated, for example, that gender is a fundamental principle or basic structure of most, if not all, human societies. Gender is thus a significant element of society's organization, and it is used as a basis for further divisions and categories. The implicit argument is that to know and understand society, we must understand its gender structure. Furthermore, to understand historical processes it is necessary to understand the way in which people/individuals operate, and that their gender identity plays an important role in their actions. These statements make understanding gender significant at the level both of the individual actor and historical processes. In addition to such claims, it is also commonly agreed that gender is politically, socially, culturally and symbolically constituted, rather than biologically given. This means that gender is not predictable, stable or static, and through inference gender as an objective structure is rejected. In combination, the various assumptions and statements found in the literature argue that this structure, which is essential for understanding society and history, in itself must be the object of analysis. Gender is constructed by society at the same time as it is a primary structure of society. The dialectic to which this refers is entirely possible, but in praxis it challenges and undermines many existing analytical procedures inasmuch as causal primacy cannot be assigned to either society or gender. It is this complex relationship which made the integration of gender (in this sense) difficult for neopositivistic approaches (e.g. the New Archaeology). As discussed in chapter 2, this, in combination with other factors, furthered the association between feminism and contextual or postmodern intellectual frameworks. Outside archaeology, such lack of primacy has, in different ways, caused problems for, for instance, Marxist-inspired feminists and political feminists alike (as discussed in Scott 1986).

Therefore, in order for gender to play an important role in analysis of society it, as a concept, needs theorization. This, furthermore, must be done both in terms of gender's own reference points and characteristics and in terms of its possible relations and association with other entities and mechanisms. The aim of this book is therefore both to centralize the concept and to begin its further analysis as a social construct that uses materiality. A further objective is to avoid the marginalization of gender studies, which usually results when discussions take place outside the 'normal' disciplinary discourse. In this book therefore, gender, as opposed to woman, is being explored as an analytical concept carrying intellectual implications and significance. I am aware that the cost of this is the shedding of the more striking political implications signalled by 'woman', and while this can be regretted I nonetheless find it a necessary and constructive development.

In this book I explore the links between gender and material things. Archaeology, as one might expect, has been and still is dependent upon other social sciences for much of its theoretical insights into gender as ideational systems or such complex issues as those currently emerging in discussions of the social dimension of sexuality and sex. Within the ignored field of material objects archaeology is, however, 'at home'. In the social sciences generally the material effect of gender is routinely observed or commonly assumed, but it is rarely investigated – either as an effect or as a constituent of gender construction. A significant dimension of both the communication and experience of gendered difference has thereby been ignored. In particular, the ways in which practical action solidifies and gives physical realities and consequences to these differences have remained absent from analysis of the construction and maintenance of gender identities and difference. This volume is a response to this lack within gender studies generally as well as a reaction to archaeology specifically. Archaeology needs a critical text about gender. The reasons for and content of gender archaeology must be clarified, and the need for an engendered understanding of past societies further explored and argued. 'Doing gender' also needs to be more fully reconciled with archaeology as a mode of disciplinary interpretation, and it needs to consider how societies may be studied through their material records. Therefore, I intend to focus upon the potentials arising from an engendered engagement with the past, arguing that the 'gender question' has to be contextualized and embedded within the disciplinary mentality of archaeology. This, moreover, needs undertaking both for archaeology as a discipline and due to the role of the past in the present. The past plays a prominent part in identity formation – both in terms of political solidarities and personal self-perception and identity – as the concern with 'who am I?' often becomes directly linked to the question of 'where do I come from?'. It is therefore important to realize that statements about the past become statements that affect the present; our interpretations of gender relations in prehistoric societies can influence and be used to build arguments about relations in the present.

Such endeavours mean developing an analytical framework, assessing and formulating assumptions and assertions concerning significance, importance, mechanisms etc. – in short, creating a framework which begins to dress gender in layers of relational and qualitative evaluations. It also involves creating and developing analytical concepts, which will enable and empower the creation of another (pre)history (Scott 1986).

Outline of an argument

This book explores these issues in order to establish the potentials of gender archaeology for studies of prehistory and to identify archaeology's contribution to our understanding of gender relations. I engage with them theoretically in part I; in part II I focus on the materiality of gender.

Following from the argument outlined in this introductory chapter, chapter 2 consists of a historiographic overview of the recent role of gender and gender relations in our appropriation of past societies. This is based on some of the main assertions and reasons commonly associated with the development of gender archaeology. The chapter to a certain extent is also an exploration of the generation and role of myths, and of gender archaeology's need for legitimization and self-definition.

Theorizing gender, through a discussion of the central concepts and by developing an analytical framework, will then be broached in chapters 3 and 4. In these chapters the focus of archaeological studies, the materiality of social action, is also introduced. The chapters focus upon the concepts of sex and gender and the common reference to negotiation. In these chapters I am particularly concerned to relate our disciplinary interests and problems to the more general discussions within the social sciences; but I feel even more strongly the need to develop these issues in such a direction that we can engage with them archaeologically. I see this as a kind of translation. A good translation involves not only an exchange of words; it also involves a change of context. It must respond to the differences in mentality and structure between two cultures. It concerns me that gender archaeology should recognize its independent way of approaching and understanding questions of gender since otherwise it can not affect these issues in any significant way. I trust that its contribution to general debate about gender can be both strong and distinct. This involves, I believe, appreciating both the distinct nature of the societies that we study and understanding how a society may be investigated through its material culture. Developing the theoretical framework for archaeology's engagement with gender involves recognizing both the strengths and possibilities of this means of social analysis as well as its limitations. For instance, in my discussion in chapter 3 of the central concepts of sex and gender and of their relationship, I suggest that the current interest in the individual as a unique, sexually embodied subjectivity is not necessarily concurrent with how archaeology can best engage with the analysis of gender. Furthermore, the privileging of the individual over the social (the 'I' emphasized and contrasted with 'Them', rather than exploring the importance of 'We'), that is often argued or assumed in this debate, should not be so simply accepted.

The differences between these two contexts of practice should be explored constructively rather than being reduced to a hierarchy. In addition, while sex and, even more so, gender are the focal point of these discussions this, of course, should not be taken to mean that gender or sex identities are single identities, and neither should one mistake their emphasis in this particular debate to mean that they are necessarily and constantly the primary identifier. Recognizing that no single variable should be privileged, since all are contextually constituted and critically informed by each other, does not mean, however, that the variables that intersect to construct social difference and subjectivities are all equal. Interesting concepts, such as positionality (Adelson 1993), which argue for the production of identity as an interplay of many different variables, become much less useful if the potential difference between these variables and how particular contexts may enhance their distinctions are not recognized as well. The underlying central issues of chapters 3 and 4 therefore become partially how archaeology may study the construction of gendered individuals and partly how the observation of long-term structures and stability can be reconciled with notions of discourse and negotiation. This makes it obvious that the study of gender does not relegate traditional discussions of the relationship between the specific and general, between individual and society, to a past debate. This concern is as imperative as ever. Rather than making it redundant, gender sets it in sharp relief and introduces a different range of concerns and observations to such questions.

Against this background chapter 5 considers the nature of material culture and uses this to ground archaeology's role in gender studies. Arguing that it is through materiality that gender gains substance, becomes tangible and has real effect upon people's lives, this chapter is central, providing a pivotal point for the book. It is through objects as resources that gender enters political and economic life in effective and hurtful ways. Those aspects of gender that can be understood as the material articulation and effects of difference are therefore not marginal; on the contrary they are central to the existence and reproduction of gender. Chapter 5, therefore, introduces material culture as a medium for gender to operate with. To further appreciate the nature of this medium I highlight its difference from texts. I suggest that while both are discursive and communicative, appreciating their differences is vital for understanding the manner in which things can become engaged in both the construction and communication of gender. Two distinct aspects of this involvement are identified: performance and practice. Archaeology, it is argued, can be importantly involved in locating how and where gender is inserted into practical action and how it is maintained through repetition and performance. The object is not gendered, but it has the ability to become so, and the processes through which this happens and the consequences of such association are important means of engendering, and thus of the construction of gender. These are therefore issues that gender archaeology must engage with and begin to analyse empirically.

In part II a number of 'material situations' are provided to consolidate, at a different level of argumentation, the potential and possible nature of gender archaeology, as well as to illustrate how this brings about a different kind of knowledge about the past and the understanding of gender. Part II therefore turns its attention towards 'material situations' which would routinely involve gender. The intention here is to further illustrate the enabling and active role of material culture. Essentially, while part I engages with general aspects of gender and approaches its discussion in manners similar to other social sciences, part II aims to be 'archaeological'. It aims to make us think with objects and to understand their impact upon the cultural surroundings we construct and how we comprehend and survive within them. Those aspects of the archaeological record that are most directly related to individuals, such as graves or iconography, and which have therefore been most extensively used for gender analysis, are deliberately avoided in this part. In their place, food, dress, space and contact are considered in turn. Within these 'situations' we find basic concerns and practices that are expressed materially. It is argued that such combinations of materialities and practices lend themselves to the expression and creation of difference. This, furthermore, would create a dependence upon the repetitive performance of difference for these to remain in existence. These are therefore areas of practices and material resources where gender negotiation takes place. Thus chapters 6 to 9 engage with the link between gender and materiality in terms of the former's existence as a material reality with real-life consequences.

Finally, before the concluding chapter 11, I discuss, in chapter 10, archaeology's central role in the study of the origin of human societies and presumably also of gender. The aims of this chapter are two-fold. First, archaeology's unique access to the time-depth and variability of human society cannot be ignored as an additional important contribution to gender studies generally. Second, the importance that gender studies consistently have given to the link between gender and culture forces us to recognize that culture is a social dimension that cannot only be approached as continuously changing and in perpetual redefinition but must also be accepted as coming into being at some point. Recognizing how studies of origins unavoidably become entangled with concerns about our identity and uniqueness as a species, the chapter does not try to 'solve' these problems. Rather it suggests that this issue may be usefully considered using concepts such as reification, instrumentalization and machination: concepts that relate to performance and practices that arise in response to contemplation within the group. This shifts the attention from perception and cognition to much more easily recognizable reactions that take a certain physical form, and are made meaningful through repetition rather than content. Whether gender or its equivalence exists beyond human societies (and before a defined threshold) is not therefore the concern; rather the specific ways in which humans at some point began to respond to and cultivate differences amongst themselves is emphasized. This chapter firmly returns to the argument of chapters 3 and 4 about gender archaeology being concerned with how communities construct and normalize their members as being particular kinds of people. The final chapter brings these various strings together by presenting gender archaeology as the study of the materiality of gender due to the mutual interrelationship between objects and gender.

2

Gender and Archaeology: a History

We took Megan and Kim Michael with us to vote at the general election. It was very exciting spotting the election posters in the window, but it was a long walk. So I began to tell Megan a story about how once-upon-a-time no one had the right to vote, then some men got the right, and later most men; but still women were not given the vote until they became very angry. Megan loved the tale, and asked me for more 'election stories'.

The development of feminist critique and gender archaeology

Various disciplines have different ways of responding to general social and intellectual issues and of relating their academic discourses to developments in neighbouring fields and society at large. Such has been the case with feminist and gender issues: archaeology's engagement with the questions they have raised is distinct and yet part of more general intellectual trends. It is, therefore, essential to review the history of gender in archaeology in order to appreciate how archaeology's use of the various concepts has been shaped and what it has taken or ignored from the different debates. Archaeology, however, is not such a unified context of discourse that there will be only one version of its gender history. There are, for instance, some quite distinct differences between European and that of American or Australian archaeology in these regards (for discussion of gender archaeology in America see, for example, Claassen 1992a; for Australia, see, for example, Casey et al. 1998, Du Cros and Smith 1993). There are also some obvious differences between prehistoric archaeology and that of later periods, especially Classical, medieval and industrial. In addition, the production of genealogies will always also be affected by the interests and knowledge of their authors. A coarse outline of the history of gender archaeology can probably be relatively easily agreed upon, as it progressed in stages familiar from other disciplines, but the details of and comments on this outline by different authors will necessarily vary. The version provided here is informed particularly by its development within European prehistoric archaeology.

The introduction of gender studies into different disciplines is often discussed in terms of its progressing through different stages. Wylie, considering primarily the American literature, presents these stages as consisting of first the feminist critique of androcentrism, then revisionary statements making women visible (remedial phase), and finally the development of studies concerned with gender as construction and its relationship to power (Wylie 1991a: 31–2). In outline, the situation in Europe follows the same stages although not all countries or fractions of the discipline have participated in all or equally in the three stages.

The women's movement of the mid-1960s, the phase now commonly labelled 'second wave feminism' to distinguish it from the much earlier suffragette movement, is the important starting point of gender studies. Its influences are found sporadically in archaeology from the 1970s, and mark a change in the discipline's attention towards women. The earliest articles (e.g. Fonnesbeck-Sandberg et al. 1972, Kenyon 1969) affected by these changes, critical of the male dominance within the profession and politically self-reflexive, were primarily commenting upon contemporary working conditions. In addition, a few reflections over the representation of women within museums and the male dominance of the interpretation of the past were published (e.g. Thålin-Bergman 1975, Bertelsen et al. 1987 (workshop held in 1979), Gejvall 1970, Gimbutas 1974, Næss 1974). The *absence* of women, whether in the profession, in representations or in interpretation, was, however, the consistent theme, and the emphasis was therefore upon gaining visibility. The concern was to give women access to the production of prehistory and to recognize that women in the past had been actively involved in the historical process. It was felt and argued that the past had consistently been presented with women as the passive bystander. History happened to her, while men made it happen. Increased awareness of androcentric biases, fuelled by debates in social anthropology in particular and discussions within the social sciences generally and in society at large, also began to reveal how interpretations of women had automatically downgraded her in terms of her contributions, abilities and importance. For instance, pottery production, when ascribed to women, was consistently considered a domestic activity, while it became a craft or industry if associated with men. Through this kind of critical deconstruction of the taken-for-granted evaluation of men and women, gender interests within archaeology moved during the 1980s (again heavily influenced by the social sciences) from being focused on the present to include a strong argument for the need to rewrite and reinterpret prehistory: a new version of our past was demanded. It had by then become clear that we do not know the gender arrangements within the prehistoric societies we study and that they cannot be thought of as static and unchangeable. At this point the notion of gender as a social construct, as opposed to sex as a biological given, was introduced to archaeology. While this distinction may have been quite widely known at the time due to a general familiarity with anthropology, the paper by Conkey and Spector from 1984 is nonetheless seminal as it firmly introduced *gender* as a distinct concept within the archaeological vocabulary. Their paper is therefore often seen as the 'start' of gender archaeology as a sub-discipline (e.g. Hager 1997a: ix, Wright 1996a: 1). The significance of the introduction of a sex/gender distinction was that gender, as a cultural construction, became an essential part of what archaeologists study. This challenged the view of gender as an objective, biologically determined identity and thus as a natural phenomenon.

This, however, was initially often done through empiricist arguments that were familiar to traditional scientific practices and, in particular, to the verification principles of logical positivism, rather than being based on political arguments. Dommasnes, a Norwegian archaeologist who early became interested in women's issues in archaeology (e.g. Dommasnes 1976, 1982), has provided some pertinent and very insightful self-reflections upon this relationship between the traditional criteria of science and the early gender studies. She suggests that the first phase of gender archaeology in Norway was eased and made acceptable because it closely followed processualist scientific prescriptions (Dommasnes 1992: 6). Otherwise archaeologists have mainly left these issues and insights to philosophers such as Wylie (1991b, 1992b, 1997).

The increasing tension between, on the one hand, established scientific methodology and epistemological rigour and, on the other, a growing interest in subjectively defined research problems was therefore mainly a significant issue during the second phase in the development of gender archaeology. The first phase, being mainly focused upon 'labour' questions, did not comment upon epistemological issues, and the notion of scientific knowledge was properly generally accepted. Nor is the tension relevant for the third phase, but in this case it is because its self-aware affinity with different postmodern epistemologies made it more self-reflexive and thus made it embrace rather than stumble over these issues. Thus, despite the now common linkage or even equation between post-processualism and gender archaeology (even though it could be argued that much of post-processualism mainly 'uses' gender as a means of being radical or as an example of multivocality) the possibility of accommodating *some* aspects of gender stud-

ies within a positivistic framework should be recognized as character-
izing a distinct phase of the history of gender in archaeology. For some
this influence, which at the time was part of the normative science
regime, was allowed for strategic reasons, but often it was also a result
of this being the scientific procedures in which the archaeologists had
been trained and with which they had learned to think. The positivistic
influence during this stage is found, for example, in the heavy reliance
on cross-cultural generalization to prove or disprove an interpretative
association and the extensive use of quantitative analysis to establish
correlates between gender and objects or behaviour (e.g. Gibbs 1987).
One can also propose that the concentration upon methodology, that
is the procedural aspects, was akin to this approach. This point does
not mean, however, that these works were entirely positivistic, but
rather that the current association between gender studies and non-
positivistic epistemologies has a more contorted history than is often
acknowledged.

The concept of gender, as it developed during the 1980s, became
increasingly difficult to avoid, and in principle the term became acceptable within the social science. The term was also now commonly
employed by archaeology, even if some maintained that these aspects
of prehistoric societies are beyond that which can be investigated.
During the late 1980s and in the 1990s gender, as a cultural construct, increasingly became recognized as part of the dynamic of past
societies and thus as a subject of analysis. The most significant consequence of this acceptance is that gender is given the potential of affecting the cultural make-up at any time. Furthermore, it follows that
since this had not been previously recognized, earlier interpretations
of prehistory must be lacking at a certain level of social analysis. The
insertion and questioning of gender in our analysis of the very varied
societies that prehistory embraces is, however, a task of enormous
complexity. For every period and range of activities being analysed
we have come to learn that our understanding of gender and of how
material objects and practices are involved in its representation and
maintenance must be reassessed and rephrased. The recognition of the
importance of gender and the somewhat reluctant acceptance of this
as a major field of academic investigation have not, therefore, by themselves secured the project of engendering the past. In response to this
problem, and being receptive to general influences from neighbouring
disciplines, current gender studies have become increasingly critical
of an inherited conceptual framework and are now concerned with
establishing archaeology's identity as a discipline of gender-informed
practices and interpretative potentials.

The relatively late inclusion of gender in archaeology?

The actual introduction of explicit gender issues (a so-called gender archaeology) has only been subject to very few studies, notably those by Wylie (e.g. 1991a, 1991b, 1992a). This contrasts interestingly with the much more prolific calls for its inclusion, including the early examples of Conkey and Spector (1984) and the 1988 volume of the journal *ARC*, which was dedicated to gender archaeology. Despite the very few investigations, certain myths about ancestry and genealogy have developed. These are essential to the construction of a distinct field of practices and concerns and in that capacity they are central to recent developments. They do, however, also have the potential to serve other needs and they easily take on the role of excuses, reasons or ammunition for current archaeologists in their attempts to define and understand their own positions. As already stated, many histories of gender archaeology can be constructed. Despite such subjectivities and the possibility and legitimacy of multi-vocality, it is constructive for a critical self-awareness to reflect upon some of the central statements that have been made and how they have functioned to create a distinct identity for 'gender archaeology'.

One of these statements has been concerned with presenting gender awareness as having arrived to archaeology *relatively* late without really making the basis of the apparent comparison clear. Another impression commonly given is one of an almost total absence of women in archaeology and prehistory prior to the appearance of gender archaeology. Such statements serve the obvious purposes of legitimizing and solidifying gender archaeology by establishing its distinctive nature compared to earlier practices and by pointing to the obvious need for it.

To me there is a dilemma here. Not wanting to undermine gender archaeology, I have nevertheless found it difficult, even for strategic reasons, to agree to the generation of oversimplified views of the nature and history of archaeology. There may be a strong desire for emotive and political engagement with the consolidation of feminist or gender archaeologies, but nonetheless I do not find such selective genealogies useful. As regards strategies, I cannot believe that they work in the long term if they have a shaky foundation. Simplifying our own origins and reasons for being are strategies that underestimate how powerful the arguments for gender-informed archaeologies are. It also ignores how sophisticated these reasons can be made, moving us beyond simplistic postulates and easy uses of our own disciplinary past. Accepting that our discipline is complex and that the reasons for gender archaeology are many and have different motivations, variously embedded within the subject and in society at large, we should dare to use the history of archaeology and the position of women and gender within it to challenge ourselves and our understanding of discipline (at various interpretative levels) and solidarities, rather than use it mainly for self-justification.

One can, for instance, usefully respond to the claim that the inclusion of gender concerns in archaeology was relatively late in three ways. First, one may ask 'relative to what?', and in doing so reveal some aspects of archaeologists' disciplinary identity and expectations. Second, the basis for this statement can be reassessed. Third, one may also wonder what importance or interest this has and how the negative impression created may affect people's perception of the discipline.

The claim that gender was late in being introduced to archaeology is found both explicitly (e.g. Nelson 1997: 15–20, Wylie 1991b) and less directly through various statements referring to general gender uninterest and inertia within the discipline. Meanwhile, the only substantial analysis of the inclusion of gender in archaeology that suggests where its beginning should be located has been conducted by Wylie. Based on primarily American examples, she argues for a certain association between the increased acceptance of gender issues and the development of a subject/subjective orientated archaeology (e.g. Wylie 1991b). She does, however, also identify an earlier phase during the 1980s when women's roles were being questioned. This, as already outlined, was a phase in which interest in equality and equity issues were articulated, while the nature of scientific practices was left relatively unchallenged. It is therefore not entirely clear what (and therefore when) one may identify as the first inclusion of gender interest in the discipline. The link to feminist concerns, as expressed in the women's movement from the 1960s onwards, is, however, unequivocal and can usefully be further explored in order to clarify our 'roots'.

A very early expression of such concerns, which probably should be included as an example of the early phase, is Kathleen Kenyon's fiery speech to the Oxford Union in 1969, in which she lamented the fate of young female archaeologists (Kenyon 1969). Other early discussions of this kind within archaeology can also be found in Scandinavia in the 1970s where they were published by women of the sixties generation. Explicit feminist comments upon equity issues within archaeology were, for example, published at this time in both Norway and Denmark (Fonnesbeck-Sandberg et al. 1972, Holm-Olsen and Mandt-Larsen 1974), while the first concise discussion of the androcentric nature of interpretations may have been the workshop *Were They All Men? An Examination of Sex Roles in Prehistoric Society* (Bertelsen, Lillehammer and Næss 1987), held in Norway in 1979. The fate of this workshop is interesting in terms of understanding the incorporation of feminist concerns within mainstream archaeology as well as in feminist historiography. While held in 1979, it did not find a publisher until 1987, although before then it was frequently referred to in writing within the Norwegian discussion of gender archaeology (Bertelsen, Lillehammer and Næss 1987: 7). For its publication it was decided to use English, thus clearly aiming beyond its original local Norwegian audience, yet it has remained remarkably ignored in overviews of the development of gender archaeology, which consistently try to place its development late and focus it upon a few seminal publications, especially the paper by Conkey and Spector from 1984. Only recently has it become more widely acknowledged (e.g. Nelson 1997) and incorporated into the genealogy of gender archaeology or its canonical history (Hodder 1997: 75). Thus as late as 1992 it was possible to write that 'Surveys on the states of women archaeologists appeared this same year [1990] for England, the United States, Germany, Australia and Norway' (Claassen 1992b: 1), and to imply that these were pioneering works – a statement which at least in the case of Denmark and Norway ignores women's voices of, respectively, eighteen and sixteen years earlier. Another disregarded indication of gender as a growing presence in the discipline is the extent to which it has been incorporated as a theme in conferences and meetings. In Britain, for instance, gender and/or feminist archaeology has been regularly discussed since 1981 at the annual TAG conference (Theoretical Archaeology Group) – but little of this has been published and this early inclusion is reduced to 'social knowledge'.

The argument that gender came relatively late to archaeology is probably meant to be in comparison with social anthropology and the social sciences generally. In social anthropology, partly influenced by an ethnographic concern with women's lives, gender developed as a distinct topic during the seventies. The volume *Women, Culture and Society* (Rosaldo and Lamphere 1974) may then be selected as the 'landmark' in anthropology against which one may compare. This presumes, however, that archaeology should or ought to develop intellectually in parallel with its neighbouring disciplines. While this *may* happen, it should of course not be treated as a must, as there are also possibilities and restraints that are unique to the disciplines. There is thus an assumption that archaeology in terms of gender studies is equal to the disciplines at the forefront of gender research. This ignores the formative role that social anthropology and sociology have played in the recognition of gender as a separate construction and in outlining its social constituencies. Archaeology did not participate in this deconstruction of what women and men mean and how they are made, and the discipline was very much on the receiving end (together with other disciplines) of a debate. It is therefore neither surprising nor particularly shameful if gender awareness developed later in archaeology than in social anthropology.

The relative lateness of gender or feminist interests in archaeology does also depend upon how these interests are defined and thus to some extent disciplined. The outline above of how concerns with equality were debated within disciplinary frameworks since the early 1970s does not support that it was particularly late compared with many other disciplines. The inclusion, or rather the development, of a somewhat definable gender archaeology did, however, take longer and was some years late compared with some disciplines but, on the other hand, compared with others it was early (see also Beard 1994).

This question of whether gender was late in being included in archaeology is therefore mainly relevant and interesting from a political point of view. The persistent androcentrism, the problems of marginalization, the self-regulative and reproductive nature of disciplines and the closure they create in terms of knowledge and challenges are interesting and important aspects of the politics of academia. In terms of the interpretative engagement that archaeology may provide, being some years late, is, however, not particularly surprising nor necessarily very important. Archaeology does not have the means of developing an understanding of gender prior to its investigation by other disciplines. In that sense gender archaeology had to be delayed: its conceptual framework and theoretical propositions had to be suggested by others. This does not mean that archaeology does not have an input to these concepts and framework; it most certainly must have, or it cannot use and expand upon them. The intellectual content of gender archaeology, as opposed to its political motivations, were, however, initially borrowed.

The above examples of neglected early engagement with women's issues is not meant primarily as a 'correction' of existing histories – probably there are many other corrections to be made. Rather they serve to reveal how some of our central statements about gender archaeology and its origin and reception easily perpetuate or create new biases and how they then also participate in creating closure. Hidden within such statements are assumptions which give gender archaeology well-defined limits, resulting in inclusions and exclusions. They also often neglect to give proper attention to the nature of archaeology, its restrictions and its potentials. On their basis we create a self-image based upon a selected view of our history and origin, and in that process we ourselves risk making certain groups (and national traditions) invisible. Statements to the effect that archaeology was slow in recognizing gender are basically meant to motivate initiatives and contemplation. Their effects can, however, range further and we should therefore expect their foundation to be made clear.

The presentation of women in archaeology and prehistory

Another prominent myth relates to the presence of women in the profession and in the past. The recent explicit interest in gender issues and its relationship to feminism has often resulted in archaeology and its product, the interpreted past and its material record, being presented as either genderless or as entirely androcentric and immersed in chauvinistic propaganda. The former characteristic is weirdly 'blind' towards how women and men have always been part of both. This is important since through such an appropriation-policy, where the discipline is made to appear in a certain way, the feminist and gender critiques themselves risk becoming an example of how the muteness of certain groups is created by the blindness of the dominator (Kehoe 1992: 23) – a relationship of dominance it sets out to reject. The latter characteristic, while possibly partly correct, nonetheless grossly simplifies the nature of gender issues as they are embedded in traditional disciplinary structures and knowledge generation. Such statements make it appear as if our generation *invented* gender, rather than recent developments being concerned with investing it with new and challenging meanings and motivations focused upon developing it as an analytical concept (and possibly an instrument of change).

For a critical development of gender archaeology these claims on traditional practices should be further explored in order to establish more fully both the genealogy of gender concerns within archaeology and the arguments for its existence. Let me repeat that these reflections are subject to more or less obvious biases and intellectual and political agendas. Meanwhile the ability to illuminate the interests of particularly defined groups and the institutionalized production of knowledge provide an essential background from which to appreciate some of the constraints built into the project of engendering archaeology and of developing this as a field of specialist knowledge and involvement (see also Kehoe 1992: 26–7). From the beginning it should be pointed out that the relationship between identity and knowledge and one's engagement in knowledge production is not easy to understand, and many factors are involved and intervene in the process. For instance, despite our consistent rejection of androcentrism, it is not yet clear what we would recognize as non-androcentric knowledge; a gynocentric replacement offers little real alternative. It also seems to be the case that androcentrism is not produced by men only, as women often learned to 'master' this more rewarding behaviour. The extent to which knowledge, as an individual project, is gendered and whether, for instance, a man's understanding is always androcentric and that this therefore is part of his subjectivity seem at present wide open questions.

In our gendered engagement with the history of archaeology, it may be instructive to learn more about whether and how women were incorporated into the discipline rather than just accepting the discipline as male-based. It is also realistic to assume that gender politics and stereotypes emerge from the socio-political contexts in which archaeology was exercised rather than assigning male archaeologists specified intentions expressed in terms of control over the past and of women. Individual examples that challenge these assumptions can then be given due attention. The embedded suggestion made here, that the suppression of and discrimination against women often happened in a covert rather than open fashion, also makes more understandable why this was so relatively little discussed and why women participated in it. Thus, the asymmetrical evaluation of the role and contribution of the sexes to society and historical processes, which affected both the interpretations of the past and the role of female archaeologists, was usually deeply naturalized and it was commonly expressed by women and men alike. Rather than conflating the complex manner in which knowledge is constructed, and in particular knowledge that may play a central role in our notion of who we are, into a notion of men deliberately stealing women's past and history, the mechanisms through which these views were generated and agreed upon must be traced and analysed. In particular, archaeology will greatly improve its self-knowledge about how it instrumentalizes these naturalized views on gender if the assumptions used to gender-stereotype the past are analysed, and if this is followed up by studies of how this has interacted with and influenced interpretations of the material evidence. Some studies have begun such critical investigation of gender as part of the history and development of archaeology. Moser, for instance, in several pieces of work, has investigated the construction and reproduction of gendered understanding in pictorial representations (Moser 1992, 1998). Another important preliminary study has been published by Hjørungdal, who investigated nineteenth-century discussions about gender-coding of a range of objects commonly found as grave goods in prehistoric graves from northern Europe (1994).

As mentioned, critique of the absence of women from our constructed past and in the profession was the first indication of feminism and women's interests affecting archaeology. The earliest concern was with visibility, and it was quickly applied to the practice of archaeology at several levels. These interests, which can be grouped as (1) visibility of women in interpretations of the past, (2) visibility of women in the disciplinary history, (3) visibility of women in the job market (equity issues) and (4) visibility of women in representations (museums), provide us with useful starting points for reflecting upon the entangled history of gender and discipline, upon power and empowerment.

The interpretative exclusion of women from prehistory

The notion of a relatively late introduction of feminist/gender archaeology has tended to present all previous archaeological work as gender-ignorant. That, of course, is not the case. Earlier generations of archaeologists, and possibly especially female archaeologists, have engaged in various ways with the question of gender in the archaeological record.

An extensive review of the role of women and gender in the history of archaeology cannot be attempted here. A few selected examples will have to suffice to make the point that women have always been part of the past. It is the understanding of their presence that has changed, not the acknowledgement of their existence. For instance, in the nineteenth century some of the meta-histories produced gave much attention to social structures such as kinship and marriage (Arwill-Nordbladh 1998: 5). Amongst these the works of Bachofen, Friedrich Engels and Lewis Henry Morgan are of interest to archaeology as they commented upon the characteristics and changes of social organization in the remote past in a manner that would directly affect the archaeological interpretation of the past. Their influence upon archaeological thinking, and especially as regards gender relations, has as yet been little investigated. One of the exceptions is Arwill-Nordbladh's analysis of Montelius and his discussion of marriage as a historical institution (1989, 1998: 4–16). She also points out that there are obvious parallels between these works and assumptions used and topics debated by some of the most eminent nineteenth-century archaeologists such as John Lubbock (ibid. 1998: 6–8).

The point of these influences is that to some extent they introduced the idea that gender roles could be related to social concerns rather than being biologically determined. It was not, however, a question of gender as social construction, but more like gender as an aspect of social organization. Any influence from Engels, whether direct or indirect, would, for instance, tend to approach gender relations as a correlate of gross types of social organization, and in particular modes of production. In the differences between these early discussions and current debates several distinctions are obvious, such as those between orthodox Marxism and postmodernism, or between social analysis in terms of classes or groups and one conducted in terms of agency and individuality, or between gender as an aspect of the division of labour and rights or being a question of a discursive existence. These, while representing radical changes and disjunctures in how gender has been perceived and approached, do not confirm that the past has been presented genderless. Kehoe, drawing our attention to l'Abbé Breuil's drawings of scenes of men and women in the Palaeolithic, has made a similar point (1992: 26).

In addition to ideas about change in gender roles through time, which may have been the interest of only a few scholars, archaeology has also consistently been concerned with assigned roles generally and identifying gender specifically. Such roles were not explicitly problematized, and the nature of gender relations was often considered as a natural phenomenon or as predictable. Nonetheless, archaeologists have from early in the nineteenth century classified and grouped their material using notions of male and female (see Hjørungdal 1994: 143–4). Although this practice, which was indeed both andro- and ethnocentric, might hardly ever have been theoretically explicit, it did nonetheless contain a discursive element as unfamiliar material objects were processed and given gendered meanings. This practical engagement with the material remains did in fact at times involve discussions of the reasons for its gender association (e.g. Mestorf 1889, Müller 1876, both discussed in Hjørungdal 1994) and 'As time went on, the most frequently used criteria of male versus female, were weapons versus jewellery (e.g. Lisch 1840). These particular material things have acquired the status of metaphors par excellence of "malehood" and "womanhood" within archaeology' (Hjørungdal 1994: 144).

In this ordering of the material record of past societies, the early generations of archaeologist engendered the past, but their engenderment took the form of applying their own familiar gender experiences to it. Furthermore, they interpreted these as natural and as a necessary outcome of the mental and physical differences between the sexes.

To describe and reject traditional archaeology as andro- and ethnocentric very appropriately encapsulates the deeply entrenched sets of gender assumptions that influenced their interpretation of the past and the classification of its remains. To present this as there being no attention towards women or gender in the earlier archaeology is, however, to understand these problems too simplistically. It has not been the insertion of women or the introduction of gender that during the last decade has radically challenged previous approaches; it is the different meaning of gender, that we are trying to accomplish theoretically and in its application, which has drastically transformed these concerns.

Women in the history of archaeology*

It has also been argued that the past has been produced exclusively by men, that there are no female participants in the history of archaeology. One of the underlying implications is that women would have produced a different discipline and another prehistory, and that their absence is therefore regrettable. This therefore also becomes part of the disciplinary legitimization of gender archaeology. Meanwhile, although the question of equality that this raises is extremely important and valid, we see once again that the issue becomes more challenging when its basis is more fully explored. As part of a strategic statement the nature of the discipline may justifiably be simplified, but when we aim to understand the role of women in archaeology and to use this constructively it is essential to go beyond a simplistic account. It is particularly important that the selective nature of disciplinary history is recognized and that this history is not treated as a truth. The history of archaeology with its exclusion of women and gender politics has been produced through mechanisms of selecting and forgetting, which in their own right provide extremely interesting insights into power and empowerment (Díaz-Andreu and Sørensen 1998b, Sørensen 1998). Feminist claims about the lack of professional integration of women have uncritically accepted these versions, and until recently hardly any attention was therefore given to how disciplinary history is produced and whether it may contain systematic biases. In assuming that existing accounts of the professional role of women was a true record, the blindness of these accounts regarding women has been reproduced.

A number of volumes that aim at 'excavating' the early generations of women now exist (e.g. Claassen 1994, Du Cros and Smith 1993, Díaz-Andreu and Sørensen 1998a). These volumes clearly show how systematically women's contributions and participation in the discipline has been ignored and erased from our disciplinary memory.

---

* This section is based on the volume *Excavating Women: A History of Women in European Archaeology* (1988), edited by Margarita Díaz-Andreu and myself. My brief synopsis of the points emerging from the volume owes much to our many discussions.

Women's absence from disciplinary history is a common phenomenon. Their participation in academia has been little analysed and, as a distinct concern, gender politics is largely absent, or alternatively when unavoidable, women's presence is individualized and isolated by consistently referring to them as outstanding and unusual. Such individuals become detached from a coherent appreciation of the underlying tenets of gender in academia. The gender issues remain hidden – outside both past and present discourse. This separation of the individual from her peer group participates in a mutually enforcing stereotyping of women which negates their abilities, intellects and roles in society. Until recently, statements about women's roles in archaeology participated in this. The project of reinserting this muted group into our disciplinary ancestry therefore fulfils both the need for role models and case studies as well as providing more general gender-critical perspectives upon discipline and knowledge. Studies so far have proved highly rewarding, revealing, for instance, how existing disciplinary histories are based both on well-documented accounts and on myths, thus demonstrating their underlying character as a narrative about identity and closure (Díaz-Andreu and Sørensen 1998b). The studies also begin to make transparent the specific expectations and values used to grant importance to academic work and individuals. The inclusion of gender issues in the history of archaeology therefore provides an important contribution to debates and analysis of the discipline, its origin, intellectual development, social contexts and the basis for its knowledge claims.

Despite the unique and distinct histories of individual women it is possible to identify characteristics that are common to their role in archaeology. These provide significant points from which a wider social and political history of archaeology can emerge. There are, for instance, several similarities in how and when women became accepted and integrated within the discipline. Another consistent theme is the discrepancy between apparent possibilities and the practical restrictions upon the choices they had. Such restrictions are seen in the career choices of individuals, and are also indicated by institutional rules and regulation of memberships. The most pervasive tension was, however, probably between the demands of professional life and the expectation of the mother-role (Díaz-Andreu and Sørensen 1998b). Despite such tensions, women have been involved with archaeology from its beginning, even obtaining the highest jobs of professors and senior curators. This does not mean, however, that they were necessarily considered equal. Studies of the situations in different parts of Europe (Díaz-Andreu and Sørensen 1998a) and in America (Claassen 1994) show a recurrent practice of 'labour division' within the discipline. Women had, for example, easier access to museum posts and sometimes to managerial jobs than to prestigious academic positions. In practice women's engagement with archaeology was therefore often different from men's. In addition, women often explored and developed specific 'niches' within the profession. It seems, for instance, that women from early on focused their research on particular periods: Iron Age and medieval studies in Norway, Anglo-Saxon studies in Britain. Alternatively, they worked abroad in areas such as Egypt, the Near East and Crete. It also seems that women's participation in the discipline was often facilitated by their becoming involved with research topics that may have been considered feminine and thus traditionally ignored by men, so that from early on women carried out pioneering research on textiles, jewellery, pottery and art.

Male and female archaeologists thus became distinct kinds of professionals as they engaged with the discipline in different manners. As various restrictions were put upon women's participation, such differences became a matter of inequality. In fact, restricted access to fieldwork can be identified as one of archaeology's special means of differentiating between its male and female practitioners. Fieldwork, particularly early on when no formal degrees existed, was an essential part of archaeology, and access to it was a crucial step towards becoming an archaeologist. Similarly, their exclusion from committees and societies removed women from important networking, and from a central forum for the exchange of information and the creation of discourse. A particularly interesting result of the recent studies has therefore been to discover that women at times created their own, albeit informal and personal, networks and work teams. Due to its private character this alternative support system, and the role of a few men within it, has not previously been granted importance but has been written off as friendship (Beard 1994, Sørensen 1998).

Studies of women in archaeology show how different focuses, perspectives and specialities have systematically been associated with and exercised by men and women respectively. It is hardly surprising that this was often the case in earlier periods, when gender roles were thought of in rigidly binary terms and men and women were brought up and educated in radically different ways. That was also a time when women, as a means of establishing a space for themselves, may have explored such stereotypes through topics and activities traditionally thought of as feminine. It is, however, important to recognize how, despite changes in society at large, these differences have become embedded within disciplinary practices and expectations and have thus affected its mentality and self-identity (Díaz-Andreu and Sørensen 1998b).

These studies of women in archaeology forcefully demonstrate that the discipline needs to know and to come to terms with its broad social history and how it was 'shaped'. Visibility can, however, not simply be granted and the question of inclusion and exclusion in itself becomes a challenge to our concern with visibility. The attempt at re-evaluating roles and importance makes it clear that the reasons for assigning any work prominence are so profoundly shaped by the authoritative nature of disciplinary culture that it is exceedingly difficult to challenge these reasons and to go beyond the accepted notions of knowledge and value (Díaz-Andreu and Sørensen 1998b). Such challenges, emerging from the effort to give voice to one muted group, will affect reassessment of archaeology beyond its gender politics.

Women in the job market – equity issues

Another central concern has been the presence of women within the profession of archaeology. One of the roots of gender archaeology is clearly the women's movement from the 1960s with its emphasis upon 'the personal is political' and the corresponding changing views on women's public lives. This focused attention upon women's access to various ladders of employment within archaeology. Many of the earliest articles about women and archaeology from the 1970s are thus typically about women and the job market, showing the now familiar picture of women decreasing in numbers at the higher levels of the career structures (e.g. Fonnesbeck-Sandberg 1972, Holm-Olsen and Mandt-Larsen 1974). This type of survey and associated research into attitudes and behavioural patterns and disciplinary strategy choices has in Europe been used in particular in England, Norway, Spain and Sweden, and it is also prevalent in North America and Australia. The aim of such research has been partly to create ammunition for changing the pattern of employment by documenting how extremely unrepresentative and thus unfair the existing situation is, and partly to reveal how men and women participate in different behavioural strategies that reward them differently. The presence of women in most parts of the profession has been slowly changing in recent years. Meanwhile, research from both the USA and Norway suggests that there remain 'invisible' barriers to women and that they and their academic products tend to be assigned lower status and prestige even when they are formally placed at the top of the hierarchy (e.g. Engelstad et al. 1992). The impact of different reasons for and means of placing women in high academic positions is interestingly illustrated by comparison between Norway and Portugal (Díaz-Andreu and Sørensen 1998b). Both countries have numerical parity in the employment of men and women, but in Norway inequality persists in the evaluation of their work, while in Portugal this seems not to be the case or at least their products are assessed in very different manners. An explanation of this difference may lie in the situation in Norway having been created through legislation, which does not necessarily correspond to changes in cultural expectations and behaviour, while the situation in Portugal rests on a traditional system of patronage, in which social class and belonging count far more than gender (Díaz-Andreu and Sørensen 1998b, S. and V. Jorge personal communication). This demonstrates how closely gender ideologies are invested in and affected by politics.

The desire for visibility has been a motivating factor in many of these debates; but while this is a legitimate and important demand such emphasis has also introduced delimiting expectations. Primarily, it usually means that the question of gender is collapsed to being about the presence of women, and, at the same time, it focuses upon equality in terms of numbers. As a result 'Participation and incorporation into the discipline are reduced to questions of quantity and hierarchy' (Sørensen 1998: 36).

Visibility of women in representations

Equity issues were expressed early with regard to the presentation of women. This debate has particularly focused upon pictorial representations of women and the way museums create meaning and significance about gender. The concerns expressed with regard to museums are well captured by the agenda of organizations such as Women in History and Museums (WHAM), which was founded in London in 1984. The aims were to promote positive images of women and to combat discrimination through collecting for museums and mounting exhibitions and to encourage informed museum practice, including campaigning for equal employment in museums and related fields (Pirie 1985). Most analyses of women's roles in museums have accordingly focused upon questions of stereotypes and bias (see also Butler 1996) as well as equity concerns (e.g. Anderson and Reeves 1994, Grab 1991, Høgsbro 1994, Texeira 1991). The invisibility of women in traditional museum displays has consistently been demonstrated, as has their stereotypical depiction as mothers and housewives, cooking and caring through (pre)history, and the simultaneous downgrading of these activities (for preliminary studies see Chabot 1990, Horne 1984, Jones and Pay 1990, Jones 1991, Mandt 1994, Moser 1992, Webb Mason 1995, Wood 1996).

Focusing upon androcentric biases, some have asserted that women are absent from our past and made invisible in our presentations (Horne 1984, Jones and Pay 1990, Webb Mason 1995). Despite the importance of these studies, they have further solidified the focus upon visibility/presence which easily gives a limited understanding of the issues involved. The problem arises from a lack of clarity of what gender means, and as a result the question of gender becomes conflated (as in the case of equity research) to the presence of women. In addition, the in/visibility of women is usually assessed in terms of a quantitative presence. Women in representations or interpretations are not, however, merely made invisible in terms of not being present. Their invisibility arises out of their assigned insignificance in terms of the interpretative engagement with the display, that is you don't need to engage with the women to understand what is being said about the past (Sørensen 1999).

Porter has described some of the factors involved in creating this effect. She writes:

> In exhibitions . . . women and the feminine become, literally, the frontiers by which space and knowledge are defined: they are the more distant and imprecise elements, in the background and at the edges of the picture. The figures and activities in the foreground, more fully developed and with greater consistency, are those of men and the masculine attributes. . . . representations of women did not 'fit' together coherently, whereas those of men were relatively congruent. (Porter 1996: 112–13)

Men are used to 'carry' the narrative of the past through the exhibition space. It is through men that history is articulated and they therefore become the history. To understand how meaning is produced within the context of the museum it is important to recognize that such connections are not made discursively but are created through the structure of the 'narrative'. The meaning, furthermore, is constructed by drawing connections between objects as well as statements and through the creation of difference and significance. This means that the addition of the unconnected woman does not really challenge or alter the message; they are merely ornamental and not essential for understanding (Sørensen 1999). For women to become part of history, its active practitioners rather than its passive bystanders, they must become connected to the narrative, their contributions and lives must be incorporated and made essential for a satisfying engagement with the display.

Increasing the visibility of women (in particular within traditional male-associated activities) has been called for. But visibility should not become so highly regarded that we ignore how it is obtained. We often desire the past to provide us with specific narratives, but in doing so we risk neglecting women's real lives. We will then still be inserting women, rather than connecting them to history, and at the most they become sidelines, a kind of complement to history. We are also still too focused upon *woman*, rather than understanding the variability of *women*. Despite the best intentions, our analyses of gender representation in museums have, with a few exceptions, continued to focus upon visibility and the implied connection between this and significance. Lind has characterized the concern with women in museums as polarized between two different needs: misery research and dignity research (1993: 6). I suggest that the engendering of the archaeological exhibit could provide far more exciting and constructive challenges to the ways we think about and assume gender differences by moving beyond these simple (albeit at their time important) presentist motivations. We need both more subtle understanding of how significance is gained within exhibitions and greater awareness of how gender must be both problematized and connected to the narrative of change and development.

Epistemology, gender and archaeology

Archaeology, due to the distance from the society it studies and the fragmentary nature of its evidence, has always been vulnerable to the questioning of how its knowledge is produced. Insecurity about its knowledge claims and defence of its analytical and interpretative abilities have, therefore, been part of the discipline's self-awareness since its academic foundation early in the nineteenth century (e.g. Müller 1884). The status of knowledge claims has become even more problematized with the development of post-processual archaeology and the increased influences from critical theory, post-structuralism and postmodern philosophies which introduce notions of multi-vocality and the slipperiness of knowledge/meaning. The feminist critique of science (e.g. Harding 1986) has played an interesting, but complicated role within this development. Its influence upon archaeology generally and gender archaeology specifically has, however, remained limited for reasons that I shall briefly consider below. At the same time, the feminist critique has been empathic to archaeology's epistemological insecurity, and this has produced a clear niche for it to fit and from which a further wedge could be put between the archaeological past (and record) and its current male-produced interpretations. In this separation between data and its interpretation the feminist critique of science has introduced a complicated twist to post-processual claims for multi-vocality since, on the one hand, it makes data appear neutral or unresisting and, on the other, often makes claims of more truthful feminist interpretations. Thus, at one and the same time, feminist-inspired epistemological critique within archaeology strongly supports the notion of multi-vocality and the constructiveness of knowledge and yet separates the objects from its interpretation in a manner that presents it as potentially neutral or even objective. There is, thus, a curious tendency of referring to a need to rewrite prehistory in order to rectify previous biases, stereotypes and unrepresentative accounts of the past as if a feminist version would not be biased. Thus an extremely interesting conflict is arising, it seems, from the clash between politicizing our work and yet wanting to lay claim to an authoritative interpretation. Only more recently has a more fully subjectivist approach become marked within gender archaeology (e.g. Conkey 1989, Spector 1993).

The concern with androcentric knowledge production has, not surprisingly, to some extent been bound up with the project of analysing and challenging the politics of control over knowledge and epistemic authority (Wylie et al. 1989). It is worth noticing, however, that within European archaeology the critique of the discipline in terms of control has mainly been articulated by males and has been formulated within a post-processual agenda heavily influenced by critical theory and post-structuralism (e.g. Bapty and Yates 1990, Tilley 1990, 1991). These critiques have not considered androcentricity a particularly central problem (one may even argue that they have perpetuated it), and the gender bias in knowledge production has generally been ignored or only paid lip-service (see also Engelstad 1991a, 1991b; but see Tilley 1993: 22 and Thomas 1995: 352 for a partial response). Thus, while it is now widely accepted within archaeology that knowledge is socially constituted, the discipline still effectively disregards gender as part of that social influence. From a gender-critical perspective it can be argued that recent concern with the politics of knowledge (Wylie et al. 1989) has been used to replace rather than to challenge the nature of existing power structures.

The limited epistemological debate within gender archaeology has until recently mainly been concerned with avoiding relativism (Engelstad 1991a: 505, Wylie et al. 1989, Wylie 1992a, 1992b), but the ability to do so is dependent upon what is considered to constitute female knowledge and what distinguishes women's practices. If the issue is merely setting biases right, erasing stereotypes, including ignored data in our analysis and making women visible in the past, then it may be possible to do this within existing epistemologies. This is probably largely what happened during the first stage of gender archaeology, as argued by Dommasnes (1992: 6). Such procedures, however, reduce the effectiveness of the questions that can be asked. Meanwhile, if bias is also considered to affect the notion of objectivity and scientism, then a more radical revision of the ways knowledge claims are evaluated is needed. Wylie is currently one of the few to have considered these issues for archaeology. Using the critique of science as androcentric, especially based upon Harding's work (1986), she argues that any effective critique of patriarchal science depends on constructive insights about what it is that traditional theories and methodologies miss when they ignore gender and demean women (Wylie et al. 1989).

According to Wylie et al. (1989) this implies that women scientists must both develop models of scientific rationality that take gender into account and articulate regulative ideals for research practice so that it can incorporate feminist values. Since, at the same time, Wylie supports the view that women cannot be presumed to possess a distinctive set of cognitive capacities, 'female values' implies 'doing science as feminists' rather than representing other ways of thinking, that is this becomes a matter of politics rather than cognition. It is, however, difficult to see how this will avoid relativism, nor is it clear how feminism as such can provide a starting point for developing models of scientific rationality. These may in fact be more separate fields than Wylie presents them as, and some, such as Strathern (1987), hold and accept that the aims of feminism are incompatible with the objective study of society. Another problem arises from the danger of marginalization. If women's knowledge acquires its existence through feminist practice alone, then it may easily become reduced to just another 'voice' amongst other marginal or minority ones, one that is relevant only to feminists. Furthermore, if one of archaeology's aims continues to be – in addition and not unrelated to its various contemporary purposes – to understand the variability and dynamics of gender relations over time and space, then a feminist agenda may not alone provide sufficient guidance for its development.

In contrast to Wylie's position, which attempts to unite feminism and a non-relativist rationality as a foundation for knowledge claims and scientific practice, others have explored the idea of difference as a means of creating a place for women's contributions. This is often expressed in assumptions that accord women different intellectual abilities: assigning them greater sensitivity, making them more intuitive, suggesting that they have a different empathy with the past or stressing their different experiences generally (e.g. Gero 1996). This approach has also been used to argue that women's ways of thinking are incompatible with, and accordingly suppressed by, notions of objectivity and scientific rigour. Basically, women are assumed to have the ability to 'know' differently, reaching alternative and complementary understandings to those of males. The reasons for such differences are also debated, and it is common to see them explained either as biologically determined or socially constituted. Whatever their reasons, they are considered to affect how we think. Depending on how strongly these differences are maintained, and the extent to which they are seen to express cognitive abilities, they will affect how men's and women's knowledge claims can be compared. If a strong cognitive separation is argued, it does not necessarily follow that the traditional criteria for evaluating knowledge claims are false, rather that they apply only to men's thinking. It could thus be argued (as at times it is) that knowledge claims by men and women should be assessed within different epistemological frameworks, replicating ideas of the rational, logical male versus the irrational, emotive female.

Another line of argument is a concern with language itself, and how our existing disciplinary terminology enables certain interests and ways of speaking, while suppressing or silencing others. Similar concerns have also been expressed in anthropology (Caplan 1992: 83). This demonstrates both tension and strategy in the use of language, such as women using men's language including its meaning and power. It also hints at the problems of comparing knowledge expressed through a learned language and within disciplinary rules of discourse with that expressed in our other voices. Arwill-Nordbladh has also questioned whether our analytical and interpretative concepts are formulated in such a manner that they perpetuate contemporary gender asymmetries and make certain issues difficult to see, or even hide them (1994: 35, 45). This may automatically make women invisible or at least decentralize them (Arwill-Nordbladh personal communication).

The nature of gender archaeology: contextualization

The prehistoric past has, of course, always been presented in terms of people, including men, women and children. It is therefore not the presence of these groups that is the problem but rather the assumptions we have used in assigning them roles and importance. Until recently these were based on androcentric notions of gender roles, causing the past to be reconstructed in the image of the present and treating the relationship between the sexes as entirely unproblematic and given, and therefore outside the area of research. Gender relations were approached as known and their roots and reasons as understood.

From its very beginning European archaeology has been strongly affected by the world-view of the nineteenth century. Its understanding of the past was in many ways, and certainly regarding gender, an extension of the present. The view of the past which developed with evolution saw everything as having a natural place in society. Within this framework it was not so much the case that other views of the past were suppressed; they were unthinkable. For instance, neither the interpretation of women's changing role through history that Friedrich Engels (1884 [1970]) proposed, nor Montelius's 'typological' series of prehistoric marriage arrangements (Arwill-Nordbladh 1998: 8f) were drastically different in their world-view, despite both arguing for forthcoming change and both presenting women in the remote past as living in equality with men. The reasons and assumptions used to make such arguments were entirely rooted in contemporary ideology and had no foundation in actual analysis of the social organization of past societies (Arwill-Nordbladh 1998: 8f).

The important difference is therefore the way women are conceptualized: how they are recognized as subjects of study and the range of issues associated with this recognition. Earlier works saw women's role as naturalized, although it usually was a question of historical or cultural naturalization rather than merely playing out biologically determined roles. This distinction is not always recognized, and the manner in which 'gender archaeology' is a radical departure from earlier approaches therefore not fully appreciated. In their otherwise outstanding paper Conkey and Spector, for example, present archaeology as building on an assumption of cultural continuity in gender arrangements from the earliest hominids into the present (Conkey and Spector 1984: 14). This ignores the different evolutionary assumptions that have been used and debated by archaeology. While a major approach has, as they imply, been inspired by biological determinism and therefore interpreted gender arrangements as unchanged through history, other works were influenced by social evolutionary thinking, seeing gender organization as a result of specific types of social organization and part of a historical development (see also Boye et al. 1988: 84).

Engels's work *The Origin of the Family, Private Property and the State* (1884) marks an important point in this historical-evolutionary understanding of gender. It argues that basic social elements of society (including the social relations between men and women) come into being as the result of historical processes. It also introduces the idea (later somewhat distorted in various stories of an original matriarchy) of 'the world historical defeat of the female sex', the event through which women's original positions of equality and independence was replaced with male dominance. Although presented as a universal evolutionary sequence, this nonetheless explains male dominance as the outcome of a particular historical process rather than as a natural situation. Such social evolutionary ideas are common in European prehistoric studies, which in general work with a simplistic notion of connection between gender and social organization, so that, for instance, the introduction of agriculture commonly is associated with changes in social organization, including the gendered division of labour.

We have now reached a position where it has become clear that prehistoric women can be analysed and displayed in a variety of ways including different feminist versions. There are several potential voices and different agendas. The focus upon visibility *per se* is, however, increasingly recognized as a limiting agenda and a growing emphasis upon the contextualization of gender relations has emerged. I tried to argue for this change in approach in a short paper on women and metalworking in the Bronze Age (Sørensen 1996). An emphasis upon visibility would make a 'traditional' feminist investigation of this topic want to argue that women were metalworkers. The aim would be to make women visible in a part of the archaeological record that has hitherto been denied them. This, despite its immediate appeal, is nonetheless an analysis phrased in terms of sexist views of labour organization that may be both andro- and ethnocentric. Metal production will emerge from such an analysis as either male or female, but it will not emerge as contextual and constituted within social relations. A more ambitious approach would consist of considering women *and* the particular sphere of production and involved activities. This approach is similar to Conkey's argument about contexts of action (1991), and it is also used by Arwill-Nordbladh (1998) in her analysis of the Oseberg Viking Age burial. This approach by its very nature cannot produce such absolute conclusions as the first might, but the contemplation it empowers makes this in the long run a far more constructive and challenging way of engaging with the past. Approaching the research in terms of women and their involvement with a set of practices, in this case metalworking, means we start from a point of knowing that both of these existed, and that in their coexistence they must in different ways have influenced each other. It is furthermore possible to investigate these relationships further, and in particular to explore how and in which ways the various activities and production sequences involved affected people's lives. The central question of this approach becomes how women integrated with the social and material aspect of any particular technology.

In terms of a feminist archaeology the obvious strength of such an investigation is that prehistoric women can be maintained centrally in our research independently of whether they were 'central' to a particular activity such as metalworking. It avoids the absolutism forced by associating from the outset social membership with particular roles. Approaching these as separate identities, rather than hierarchical ones, it will succeed in finding both. Centralizing women in this manner, and securing their presence in our research agendas and interpretations of the past, will, however, have certain costs. Primarily, this approach will be less about taking over the past or replacing men. Prehistoric women will not necessarily and always emerge from it as 'equal' (whatever that means) to men in the past; but they will share, if not take the centre stage, in the analysis. In other words, a prehistory of extremes where women either 'are' or 'are-not's' (which can produce very effective politicized interpretations) is replaced by a multi-dimensional past in which women participate by definition but are not guaranteed access to all roles and values. I have contrasted these two emphases – visibility or presence – as an identifying, as opposed to an inclusive, approach, believing that the latter will be increasingly needed in archaeology.

As we variously respond to and react against traditional practices and politics of archaeology, we must be aware of the danger of closure and how easily (and unknowingly) this is created through strategic action and statements. Our task should not be to demonstrate that women were present in (pre)history because, of course, they were there; nor should we painstakingly try to appropriate certain practices and technologies for women. Rather, knowing that both women and men were present, we should aim to explore and understand how they interacted and how social structures and ideologies affected this interaction and were themselves shaped by it.

The desire and demand for visibility, incorporation and recognition run as a theme through many of the earlier feminist arguments. This makes presentist reasons, rather than the need to understand society, appear as the main motivation for the attention towards gender. Without compromising the feminist emphasis upon change, the investigation of the past can nonetheless be reasoned far more broadly – including its ability to study a variety of gender formations. There are, however, also very fundamental issues about the production of knowledge and how it is authorized that have emerged from these concerns. Discussions of equity, of visibility and of presence are, therefore, never trivial. On the contrary, they are fundamental for understanding the nature of disciplinary culture and for our ability to insert gender as an explicit topic at its many levels of practice.

3
Theorizing Gender: Sex and Gender

I spill some milk. Kim Michael, who was then two, looks at me sternly and says 'Naughty boy!'.

From its beginning gender archaeology has had its own specific aims and concerns; it is, however, only fairly recently that it has also begun to contribute to the general development of archaeological methods and theory. Despite this maturing it is nonetheless obvious that it is with respect to its theoretical foundations that gender archaeology is least secure and where it is most lacking in autonomy. This and the following chapter will therefore discuss the main theoretical components that are embedded within gender archaeology, their status and importance for the future direction of the field. My concerns are both to acknowledge how our understanding of these issues are part of and deeply affected by the discussions in the social sciences generally and to explore how archaeology may establish its own position within these debates. Basic to such an approach is the knowledge that gender is not a stable, objective identity or structure. Gender has several facets and dimensions that may be differently explored by the varied abilities and techniques of different disciplines. This means, furthermore, that archaeology should not simply borrow its understanding of gender from another discipline, be it anthropology or psychology. Archaeology must explore and develop how it, as a distinct discipline (understood as a specific and distinct manner of engaging in observation and interpretation), understands gender.

Thus gender may be differently defined depending on the interpretative context – and it may shift from being understandable as, for instance, a psychological state of being to a range of material effects. This is not, however, a matter of alternatives: it is not a question of different definitions of gender but rather of how we in our diverse practices respond to the fact that gender is expressed and affected in many different ways. Emphasizing one dimension of gender – let's say the ways gender difference affects the distribution of resources – does not deny the importance of, for example, sexuality in gender discourse.

As a social construct the relationship and dependencies between such different dimensions may, however, be drawn upon and recognized in different ways. Rather than finding the nexus of gender in one particular dimension, the social sciences should recognize and investigate its different expressions. It is for these reasons that the concern in the following chapters is with establishing a particular disciplinary discourse for the study of gender, rather than approaching it as an entity existing outside disciplinary contexts.

The sex–gender discussion

The reference to a sex–gender division is a relatively recent phenomenon in the social sciences. It arose with the influence from the women's movement, which from the 1960s inspired and provoked disciplinary self-reflection and the development of new and more 'appropriate' analytical frameworks. It has furthermore been influenced and its arguments expanded by feminist and gender-informed ethnographies. During the 1970s and 1980s social anthropology became increasingly interested in the diversity of gender arrangements contained within the ethnographic record. This showed that gender arrangements within some societies do not match sexual divisions. Other disciplines, such as sociology, began to explore the socially constructed values and meaning ascribed to individuals through gender ideology and politics. These interests led to the conclusion that sex and gender are neither necessarily the same nor absolutely overlapping identities, statements that initiated much debate about their difference, including arguments about the separateness of sex and gender identities.

Scott, outlining this development for history, argues that different reasons, variously associated with or disassociated from a feminist political agenda, can in fact be traced in the introduction of the term 'gender' within different contexts (1986). Despite the various routes towards the appropriation of this distinction and its accompanying concepts, the outcome has in general been similar. 'Sex' was maintained as the reference to biological characteristics, in particular reproductive capacities and external genitalia, while 'gender' was introduced to refer to and emphasize a social/cultural construction. The aim was the insistence on the fundamental *social* quality of gender and the distinction between these two aspects (the social and the biological) of a person.

With the term *gender*, an analytical concept was introduced that gave a new meaning, reasons and possibilities to women's studies. It did, however, also more or less explicitly emphasize society rather than women or woman. There were therefore political implications associated with its introduction. Scott argues, for instance, that while, on one hand, gender was a powerful analytical concept which could permeate established debates and challenge taken-for-granted assumptions about sex and social behaviour, it, on the other hand, removed *women* (at times consciously due to political pressure) from the vocabulary and analysis, replacing it literally with a neuter (Scott 1986). Such replacements, furthermore, were not merely cosmetic; they did in fact signal a turn from attention towards women *per se* as a focus for our investigations to an increased appreciation of the relationship between women and men as a necessary part of social analysis. In this development gender studies have severed their links to the earlier women's movement and also sometimes collide with explicit feminist politics. They have, however, also introduced a forceful, analytically well-formulated concept and associated subject matter into mainstream academic discourse.

The distinction, as first articulated, presented sex as a biological given and gender as a social or cultural construction. The former was therefore non-cultural, static, scientifically measurable and unproblematic, while the latter was a specific contextual construction. The substantial challenging, and to some extent even revolutionary, implications of this separation was that gender – as culture – obviously can be understood only through analysis and study. This was a powerful analytical statement. It could, furthermore, be made to appear scientifically acceptable relatively easy (see also comments on the relationship to positivism in chapter 2), which made possible its permeation of established debates challenging naturalized assumptions about sex and social behaviour. Through this, an aspect of individual and societal behaviour that had previously been taken for granted was now problematized and included in our studies. In addition it was accepted – largely due to influences from neighbouring disciplines – that gender is a structuring principle within society and thus is a fundamental element of social organization and of societal change (Claassen 1992a, Conkey and Spector 1984, Sørensen 1992). Although little real debate about what this means has been conducted, these two 'breakthroughs' have nonetheless been influential and expansive for the discipline.

While there was no agreement as to the exact nature of the relationship between sex and gender, gender archaeology has nonetheless almost universally taken this distinction for granted, and to some extent defines itself by arguing that these are separate categories, and that their separation should be maintained in and inform our analysis of the past. This has been one of the most central theoretical statements of gender studies. Recently, however, obvious concerns have emerged regarding the practical application and political ramifications of this distinction, and, more particularly, the ontological status of sex, due to its arguable cultural dimension, has become questioned. The distinction between sex and gender, which has been one of the central premises of gender archaeology, is therefore currently being reassessed in a manner that may drastically influence our understanding of the nature of sex and thus its role in social construction. Further attention to this distinction, and how we may apply it constructively and analytically in studies of prehistoric societies, is urgently needed.

Prior to further consideration of these issues it is useful to recognize that the distinction that has been made has tended to express itself in terms of, and is being analysed as representing, a dualistic conception of body and mind, as discussed, for example, by Gatens (1996: xii). This point is significant for gender archaeology in two ways. First, this point provides some of the background for understanding the characteristics of current discussions of sex, sexuality and gender in so far as they commonly are embedded within or at least affected by that same duality. Being aware of the dominance of this world-view and how it in itself is a construction may help to produce a critical distance to such notions of duality. This amongst other implications may assist us to salvage the feminist focus upon the construction of difference and at the same time deconstruct the ways in which we think about and analyse this (Scott 1990). Recognizing that a dualist notion of mind–body has been embedded in gender studies makes obvious how these identities have lent themselves to easy categorization whereby the notion of both gender and sex as continuous components of changing lives – both individually and as social norms – has been lost (see also Meskell 1996, Sofaer-Derevenski 1998). Second, being concerned with societies other than our own, archaeology should be particularly wary of basically ethnocentric (as well as androcentric) ontologies. If what is commonly presented as an essentially Cartesian mind–body duality is a result of the ways in which Western philosophers have dealt with difference, and if, furthermore, the notion of this as a clear philosophical distinction has been further exaggerated by feminism in its need to create opposition,* then this should make us wonder about how other societies think and construct difference, rather than assume the same duality to be universally relevant. However, while this point is rela-

* The philosopher S. James has argued that the often repeated reference to the sex–gender division as a continuation of an essentially Cartesian mind–body split misrepresents some of Descartes' argumentation (S. James, unpublished paper presented at the 'Symposium on Gender Studies at Cambridge', 7 March 1998). It is therefore interesting to reflect upon why feminism has so consistently referred to Descartes (e.g. Gatens 1996, Grosz 1994, Meskell 1996) and furthermore why in interpreting this 'inheritance' from Descartes it has so far

tively easy to make it is far more difficult not to think and analyse societies in these familiar terms.

The distinction between sex and gender has not affected all archaeology, and the terms are still at times used interchangeably or misleadingly. There is, however, a common and generalized notion of a difference between sex and gender, which is now widely held. The increased use of the word 'gender' also attests to the subtle and widespread influence of this debate even amongst archaeologists not actively engaged with it. One may therefore argue that the clarification of how gender archaeology understands these terms and how their recognition and interrelations should be considered is currently one of the main tasks of gender archaeology. Participating in the discursive development of the analytical framework and, in particular, adapting it to the specific discursive milieu of archaeology is also, I would argue, essential. If the discipline begins to engage critically and constructively with the 'translation' of general gender concerns into a specific archaeological enterprise, then this may enable gender archaeology to study past societies in a manner that aims at challenging and elucidating our knowledge about the nature and mechanisms of various gender arrangements. Through this, archaeology can also look beyond immediate presentist objectives, that is, objectives which have a clearly perceived and predictable contribution to current conditions, and aim to enrich our understanding of gender as a general social phenomenon by pursuing its diversity, including unfamiliar or unforeseen characteristics.

What is sex? – current discussions within archaeology

The term 'sex' has usually been used to refer to biological characteristics, which on a general level relate to people's reproductive abilities. In this sense sex can be established through DNA, chromosomes or external genitalia. The latter two are currently variously emphasized or questioned in discussions of what constitutes sex, sexual differentiation and sexual identity.

In archaeology, sex, as biology, at the most fundamental level is based entirely upon observation of physical characteristics of the body.

---

ignored the possibility that his argument constituted a more subtle understanding of the relationship between the mind and its body. It is tempting to understand this reference to and reaction against philosophical 'fathers' in terms of a developing approach's need to position itself in opposition to earlier and arguably fundamental views.

The characteristics selected are founded upon assumptions of sexual difference in shape, stature, build, solidity of particular parts of the body and on the notion of two sex categories. The sex determination of prehistoric skeletons is furthermore based on the assumption that they are sexually dimorph in a manner similar to modern humans, an assumption made even for the earliest fossil record (e.g. Hager 1997a: 10–15). The criteria employed in such determination may be expanded to include more disputed features such as, for example, skeleton wear patterns that some consider evidence of childbirth (e.g. Gejvall 1970), while the use of DNA as yet plays a limited practical role within archaeology.

Recently this stable, apparently scientific and objective, notion of sexual division has been criticized and questioned within various subjects (for discussion see, for instance, Laqueur 1990). The theoretical arguments found in these discussions have certain bearings on the question of whether and how archaeology should and can maintain a distinction between sex and gender and what it would be about. The most fundamental critique has focused upon the question of whether sex itself is a cultural construction. Variously influenced by psychoanalysis, feminism, postmodernism and queer-theories, it has been argued that the binary notion of sex and gender disregards the reality of sex as experience and behaviour and thus excludes from its analysis groups such as homosexuals (and third or fourth genders or other specially constituted groups). In effect, it is argued that sex is a contextual issue (Laqueur 1990). This, on another level, has led to discussions of how our social studies in their disregard of this diversity have become framed within established structures of power and dominance.

Within archaeology the first substantial critique of the use of biological variables for sex classification was made by Nordbladh and Yates (1990). They argue that from a biological point of view there are not just two sexes but in fact a range of differences between two poles, which means that the polarized classification 'male' and 'female' is arbitrarily decided in disregard of the variability involved. Their point is that sex is experienced and learned, rather than either a duality or discrete and non-overlapping categories, and that each culture constructs its own sexual categories, relating them differently to the life cycle of the individual. They suggest that the binary opposition should be replaced by the concept of spectrum (1990: 222). This, however, mixes biological differences with the social recognition and response to them. Thus, the idea of spectrum may well be very appropriate as regards chromosome composition, but it is not relevant to social analysis unless the society studied structures its recognition of sex in a correspondingly undifferentiated fashion. Even if a society produces three or four sex categories out of the biological differences, then the concept of spectrum regarding the constituting variables is still only relevant in terms of what that society denies, suppresses or is unaware of, that is, how it creates categories out of a continuum. The approach that they propose is therefore probably rarely, if ever, relevant in terms of social practices and cultural reality. This is exactly the point of gender in its relationship to sex: it creates its structures or categories in accordance not with any specific biological realities but on the basis of a social conception of what these biologies are about and how they should be classified. Nordbladh's and Yates's argument, rather than introducing a concept of sex that is reflexive in terms of variations in cultural practices, seems to suggest that sex *is* constituted as a spectrum, which basically argues that detailed biological differences, that are not necessarily either observed or clearly experienced, constitute sex. Thus in part of their argument they seem to be referring to a concept of sex that is directly informed by detailed biological variation. In this argument, it is therefore not the existence of sex that is at stake, but rather our ability to classify it. Their approach is at the same time also clearly influenced by Lacanian psychoanalysis which questions the ontological stage of sex and sexual identity and thus problematizes their construction at an existentialist level, rather than merely a formal one. In this part it is the independent existence, and thus the ontological status, of sex that is being challenged. The same influence is also present in Yates's interpretation of Scandinavian rock carvings (1991, 1993). There he outlines how the constitution of the self happens as the individual child acquires language, arguing that sex – its recognition by the self/its experience – is a cultural construct just as gender is. One does not learn, it is argued, one's sex independently of acquiring the language to express it (1993: 53ff).

Influenced by Foucault's work on sexuality (1978), which argues that our understanding of sex has been shaped by our discourse on it, a wider tendency towards locating sex as experience and a corresponding tendency of being concerned with the body and sexuality rather than gender has recently emerged in archaeology (e.g. Knapp and Meskell 1997, Meskell 1996, Thomas 1996). The argument, as it gets perpetuated within various debates, seems to be that since the category 'sex' in itself is a regulatory ideal (after Foucault 1978) it is a fallacious concept. This seems a problematic interpretation of the point emerging from the observation of regulatory ideals; in particular, it appears that different levels of analysis become confused in this critique. There is a distinct difference here between using the term as an analytical category, employed to understand an aspect of human identity formation that societies commonly regulate and normalize, and the assumption that the term describes the experience of sex or that it can be an objective, unaffected account of what sex is. The regulation of sex and sexuality is a social reality that our analysis aims to study and elucidate. If sex is also social, rather than merely biological, then it, as a term used in analysis of society, will unavoidably imply regulation. We must accept that, having revealed the social dimension of sex, we are not at liberty to deny or ignore the extent to which this is about regulation. Sex as an analytical concept is not *per se* a prescriptive term establishing either how societies should be or necessarily revealing the variation which social concepts of sex suppress, rather it is a term aiming at understanding social categorization and practices that are prescriptive in terms of how bodies are understood. Discussing other dimensions of sex means a change of focus aiming, for example, at analysing how tensions between individual experiences of sexuality and their social sanctioning are expressed. Critiques of the concept and usage of the term 'sex' as referring to a regulatory ideal are, therefore, frequently misleading inasmuch as sex often takes the form of regulatory practices and categorizations while the arguments seem to imply that it should rather be concerned with the individual understanding and experience of sex and sexuality; that I think is another matter. The problems arising from sex as a regulatory ideal are therefore primarily relevant at another level, since we must question whether we can critically analyse normative and regulatory practices through concepts which already have these regulations built in. This, however, relates to a more general epistemological problem about the possibility of knowledge. The solutions to the problem that meaning and expectations are already embedded in language and are within the terms that we bring to our analysis is not, however, simply to deconstruct the category of sex, as this shifts the focus of analysis to that which is suppressed, rather than providing a more complex understanding of the construction of regulatory mechanisms and ideals.

Such a shift in emphasis is, however, currently taking place. The growing attention towards sexuality, rather than gender or sex, risks privileging the latter as the individual experience of sexuality rather than social practice and in doing so it may ignore the critical question of how socially sanctioned 'normalities' are created. This shift ignores that conventions *are* created, and how strongly they affect both expectations and behaviour, that is, it risks presenting all sexual feelings and experiences as socially equal and sees them in terms of a sameness desired by current political ideologies, despite the social reality of close but complex associations between sex, sexuality, violence, suppression and dominance. It also easily assumes that sexuality, that is sensations and practice, dominates over and above physical characteristics in the assignment of sexual identity. This moves attention from gender, which (although also a dynamic between individual and society) is primarily a social and cultural construction, to the individual construction of self and identity. Recognition of both biological/physiological and psychological variations in our sex identity and sexual make-up should not make us disregard the strong social influences and normative tendencies that people are also affected by. The individual and society are not, of course, unrelated, but they provide different foci of understanding (and thus of research). The current interest in, almost obsession with, the individual may respond to the modern person's sense of self-identity (Shilling 1993), but it may not be the most constructive approach for social analysis generally and for historical studies specifically. In particular, it provides inherently limited understanding (in the sense of critical engagement with a set of evidence and associations) of other cultures and places, such as the past. Thus, while current debates about sexuality and the critiques of sex as given biological categories are extremely useful and vital, they must also be recognized as causing a not entirely desirable tendency of replacing social assignment of sex roles with the individual experience of sexuality. In this shift of emphasis we risk two different kinds of reality being confused.

Archaeology, I would argue, can constructively hold on to the recognition that sex is commonly constructed, understood and reacted to in terms of distinctions between people, and that these are often construed in terms of a few or only two sexes. It is interesting here to consider the implications of Laqueur's argument that the notion of two distinct (or, one would assume, any other number of distinct categories) sexes is explicable only within the context of battles over gender and power (1990: 11) and similarly to recognize the social emphasis in Foucault's statement that the construction and understanding of sex cannot be isolated from its discursive milieu (1978). While these two texts are used for different arguments, their common emphasis upon the social and discursive aspect of sex suggests that the critique of sex as a biological given does not have to result in sex as a fluid identity or an entirely existentialist matter. In fact, the various discussions tend to return in one manner or another to a notion of constructiveness. The essential issue is therefore not whether sex is subject to social categorization, but to what its construction refers, and therefore also how sex may have different social foundations and emphasize specific differences between people as it is created and recognized personally and socially. Therefore, arguing, as some do (e.g. Butler 1990, Laqueur 1990) that both sex and gender are socially constructed and similarly constituted does not mean that they are necessarily the same, and nor does this directly inform us about their dependencies and interrelations (Laqueur 1990). As a practical, mundane example will show, pink frills are in many contemporary societies strongly associated with femaleness but this has no obvious pre-existing relationship to sexual identity. The ways in which the two identities are interwoven and yet separate become clear if a person wears pink frills. Depending upon the socially recognized sex of the person, this will give rise to two different interpretations: a woman dressed in a female outfit or a man dressed in a female outfit, but it will not be seen as a man dressed in a man's outfit. Thus, while interrelated, gender and sex are also different and, in particular, they relate to and affect different aspects of our behaviour.

Another point is that while this critique is an interesting development it does potentially threaten the core issues and reasons for gender studies, whose political agenda is often radical but nonetheless always also social. An additional problem arises from how the investigations into sexuality, in the form that has recently informed the social sciences, is curiously male-centred and easily provides a disturbing sense of privileging androcentric (whether homo- or heterosexual) experiences as an undercurrent in discourse and interpretation. It has, for example, been pointed out that some approaches, like those influenced by Lacan, arguably reintroduce an Aristotelian notion of women as 'lack' (Gatens 1996: vii). The current critique of sexuality thus both furthers interest in gender studies and at the same time potentially threatens them by changing their reasons and reintroducing male experiences – albeit this time individualized – as the central view of the world. In response to this collision between feminist interests and the male 'appropriation' of the understanding of sexuality, gender studies and feminism have begun to explore a number of alternative avenues. Gatens and others have, for instance, introduced the notion of corporate bodies. As corporate bodies cannot be constructively analysed through the individualism of psychoanalytic theory (Gatens 1996: xii), the social is maintained as the basis of analysis.

A further concern for archaeology is whether this notion of sexuality, disembodied socially and eminently individualistic and fragmented, embedded within the psychological experience of postmodernity, is appropriate for prehistoric societies. Appreciating the cultural dimension of our discussion of sex and sexuality we must also accept that our own obsessive interest in the sexualized individual – rather than the sexed person – might be incompatible with prehistoric lives. The andro- and ethnocentric dimensions of current concerns with sexuality, combined with the interests in the individual rather than the social, make some of these debates only peripherally relevant to gender archaeology, although they should neither be ignored nor totally rejected – just 'handled with care'.

It is therefore interesting that sex and its social importance can also be reconsidered in manners different from those inspired by psychoanalysis. Some of the social science discussions that maintain a focus upon gender as a social construct may therefore be more instructive for archaeology's further development of its gender studies. For instance, Gatens's discussion of the social or corporate body provides an interesting alternative view (1996). She points out that the 'privileged relation which each individual has to her or his own body does *not* include a privilege over its construction' (ibid.: 35, original emphasis). This means that bodies are sexed, and that society recognizes 'its' bodies as differently sexed. She also shows that it is significant to accept that societies, despite transgressionary practices and contrary to personal experiences, in general see bodies as variations upon male and female. This, amongst other points, shows that for most of our analysis of society, such as the investigation of the maintenance of gender difference, the diversity suggested by variables like either chromosomes or individual psychology may be essentially irrelevant. This notion of the sexed social body can usefully be explored in interpretations of gender, as sex understood like this is neither neutral, and thus easily separated and categorized, nor personal. Gender will therefore be firmly attached to sexed bodies although it will also, as will be discussed later, go far beyond their biologies.

In addition to physical sex determination of skeletons, archaeologists also routinely assign sex to prehistoric individuals by inference due to assumptions of correspondence between sex and cultural practices or objects (e.g. Gibbs 1987). One may call these contextually determined sex markers. That practice is, of course, based on an assumption about normative associations between sex and behaviour. This is not a new aspect of the discipline, and intensive debates about the attribution of various objects to 'the sexes' are already found in the archaeological literature during the nineteenth century (as discussed in chapter 2); normative categorizations have affected the entire discipline ranging from its displays to the identification of objects. The assumption of association between sex and objects is therefore deeply embedded within the discipline, and in practice archaeological determination of sex is often given greater authority than a biological one. The presence of a sword in a grave thus makes this a male grave, and extremely convincing biological arguments are needed to change this identification. This, amongst many other examples, is illustrated by the famous Mesolithic burial from Barum, Sweden. The presence of a flint blade meant that the grave was consistently interpreted as a male grave, despite the 'fragility' of the skeleton, until it was argued on the basis of the skeleton that the person had had multiple pregnancies (Gejvall 1970). A similar example is provided by the rich Iron Age burial from Vix in France, where there has been considerable reluctance to accept that this was the burial of a woman, despite the presence both of a 'female' skeleton and objects traditionally associated with women. Alternative interpretations, including the proposal of this being the burial of a transvestite priest, have accordingly been attempted (for discussion see Arnold 1991, 1996: ·156). This common assumption of a link between sex and material culture suggests that, on one hand, the notion of gender, that is, an identity expressed through practice and norms, suits archaeological practice and, on the other hand, it causes some confusion about whether it is gender or sex that is being referred to and studied.

Finally, recognizing the range and complexity of the issues raised, it seems important to accept that the response of the discipline to these different arguments neither should nor can be dictated centrally. We must, however, understand that sex is not as easy and straightforward an aspect of either our biology or identity as was previously assumed. It seems now convincingly argued that sex in itself is at least to some extent affected by discourse and thus is constructed culturally. There is also, however, wide disagreement both about how this may relate to physical and biological characteristics and about how this affects the distinction between sex and gender.

What is gender? – current discussions and archaeological practice

Gender is best understood as a set of values that assign gendered meaning to behaviour and affect that behaviour. Through such meaning, culturally specific notions of femininity and masculinity, of what it means to be a woman or a man, and various variations on these themes are constructed. Such meanings are created through rules, in particular those concerned with exclusions, notions of normality and values, and they are articulated and maintained through objects as well as through discursive, especially ritualized, and non-discursive practices. It is also a characteristic of gender that it is the subject of subversion and provides a focus for 'deviations'. Gender, therefore, is not static; it needs to be continuously renegotiated, confirmed and maintained. All its forms and meanings can be transformed and may be considered transitional. This means that gender is dynamic, and it gives rise to gender identity, roles, relations, ideology and politics. It affects actions and understanding and it uses objects; but in itself it has not any form or matter. Nor is gender exclusively about women or men; it is about people's relationships in terms of dynamic and negotiable differences. Gender is then a basic aspect of how societies organize themselves and of how individuals understand themselves. It is also a fundamental influence behind the organization of different types of labour and for relationships between differently constituted people. Gender is therefore basic and fundamental to how society appears and functions, although it is neither deterministic nor necessarily primary as it itself is constituted by society. Therefore, although we commonly refer to gender as a structure, it is probably more constructive to recognize it as a dynamic within communities. Gender cannot be observed; only the effect of gender can be felt, traced and studied.

The most common critique levelled at gender has been that it privileges gender as a structuring principle before class, age and race differences. There has also been considerable concern with whether gender relations have universal characteristics, such as the widespread subordination of women. A less explicit but nonetheless relevant question is whether gender is always in discourse, what is its purpose and how is it constructed?

Within archaeology only some of these concerns have been widely debated. Amongst these the current emphasis within sociology upon the self-recognition of gender identity and the interest within psychoanalysis and sociology in notions of subjectivity and embodiment have gained some attention. The reactions to these debates are so far limited, but one can nonetheless discern different views within the discipline. Sofaer-Derevenski, for instance, considers this emphasis a problem for archaeology, as it cannot fully employ a concept of embodied subjectivity focused upon the individual. With regard to mortuary practices (the contexts where archaeology arguably meets the individual most directly), she supports the position that views burials as social arenas where society's perception of the individual is constructed, rather than seeing the grave and its context as directly relevant to discussions of subjective identity. Thus the gender relations that may be observed in burial practices would largely relate to 'corporate notions of gender identity and gender appropriate behaviour' (Sofaer-Derevenski 1998), an archaeological approach to gender that has some similarity with, for instance, Gatens's notion of the corporate body. On the other hand, others, such as Meskell, have tried to embrace the notion of the individual, and she proposes that burials may be understood as expressions of embodied subjectivities (1996, 1997).

Before moving on to further consideration of archaeology's understanding of gender, it should be stressed that we cannot excavate gender – and that this is not a matter of methodology but of its ontological existence. There is not a particular feature of the body that constitutes its gender nor a particular object that contains it. Despite this, the nature of the cultural construct, gender, that we aim to study is rarely considered, and gender is basically assumed or inferred from other characteristics. This is well illustrated by mortuary studies, where archaeologists are confronted with individuals who had both sex and gender: how can these dimensions be identified and understood? And how do we avoid either collapsing them into each other or identifying them through assumptions about cross-cultural universals? In practice there has been an obvious tendency of either accepting that sex is the only variable that can be observed or of using differences within, for example, grave goods or burial practice to identify gender. Thus, the same variables are often used to establish both the sex and the gender of the person. This is obviously problematic. It is, of course, possible that grave goods or other variables were used simultaneously in the construction and communication of several different dimensions of a person, but as these identities were formed through distinct discourses the objects are likely to have been explored in different ways. The critical questions are, therefore, on one hand, the relationship between sex and gender and how this involves materialities, and, on the other hand, how the same variables within a context may be making references to and commenting upon several dimensions of the person.

On the relationship between sex and gender

The relationship between sex and gender has never been properly clarified, despite the prevalent acceptance of their distinction. It is in fact often presented as an under-theorized relationship. There are, of course, many views about it, but basically it can either be a question of total dependency or of different degrees of separateness. Sayers has characterized these two poles as 'biological essentialism' and 'social constructionism' respectively (1982: 3). The former proposes a direct relationship between sex and gender and argues for the existence of an essential woman, whose feminine characters may be expressed at different levels. This is, for example, expressed in notions of gender as a system of cultural codes inscribed on biological sex (Maurer 1990: 414, Lesick 1997: 34). Various views within social constructionism, on the other hand, argue that the influence of biology (sex) is indirect and is mediated by the way sex is interpreted and construed within society. Feminists have expressed both views.

A third view has recently emerged, proposing that there is no distinction between sex and gender. Butler, for instance, stresses that sex is always already gendered (Butler 1990: 7). Within archaeology a similar argument is found in the psychoanalytically informed part of Nordbladh's and Yates's discussion of sex (1990). A slightly different argument, which nonetheless has a similar effect, has been mounted by Moore, who suggests that the embodiment of sex and gender means that they affect all things and thus are indistinguishable; in effect they are the same (1994: 14). Meskell represents a similar view within archaeology (1996). She argues, after Moore, that using sex to differentiate between bodies and gender to indicate the variable social constructions placed upon those differentiated bodies obscures rather than clarifies cross-cultural analysis (ibid.: 3). In her comments upon the various feminist approaches to the body and their relevance to archaeology, Meskell criticizes social constructionists, Marxists as well as psychoanalytical feminists, for presuming that sex is fixed and for focusing upon gender and its corresponding cultural meanings and values (ibid.: 4). She further criticizes the group concerned with the lived body and sexual difference, exemplified by Butler and Gatens, for not acknowledging that the body is also recursively engaged with culture. Her review of these different developments is obviously interesting to archaeology, although her comments and critique may not be as clearly informed by archaeological concerns as may be desired, neither do her arguments escape critique. For instance, the analytical emphasis upon gender that she associates with social constructionism does not necessarily imply that the body is seen as biologically determined and fixed. Rather, it argues for difference in the relationships in which these two dimensions can be placed and how they are formulated and enacted. It has, for instance, increasingly been recognized that in addition to social and cultural influences on the construction and recognition of sex there is also an individual temporal dimension to this construction, as sexual identity usually varies through the lifetime of the individual. Clearly, the variability within sexuality is not unacknowledged within the above-mentioned approaches. The main difference arises from what importance is given to the recognition that sex and gender are not independent identities, even if it is not clear how they relate to each other. For archaeology, the ability to consider gender without sex is, however, an important option. Gender, despite its association with sex, is also different from it because it is differently embodied. Furthermore, the manner in which it can affect behaviour and permeate meaning in areas not immediately reachable by sex or sexuality underscores such differences.

Meskell's critique of approaches that focus upon the idea of the lived body starts from a particular level of application: the individual. As argued earlier, it is, however, doubtful whether and how the current attention on the individual can be constructively employed in essentially historical studies and what its usefulness is regarding the potentials of archaeological data. Her arguments, while a challenge to archaeology, are therefore probably not pointing towards a lasting resolution regarding the discipline's understanding of gender. Responding to the problems arising from our concern with sex and gender by replacing society with the individual ignores the challenge emerging from how difference may be understood. We should rather look towards the deconstruction of the dualism associated with gender and sex identity that is emerging from various recent explorations of these concepts. Arguments by, for example, Butler (1993), Gatens (1996), Moore (1994) and Scott (1990) suggest that we can aim to understand and investigate difference in such a manner that this does not return us to a traditional notion of oppositions.

This emphasis upon understanding and developing our conceptualization of difference provides an interesting challenge for the further development of an archaeology of gender. It suggests that we may develop a conceptual framework that enables a constructive social analysis of difference(s), rather than denying or diluting both its/their presence and relevance. It may also help towards avoiding comparison and relationships automatically becoming a matter of hierarchy. This is also an emphasis upon diversity and structure that corresponds well to many vaguely recognized patterns in the archaeological record. Not structuring our analysis in terms of oppositions and symmetries but through the recognition of different kinds of difference, and their evaluation and manifestations, provides gender studies both with new freedom of thought and the practical potential to investigate such expressions. From the position of archaeology, and concerned as I am with its ability to claim relevant knowledge about prehistoric gender relations, I suggest that difference is still the central question, rather than proposals such as 'reclamation of individual contextualised bodies, rather than universalist collectives, may provide a more appropriate level from which to conduct our analysis' (Meskell 1996: 5). Foregrounding the individual in this manner, even if the dynamic dependency between individual and society is still acknowledged, can provide 'hot' interpretation, and it may, in particular circumstances (such as Meskell's Egyptian burials), allow us to examine how individuals are variably constituted within specific contexts (Meskell 1996: 6). It is, however, problematic in that it artificially isolates the individual (the 'I' is not studied as part of the 'We'). As an approach it is also limited in that it offers no guidelines for (and little recognition of) the analysis of society as institutions and structures, or of gender as ideology and as normative and regulatory processes.

The critique of sex as a biological given has made it apparent that current gender studies must forge an understanding of gender which neither underestimates nor neutralizes its relationship to sex, while, at the same time, neither reducing nor negating its social dimension. Thus it seems that we have come to a point within the discipline where the earlier feminist distinction between sex and gender cannot be maintained on a theoretical level, at least not in terms of a biological given versus a socially constructed identity. Both sex and gender will probably have to be recognized as affected by social context and as being closely aligned and associated. It does not, however, seem constructive (or accurate) to argue as, for example, Laqueur (1990) and Butler (1993) do, that there is no distinction between sex and gender. Even if no other argument could be mounted in defence of their difference it would be sufficient to acknowledge that we need this distinction to make better sense of the complex web of meaning and significance surrounding our gendered and sexualized lives. Furthermore, focusing upon the materiality of gender, that is, the practical and physical effect of gender upon people's lives, it is also quite easy to show that despite their interwoven existence the relationship between these two dimensions of our being is not straightforwardly apparent.

It is also important to recognize that the relationships between sex and gender are not clarified by introducing, as is often done, observations of what appear as alternative gender arrangements, such as some cultures having a third gender, that hermaphrodism exists, that gender ideologies can be polymorphous rather than dimorphous, or that not all cultures are shaped by the masculine–feminine division. Such observations are usually used to argue that, due to these alternative arrangements, sex is not relevant for gender (e.g. Lesick 1997: 34, Lingis in Meskell 1996: 3). Such arguments are, however, relevant only if it is assumed that a sex–gender dynamic must necessarily be dualistic. This limitation is not built into the concepts, rather it is due to our failing imagination and the extent that we are embedded in our own particular cultural context. That, not social realities, is what makes us so easily interpret sex–gender relationships in this simple, dualistic manner. The differences referred to in such arguments against a relationship between sex and gender merely demonstrate the variability of sex–gender arrangements; they reveal differences in norms rather than comment upon the relationship between sex and gender in any detailed manner. In this, the analytical ability of the concepts is being confused with how we have tended to interpret them (e.g. Lesick 1997: 33). It is important to recognize, however, that archaeologists who reject a sex–gender relationship on the basis of such varied empirical observations use a fundamentally different logic from those who ar-

gue that archaeology (currently) can not recognize gender independently of sex and sex roles and that therefore the discipline should not
maintain their separation (Claassen 1992b: 3).

Some clarification of archaeology's position in this discussion may
be reached by further investigating what are common assumptions
about the relationship between sex and gender. Do we believe that
these dimensions have different purposes, different reasons for their
existence? Why do we have gender? Is gender necessary? If we approach the literature with these questions in mind, a range of variations predictably appears, but within them certain patterns can be
extracted. There is, for instance, a strong tendency to ascribe to gender some social purposes, which are of a different kind to any role
that we may assign to sex. Although this is not clearly stressed, in a
certain sense gender is interpreted as functional; it has a reason. Conkey
and Gero, for instance, propose that gender is a social structure with
the primary purpose of dividing work between individuals in the society (Conkey and Gero 1991). The emphasis upon gender and labour
division is in fact extremely common, although the reason for the
association is differently perceived (for a detailed discussion see Sofaer-
Derevenski 1998). Others see it as a means of finding appropriate sexual
partners (Claassen 1992b: 3–4). The focus upon the creation of difference, the argument that gender ideology aims to make people different
(e.g. Sørensen 1997), may also be linked to this view. The assumption
that gender has a function or a reason brings up a certain tension,
however. Assuming that gender has a function it is easy also to accept
that these are universal functions, which means that the social construction of gender is not necessarily about gender itself, as it is already there, but about its forms and expressions. Is it then the case,
one must ask, that gender is a universal characteristic of society closely
associated with its recognition of sexed social bodies, and that it is
only the expression and form of gender, that is, its contextual construction, that are depending upon discourse? Gender is then both
structure and social practice, and these two dimensions are evoked
differently. The complexity of the concept of gender, as we have used
it, has, I believe, not been explicitly acknowledged. Its complexity may,
however, nonetheless emerge from how it has influenced interpretations.

Another tendency is to see gender entirely as reflexive. This view is
also commonly found within archaeology, where, for instance, Conkey
and Spector (1984) have emphasized gender in terms of symbolic behaviour and, like Gibbs (1987, 1990), see gender as society's articulation and cultural elaboration of sex roles. This approach can easily
lead to gender becoming subservient to sex, and it has at times led to

the argument that gender is an effect rather than a structure or a principle. This furthermore implies that it is an effect of something, and this tends to become sex, rather than it being recognized as rooted in practice or power relations. This moves gender much closer to sex as it becomes the social acknowledgement and reflection upon sex. Gibbs, for instance, argues for an inextricable link between sex and gender. In her approach the cultural construction of gender arises as a result of society deeming sets of behaviour, attitudes and concepts appropriate for the two sexes and hence defining gender for them (Gibbs 1987: 7). It is important to recognize that, while such approaches easily lead to sex and gender in effect becoming the same, they are based on a conceptualization of sex entirely different from the current arguments about the sameness of sex and gender. The absorption of the two dimensions is in the former arguments entirely due to the reflexive 'servicing' role that gender is assigned, while in the latter it is caused by the concern with the ontological status of sex and its dependency on culture.

Amongst other archaeological reflections upon this relationship Hjørungdal's discussion of the concept should also be pointed out, as she argues that sex should be seen as a metaphor for gender (1994). There is also a growing and very interesting emphasis upon variability and difference where it is argued that gender functions differently in different contexts (Joyce 1996), or it is proposed that gender has several points of reference of which sex is just one (Sofaer-Derevenski 1998). Meanwhile, the maintenance of some kind of separation of sex and gender is generally agreed upon due to the universal fact that there are biological differences between men and women and that societies react differently to those (Moore 1994: 71ff, Sofaer-Derevenski 1998).

4
Theorizing Gender: Negotiation and Practice

Gender negotiation

A central premise of gender archaeology has been that gender is negotiated. This implication has been part of its theoretical foundation at least since Conkey's and Spector's seminal article of 1984; but before then this aspect of gender had been little acknowledged in either feminist or traditional archaeological writings. The new emphasis, arguing for gender as a negotiated difference, a social construction and a question of agency and discourse, shows the emerging relationship between the developing concerns of gender archaeology and various postprocessual and postmodern approaches, as also discussed in chapter 2. It is, however, an aspect of gender which has been given relatively little attention in the archaeological literature, despite its clearly being assumed in much of current gender writing. The root of the statement is clearly to be found in the women's movement. Gender as a social construction is also gender open to change, challenge and difference, and thus to negotiation. There is, however, a striking discrepancy between the theoretical recognition of this dynamic, inherently unstable, aspect of gender relations and the manner in which this has informed interpretation. This disjunction between theoretical insight and practical analysis constitutes an area of obvious conflict. The problem may to some extent be particular to archaeology, or at least particular to the clearly inferential nature of all its claims about social, as opposed to material, conditions. The frequent fall-back to what are essentially structuralist interpretations within gender studies in general suggests, however, that the problem of recognizing and studying negotiation as a real phenomenon may be shared more widely.

Let us, however, as a beginning clarify what social practices it is we are trying to capture when we refer to gender being a negotiated difference. At what levels may this take place, and how may material objects become involved? Negotiation refers to social life being affected by competing interests, which express themselves as rights, obligations and needs. It therefore affects resources and their (re)distribution, invoking, for instance, bargaining and contracts. Our description of what negotiation involves evokes a language of practices and objects. Negotiation is the continuous maintenance of, or attempts at maintaining, an agreed view of rights and obligations. These relationships and appropriations are commonly expressed in terms of resources, and they are often naturalized by associations between objects and categories of people. There is thus frequently a substantial material aspect to negotiation, both in terms of what is being negotiated and of how the result of that process is communicated and rectified. These views about rights and responsibilities are socially and historically specific and they are deeply implicated and affected by contextually created ideologies about the roles and identities of particular groups of people. This means that negotiation about resources is not merely about economic redistribution but also about reinforcing and articulating socially constructed differences between people (Moore 1994: 87). The negotiation that gender studies refer to (or should refer to) therefore embraces more than the explicit creation of male and female appropriate behaviour, as it also informs other practices including political and economic ones. These relationships are not, however, either hierarchical or causal; rather they appear as part of each other insofar as, for example, the political and economic implication of membership to gender is immediately affected by the social significance of gender. In fact, one may propose that the ability of (and need for) a continuous on-going negotiation of the meaning of gender may be due exactly to there not being a single focus for its construction. As the identification, interpretation and valorization of gender arise from many dimensions it becomes a fluid, stretchable identity which in the social arena needs to be agreed upon. And it is as an agreement that it becomes a cultural construction.

Thus, gender archaeology should both explicitly incorporate and explore how, despite the apparent problems of instrumentalizing studies of negotiation, real physical actions are involved in such practices. The recognition of these practical elements – products of processes of agreement, maintaining, change, resistance and alternative actions – are essential for the location and observation of negotiating strategies. In response to traditional Marxist discussions of ideology and suppression it has become increasingly argued that people are not necessarily passive and ideologically duped. They recognize that they participate in negotiation of rights and responsibilities, and they may consciously and strategically explore the possibilities provided within contexts and their particular constraints. This active participation and conscious recognition of discourse is not, however, to be simply taken to represent 'free will'. It is rather a question of abilities, of knowable people understanding some of their own situatedness and of making 'the best of it', and also of recognizing how affective space is also created through the influence and power of emotions such as desire and duty. Negotiation goes beyond these personal understandings, however, as it is also about the practices through which people arrive at an agreed understanding of meaning. Moore, in discussing households, emphasizes that

> The ability to provide an interpretation of the terms of . . . [a] contract, or indeed of any set of normative practices and understandings, is, of course, a political ability. Definitions of terms, and interpretations of normative practices and understandings, are political definitions. They are political because they can, in principle, be redefined and contested, and because they will always have material consequences. (Moore 1994: 91)

As negotiation is often about definitions and interpretations of rights, gender negotiation (and thus the maintenance of gender itself) is involved with power (Moore 1994: 92). Gender is, however, also involved with power because the definition and recognition of identities are connected to normative ideas of a particular social order. Thus, it is on the basis of naturalized differences between identities that the rights and needs of particular individuals are established. Needs claims always have a contextual and contested character, and arguments about them necessarily involve discussion of rights which immediately invoke social identities. Such contestations, furthermore, are not just interpretations but practical acts and interventions (ibid.: 100). This means that understanding negotiation involves also considering how politics, power and authority are critically involved in the agreement of meaning and value, and thus affect how they are acted upon (ibid.: 92).

Having theoretically and in the abstract recognized how central negotiation is to the formation of normative agreements about value, meanings, rights and needs, we are still left with the problem of assigning this phenomenon a form through which it can be studied: what does negotiation look like? Such questions, despite their apparent banalities, are central inasmuch as the powerful potentials of these points are only fully released if applied analytically. Basic to the argument is the realization that social reproduction is always about the reproduction of particular sorts of people. As an example of these relationships

Moore's outline of gender involvement in redistribution is useful. She shows how sexual division of labour creates the necessity for redistribution. That means that the system of redistribution will be gendered, and it will be partly gender ideology that bestows the rights and entitlements that provide the framework for bargaining and negotiation about this redistribution (Moore 1994: 102). Accepting this argument means that the struggle over access to economic resources simultaneously becomes a struggle over definitions and meanings, including gendered ones. 'It is through the negotiations that shape the outcome of the system of redistribution that social identities are themselves reproduced and opened up to potential change' (ibid.: 105). While many traditional views of gender division of labour can easily be criticized for their stereotypes and ignorance of cultural variations, it can nonetheless be argued that, at some levels, labour divisions will always exist, since people can neither logistically nor physically do the same things. It is also clear that gender is one of the variables that systematically inform labour division. Moore's argument about the interdependency between the nature of labour division and the politics of redistribution is therefore central to social analysis and in particular to the analysis of negotiation and change within the gendered allocation of resources. Moreover, in this view gender is not merely attached to or being reflexive of these other processes as it in itself is constitutive of economic and political processes (ibid.: 92).

Therefore, for an archaeology of gender the important initial step is to recognize more fully and to explore further how the negotiation of gender implies that a focus or a 'material locus' is needed. It is through this connection that materialities become central. It is obvious that material objects lend themselves well to such discourses about rights and obligations. We may thus suggest that while gender negotiation at a certain level is concerned with establishing normative views upon rights and responsibility, this will in fact commonly be expressed in terms of material resources. The material world is thus often deeply implicated in gender policies.

Agency and gender in archaeology

The focus upon negotiation means that the role of the individual gains some actuality, and a brief consideration is needed here. The concerns with the place of individuals within society and their relationships to each other have been greatly affected by recent discussions in social theory. For archaeology, the works of Giddens (1979, 1984) and Bourdieu (1977, 1990) have been particularly influential. From Giddens the concepts of agency and structuration have been introduced to archaeology (e.g. Barrett 1988), and from Bourdieu the notion of habitus. Both concepts relate to the question of the relationship between individual and society and both have also had some importance for attempts to develop a feminist approach. The background to this interest can be located in the development of post-processual approaches within archaeology. As the increased emphasis upon contextually constituted meaning became critically interested in how this could be reconciled with the construction and maintenance of long-term structures and coherent patterns, attention became focused upon individual actions – their constituent nature and form. Recently, as discussed in chapter 3, an explicit interest in the individual, subjectivity and intersubjectivity (e.g. Meskell 1996, Yates 1991, 1993) and in the body as a phenomenic experience (e.g. Tilley 1994) have also begun to inform some archaeological studies.

Gender studies have been affected by these concerns in essentially two ways. On the one hand, feminism has become increasingly interested in the variability of *women* rather than the analysis of *woman* as a categorical identity and, on the other hand, the stable, almost conservative, character of gender arrangements forces an awareness of cohesion which goes far beyond the activities of the individual. For gender studies the question of the relationship between the individual, gender identity and the larger social context is further fuelled by their own origin in the women's movement, their political awareness and their desire to believe in the possibility of change beyond individual circumstances. The emphasis upon individuals and agency also calls into question how we interpret why women in various cultures have agreed to their own suppression and subservient positions.

Another aspect of the question is how it relates to the serious concern with understanding the position of the individual within structures of power and dominance. Two themes emerge here: resistance and complicity. These, however, as Moore points out, are both types of agencies and of subjectivity (1994: 49–50). Recognizing the relevance of both for understanding individuals within social contexts, we begin to see the roots of some of the complexity surrounding concepts such as agency. Furthermore, while, for example, resistance may be observed, its motivations argued and its effects studied, the ways in which it is made possible practically and emotionally lend itself less easily to our investigation. Actions of resistance or complicity that may initially look rather straightforward often become slippery and appear diffuse regarding their relations to and location *vis-à-vis* both the individual and society; in fact, the boundary between these becomes indistinct, despite an analytical language which locates them as different.

The increased recognition of gender's dual qualities as both category and practice, of gender identity being both constructed and lived (Moore 1994: 49) and of gender as a process of the individual life (Sofaer-Derevenski 1997, 1998) is another reason for the growing interest in the individual. The individual that has become of interest to feminism and gender studies is, however, seen as a unique, gendered person, rather than either a passive member of the category 'woman' or the neuter implied by agency. Meanwhile, the problems of identifying, let alone analysing, the individual and particular structures simultaneously with upholding an appreciation of the nature of society and the emergence of general structures have not been solved. This tension is strongly felt within archaeology where recent developments towards a focus upon the individual, contextual and experiential stand in contrast to archaeology's traditional concern with temporal changes, and arguably also to the obvious potentials of the archaeological record. Breaching this difference is, however, necessary, since interdependency and difference between individual and society have become obvious concerns that must inform our studies of society.

The agent, the individual and archaeology

In the archaeological literature, agency often appears merely as a social player or normative representative of a kind of social entity. The agent of agency is therefore often used in a manner that makes it passive, neutral and neutered, and this severely hinders a sense both of the individual and how individuals become constituted as special kinds of gendered persons.

The neutrality of this agency has been criticized both by feminists and by phenomenologists like Merleau-Ponty. The latter argues that 'Only I can live my body: it is a phenomenon experienced by me and thus provides a perspectival point which places me in the world enabling relations between me and other subjects and objects' (Merleau-Ponty in Meskell 1996: 7, see also Tilley 1994). There have been various responses to the concerns and propositions raised by such critique. In archaeology, Meskell has, for example, argued for focusing upon the contribution of real rather than abstract bodies to their own experience within the milieu of power, although she also acknowledges that there is no pure constitution of the self, since the self is always situated relationally (Meskell 1996).

This later point is related to one of the substantial critiques of the concept of agency which argues that there is not such a thing as a fully knowable actor. No one can ever be entirely aware of the conditions of its own construction; it is impossible to be fully conscious of what one does with one's body even when one has clear intentions (Moore 1994: 53). The limitations of the agency concept may therefore not be solved by a simple focus upon phenomenologically experiencing and existentialistic selfs, as currently suggested by developments within archaeology. The references to either agency or individual, and the approaches they refer to (structuration theory and phenomenology), are based on fundamentally different reasons for interest in people. Attempts at their reconciliation, as seen in some archaeological texts, may, however, easily lead to a perception of the person as either social *or* unique, rather than both. Moore has argued emphatically for the necessity of both elements in social analysis. She stresses how individuals are able to bring a considerable amount of self-reflection to bear on the practices and discourses of day-to-day living. She also argues that bodily praxis can act as a form of self-reflection that does not always enter the discursive. Analysis of agency must therefore include, for example, consideration of such ignored variables as the role of fantasy and desire (Moore 1994). While this argument is helpful, it nonetheless shows that the relationships between agency and social construction, between people's self-understanding and dominant cultural discourses, are complex and remain analytically somewhat problematic.

Post-structuralist approaches at the same time tend to see the individual as fragmented and contingent, rather than as a unified self. To describe the many ways in which individuals understand themselves, the notion of subjectivity has become extensively used in social studies. Subjectivity in post-structuralist debates includes, however, conscious and unconscious thoughts and emotions and the interaction of these with the constitution of the subject through language and discourse (Lupton 1996: 13). This, while appreciating the core elements of the subjective experience of self, may nonetheless fail to recognize or at least spell out the formative interaction with both the surrounding physical materiality and institutional structures, as these are reduced to 'discourse', forming merely the backdrop for practice.

To me it seems that in these discussions the relationship between the individual, as subjectivity and embodiment, and that which is beyond the individual (its intersubjectivity) remains rather unclear. This, however, is a central dilemma for archaeology which, as a discipline, defines and designs its contexts of interpretation materially. Rather than observing actions that result in certain effects, we infer actions from their results. There is therefore a consistent need to decide upon and validate what it is we are studying and at which level of social complexity we can locate the actions that led to the patterns and changes that we observe. This means that the ability to argue for difference between the context of self and the context of society becomes crucial for the above arguments to lend themselves to analysis.

Woman or women: the question of cross-cultural generalizations

Related to this problem, but also in itself a critical issue within gender studies, is the use and value of universal generalizations* about gender and about women specifically. As with other aspects of gender the use of universal generalizations is obviously rooted in the women's movement, which made both demands and claims which were often generalized. The women's movement (largely due to its political agenda) was concerned with women's issues, their rights and status in a manner similar to that of traditional labour movements. It was woman as a representative corporate body that was the concern, not the variability and differences amongst women. Furthermore, within academia the idea of the essential woman, who was largely to be understood through her biology, was a familiar view which epistemologically fitted the largely positivistic regime which dominated much of the sciences. For archaeology, the use of universal generalizations, whether direct or in the form of different types of analogies, was furthermore a familiar procedure and a recognized route to interpretation. Archaeology's relationship to anthropology was in this context central, as the latter provided the pool of analogies and record of human behaviour and social forms, that the former could utilize in its interpretations. Universal and cross-cultural generalizations, together with simple structures such as binary oppositions, have therefore played a significant role in gender archaeology, especially in providing a starting point for challenging existing interpretations and for reaffirming alternative ones. The increased emphasis upon gender as a cultural construction did, however, create a problem for gender archaeology since contextuality and the appeal to universals were contradictory. The further development of feminist and gender studies, with its increased interest in the relationship between the individual and society, the construction of identities and the notion of the insecure state of scientific knowledge, has furthered attention towards the contextual construction of gender (and sex).

---

* Universals do not imply that there will be no exceptions, merely that something is found worldwide in many different contexts and that in all of these the particular phenomenon is common. That women can give birth to children is thus a universal phenomenon despite some women being unable to do so.

This leaves the idea of universal generalizations highly problematic within contemporary thinking (e.g. Damm 1991: 132).

Despite the theoretically unsatisfactory nature of universal generalizations, there are aspects of gender that easily lend themselves to such interpretations. Such aspects should be recognized as critical issues for gender studies as they may indicate areas where the individual and society interact in particular ways. At the base of these generalities lies the reproductive differences between men and women. Women can give birth and men cannot. This is a universal difference (even if exceptions may be found), and it leads to recognizable patterns of differences between men and women. Women are, for example, usually differently, and often more, involved with nurturing and caring for the children. Child bearing and rearing may therefore affect women's mobility in comparison to men's, and this in itself may inform and inspire various types of labour division and collaboration within a community. In fact, various behaviours can be shown to be *in general* more associated with women than with men. Archaeologically, these differences and the generalizations they give rise to have played a prominent role in engendered interpretation. It is often assumed, for example, that men and women were differently associated with public and private domains or that labour was divided up between them. Some interpretations suggest, for instance, that women had different roles in agricultural societies and in pastoral ones, due to their lesser mobility caused by increased fertility and higher birth and infant survival rates in agricultural societies (Leibowitz 1983: 138), or that men hunt and women gather because men are physically stronger and not tied down by children. It is also common to emphasize both physical and emotional differences between men and women, associating the former with strength, aggression and violence, making men the hunters, leaders and warriors of prehistory and women their opposites. The universals may also be more specific, stating, for example, that women are likely to breastfeed for a longer duration in mobile societies than in settled ones. Examples of such generalizations are plentiful and have consistently informed the ways in which we interpret prehistoric societies.

There is, however, an unsolved tension within this way of understanding variability and sameness. It is therefore necessary to ask both how this can be reconciled with an appreciation of the cultural construction of gender, and how this use of universal generalizations is different from stereotyping? To dissolve some of the tension it is, therefore, useful to return to the discussion of gender in chapter 3. There it was proposed that gender was both a structure of difference emerging from society's recognition of its sexed bodies and a practice through which these constructed differences are made meaningful in terms of norms and values. Accepting that gender itself has different dimensions, it is possible to argue that these provide different opportunities and are of varied relevance to universal generalizations. Thus, those dimensions of gender that arise from the recognition of different bodies may lend themselves more easy to generalizations than the practices that take place in response to those differences. This, in turn, may suggest that the existence of gender itself is a general phenomenon. Thus we find universal similarities in terms of there being gender as well as there being bodies. The problem about universals arises therefore first when one recognizes that even the limitation and confinements of these categories are difficult to establish. While bodies can be generalized, attitudes to them and the practices of the body are not universal. For instance, cultural attitudes to breastfeeding are certainly not universal, neither is mothers' participation in it (Maher 1992). The ways in which the body walks, moves or is sexualized can be affected culturally and become constructed within particular contexts. The application of universal generalizations can therefore easily be problematized, and their use recognized as being limited to classification of the world rather than an exploration of it. During the early stage of gender archaeology universal generalizations did, however, provide a relatively easy way of engendering the past, as specific gender arrangements could be assumed rather than having to be investigated (e.g. Randsborg 1984).

By their very nature universal generalizations will easily lead to stereotypical statements as they ignore variations. Stereotypes emerge, however, primarily when universal generalizations become causal mechanisms of something else: 'women are usually smaller then men and they are therefore less aggressive'. Another problematic aspect of universal generalizations is that they are based on specific historic communities, while gender archaeology desires to explore gender arrangements within a much wider temporal dimension. These problems, one could argue, are shared by other explanatory approaches, such as, for instance, certain schools of psychoanalysis which, despite their interest in the unique individual, at a certain level assume an essential woman and are able to postulate universal female psychological features such as the castration complex. The use of generalizations are merely played out at different levels in these approaches. The point is that, despite our current awareness of the contextual construction of many of the dimensions involved, be it of the body or the mind, we construct and expect universal characteristics, and our interpretations are often focused upon the general or generalized versions of specific situations. Again, we notice how the tension between the specific and the general has been neither solved epistemologically nor ontologically clarified.

This, however, is not a problem specific to gender studies but one that affects the entire interpretative project within the social sciences.

The problem inherent within this tendency to generalize is of significance for our understanding of difference. The difference between the sexes, between socially sexed bodies and between gender constructions concerned with rights and values is in principle open and continuous. In practice, however, universalistic comparisons and generalizing tendencies will attempt to classify difference; they will aim to give it familiarity, to provide a key or code for it, as it aims to make the diversity understandable. The Western cultural tradition of understanding in terms of duality will further this tendency and difference will tend to be understood as binary oppositions and in terms of an evaluatory hierarchy. The political implications of this are all too obvious.

> The dominant view of women involves recurrent, although more or less explicit, images of women's incompleteness, which in turn are implicitly used to justify women's differential treatment. In the context of male privilege, female 'incompleteness' invariably amounts to male–female complementarity. Complementarity, in a situation of domination and subordination, leads to women being conceived as both conceptually and actually dependent on men – these assumptions can, however, be challenged by economic or political changes in women's status. (Gatens 1996: xi)

Much of what we associate with gender can easily be presented and thus made intelligible in terms of such oppositions. But the ease with which these variables lend themselves to dualities only helps to hide their greater complexity and their temporal dimensions. The particular image of the nature of women that they have been reproducing has furthermore served to curtail and contain our understanding of women's cultural possibilities (Gatens 1996: xi). Gender as lived is hardly imagined, let alone understood, through these principles. The use of universal generalities and the focus upon cross-cultural comparisons are therefore extremely problematic entry points for a gender archaeology, since from the start they are fixed within certain ways of understanding gender.

Gender (and) archaeology

A concern with how one may observe gender and how one would know that it is gender that one is looking at is often raised (e.g. Claassen 1992b: 2–3). Such questions cannot, however, be answered in the terms in which they are phrased – gender is a process, a set of behavioural expectations or an affect, but it is not a thing. Meanwhile, as archaeology looks at things, the discipline needs to establish how gender can appear within contexts as we define them. One of the major concerns of gender archaeology is therefore to understand how gender is affected by and uses material objects. In its response to this challenge gender archaeology has put much weight upon methods for identifying women in the past (e.g. Conkey and Gero 1991: 12–13, Gibbs 1987, 1990). This emphasis has been furthered by the early desire to make women visible, and thus apparently important in the past; an emphasis that was due first to the influence of the women's movement and later to feminism, which both focused upon woman *per se*.The results of this emphasis have, however, generally been slightly disappointing in the sense that little revision of prehistory has taken place and our understanding of the past has not been substantially changed, let alone radicalized. More significantly, this emphasis easily misleads us about how an engendered understanding of society may be reached. It has also meant that the lack of clarity about the relationship between sex and gender and the vagueness of the term 'gender' have not been critically engaged with. As gender archaeology focused upon its methodology (and indirectly upon women's visibility) it fossilized its conceptual framework, ignoring the need for its further clarification.

It is relevant and pertinent to relate the theoretical concerns that emerge from these critiques to their analytical investigations. This interaction, rather than searching for methodologies and thus indirectly for answers to assumed questions, should be concerned with what are in practice the implications of our theoretical constructions. Postulating, for instance, that gender is socially constructed we should also ask the question 'How?'. Is social agency or ideology the answer, is normative behaviour the basis for the emergence of such structures? Are they created in negotiation and how does that involve material culture? We have generally not engaged with this level of contemplation, and in place of such questions 'gender as a social construct' has become a catch-phrase that we assume we understand, but which we cannot instrumentalize in our social analysis. Central statements easily become passive, a magic wand used unreflexively in an assurance of their importance and assumed meaning while in fact we have been losing sight of their implications. Further development of gender archaeology is dependent upon renewed attention towards its central propositions. Their arguments need revision and their relevance for our particular discipline is ready for reinstating.

If the universal relevance of gender is accepted to be that all cultures construct ideas of appropriate behaviour for certain types of individuals, who are defined as belonging to groups through their socially perceived sexed bodies, commonly constructed as male or female, then archaeology can engage with the investigation of how such ideas and behaviour are manifest in different types of practices and objects. In addition, and these are some of the unique contributions of archaeological gender studies, the variation through time, including deep time, can be considered and the manner in which normative ideas of, for instance, masculinity and femininity are articulated, acted upon and contested through the material world can be investigated. This provides us with an opportunity to look at how gender affects both the material conditions of life and ideational structures. The further development of gender archaeology is therefore not dependent upon methodology or new types of evidence; rather it rests upon the ability to recognize that gender is part of a social system whether its presence is made clear through particular activities and articulated through an emphasis upon difference or whether it seems denied and is absent from cultural expression. Both versions are gendered, since gender is not about an articulation of women versus men but is rather about how society relates to and constructs cultural categories from the differences that always exist amongst its members.

Archaeology, therefore, rather than developing a methodology for identifying women's participation, must investigate the means through which different genders are constructed and how they affect the world around them. This means that gender may affect and be affected not only by material objects (e.g. food) and practices (e.g. the preparation and serving of food) but also, as Sofaer-Derevenski (1998) has argued, the body itself. A significant contribution that archaeology could make to gender studies would therefore be understanding the materiality of gender. Archaeology studies gender relations as they are expressed in material culture, and it therefore has to explore also what this means. It has become increasingly recognized that material culture is not just a passive reflection of society but also a constituent of it and of its social norms. But how does the active nature of material objects compare and relate to social action? Such issues are central to gender archaeology in particular, since gender ideologies are often expressed and maintained through symbolic association, representations and objects. In the following chapter it will be argued that this means that when gender is materialized it takes on specific forms and gains its own distinct ways of entering into discourse, not detached or unrelated to its social dimension but articulated through a different medium and transformed during this process. This, moreover, is not a secondary aspect of gender, as gender is a situated experience which refers to and emerges equally from its material manifestation and its social articulation. As they are constructed through a distinct means of communication the dynamics, stability, means of interpretation etc. created through the media of objects are particular. Looking into these dimensions of gendered practice and performance may also allow us to characterize this materiality further. These issues, and in particular the ability of objects to add meaning by their presence and distributions, are further illustrated by the case studies in chapters 6 to 9.

5

The Materiality of Gender: the Gendered Object

When Megan was about three years old one of my husband's female colleagues came around. I rarely drink beer and Megan had never seen me do so, but the woman accepted one. Megan looked at the woman drinking and asked in a child's theatrical whisper 'Is it a man?'.

Gender and the object

Archaeology's relevance and contribution to gender studies come from both its unique time dimension and its expert understanding of material culture. Thus, despite the obvious influences from the social sciences upon the development of gender archaeology, this field also has an independent character and with it a unique contribution to make. The release of this potential depends, however, upon the development of identifiable approaches to the study of gender that are based upon analysis of how gender is expressed through and with objects and actions. To a large extent archaeological studies will therefore be concerned with gender as an effect (politically and materially) and a process, rather than as an experience or state of being (see also Sofaer-Derevenski, 1998).

Within gender studies generally, limited attention has been given to investigating and understanding the material dimension of gender as an active structure rather than merely a reflexive relationship. This stands in sharp contrast to the theoretical emphasis upon both the symbolic dimension of gender politics and ideologies and their material consequences. The neglect that is identified here is significant since it means that the media and materials through which gender is enacted and acted upon have largely been ignored. For instance, anthropologists, who routinely observe and describe material objects as part of their engagement with a community, tend to understand the meaning of the objects and their role in gender politics through verbal information. Anthropology has long been aware of some of the problems attached to this information, such as the influence of the anthropologist upon the informant or how representative any one member's understanding of society is (Moore 1988: 1ff). These concerns have not, however, caused anthropologists in general to pay more attention towards how such meaning, through its status as social message, takes on and uses physical forms (whether as actions or objects) and how through these associations communication becomes attached to objects. The specific nature of objects, and the implications and impacts this has for how meaning, communicated like this, is understood, accepted and responded to, has accordingly been given little attention. While, in general, anthropology and other social sciences take the object for granted, accepting its existence and importance but not reflecting upon what it does and how this is done, a few scholars within these disciplines have considered this dimension of human and social practices more critically. For archaeology, the contemplations by Miller (1985, 1987) and Moore (1986) seem particularly interesting, probably partly because both were first trained as archaeologists and therefore use perspectives that are to us both familiar and different. Similar concerns and useful discussions are also found within design history and in the growing field of material culture studies, a subject area straddling different traditional disciplinary boundaries.

Meanwhile, with regard to studies of material culture, archaeology has a particular role due to its traditional focus upon the object and its dependency upon it for understanding the nature of society. This means, for example, that as a discipline its theories and methods have a long discursive history and have become affected by, and now contain residual traces of, many epistemological changes within the social sciences, rather than being expressed entirely within a postmodern perspective. There is thus much potential intellectual baggage within archaeology that can be brought to bear upon the further inquiry into the nature of things. An exploration of the intellectual abilities within and the reasons behind archaeology as a 'method' of investigating social conditions can therefore add to this important but largely ignored aspect of society. This also means that archaeology has the experience and expertise to confirm and consolidate material objects as a dimension of gender discourse. As the latter has been so little appreciated, while also so obviously assumed, critical attention towards this aspect of the construction of gender and its discursive existence is now of central importance. In fact, one may argue that within any society the importance of gender difference becomes most clear when it influences the redistribution and access to various material resources. Gender as an ideational system is significant, but its effects are felt and become of critical importance when the idea of difference also dictates how this corresponds with the allocation of certain rights and the prohibition of others. In its operation gender uses objects and actions, and it is through their articulation in the material domain that gender differences really hurt. Thus, in the continuously on-going construction of gender, objects have a creative role and they therefore have to be acknowledged as also having a fundamental position in social dynamics (see also Arwill-Nordbladh 1998).

One of the few exceptions to the general neglect of the object as a discursive rather than simply a symbolic aspect of gender is the volume edited by Kirkham, which considers various design items, aiming to understand the ways in which our mental and material worlds interact (Kirkham and Attfield 1996: 1). The book argues and convincingly demonstrates that

> The degree to which gendered objects are part of, and inform, wider social relations is exemplified at every level of daily life. It stretches from the type of clothes we wear to work or choose to go to bed or have sex in (by no means necessarily the same) to the types of presents we give and are given, and from the design of cars to hair-dryers and hi-fi equipment. (Kirkham and Attfield 1996: 5)

In addition, some museologists, in particular Porter (1988, 1991, 1996) and Sandahl (1995), have brought a feminist perspective to the analysis of the meaning and impact of objects in museums. They focus upon the nature of objects, in particular their emotive and evocative properties, which Sandahl uses to characterize objects as materialized emotions (1995). They, and others (e.g. Gaarder Losnedahl 1994, Jonsson 1993, Lind 1993), have also begun to discuss contemporary gendercoding of things.

An emphasis upon the material is found in another form in Butler's influential discussion of the materiality of sex (as bodily form) and its problematic relation to gender, and her proposal that attempts at controlling citational practices of gender must begin with control of the materialization of the body. Using Lacanian psychoanalysis, she stresses those practices through which the individual approximates a specific sex, calling this the materialization of bodies at an individual scale (Butler 1993, Joyce 1996).

The nature of objects

Feminist theory in general sees gender as a social construct which constitutes an essential dynamic of society. It is also assumed that this construct is maintained through negotiation. Gender, furthermore, is presented as observed through the ways in which norms, values, rules and other social principles dictate and affect actions and thinking (including the production of material culture). Feminism often presents these values as symbolic structures, but otherwise there has been minimal attention towards the relationship between them and material objects. The social and the material are, however, quite separate and distinct spheres. They do relate to and critically inform and influence each other, but their relationship is far more dynamic and discursive than a merely reflexive, mirror dependency. Accordingly, this currently 'blind spot' in gender studies needs illumination, meaning that the nature of the object and its involvement in gender construction must be investigated.

In recent theoretical discussions, objects have often been compared to text. This association has been made both within archaeology (e.g. Hodder 1986, 1989, Olsen 1997, Tilley 1990, 1991) and within other disciplines, such as sociology or linguistics (Ricoeur quoted in Hodder 1989). This argument is usually inspired by post-structuralism or semiotics (e.g. Barthes 1977). These discussions of the similarity between text and objects rest mainly on arguments stating that both have the same properties of being distanced from the author or producer (Hodder 1989: 257). Their meanings (text's and action's and here, by inference, also object's), rather than being dictated by the author, are produced in the reading and by the reader. I suggest that this comparison arguably prioritizes certain properties of the production of meaning and downplays others (see also Hodder 1989). Primarily it emphasizes the distancing from the author, the shift in meaning and the possibility of endless reinterpretations. These characteristics may, however, be a result of the project of communication *per se* (despite the argued difference between speech, language and text), rather than being an inherent property of particular media. If indeed these are the characteristics of the practice of communication, then text, actions and objects will necessarily be similar in this respect as they are all discursive and communicative. Whether and in which ways the different physical and conceptual forms of the media, through which communication takes place, may also affect communication is not necessarily clarified by the emphasis upon these common properties. It is relevant to wonder about how, for example, the different relationships to the senses that various media explore, such as feel or smell, affect the production of meaning, and at which level that effect comes through.

Hodder, primarily inspired by Ricoeur, uses the metaphor of material culture as a text to argue for a shift in analytical emphasis from the thoughts that lay behind material culture to a concern with how the material world itself contributed to the structuring and constituting of thought (Hodder 1989: 257). Material culture, he argues, derives its meaning from its specific role within the context of practical action. However, while these claims help to clarify the relationship between object and meaning and the role of the object, they remain somewhat obscure as to how meaning is actually constituted and in particular how coherent and consistent sameness in meaning can be created over long durations. Hodder acknowledges this concern and suggests that material culture meaning is also constituted through experience and partly comes about through use (Hodder 1989: 258–9). Thus, material meanings are affected in various ways by the material world and the physical properties of objects.

Objects are also, therefore, different from both texts and language, and while the textual metaphor has been important for recognizing the discursive and communicative role of objects, it is equally important to acknowledge their difference and to understand how it is that objects both enable and affect the expression of social concerns. The importance of objects, as tools to learn from and with (Bourdieu 1977), for affecting understanding of the world argues further for the significance of learning about how they communicate and thus for their analysis. Obviously, many of the object's specific qualities result from its physicality.* Primarily, this means that the object is evocative. Objects easily provoke identification; they are affective and act as an aid to memories. They play on tradition and recognition, and can be subject to fetishism. Objects also have aesthetic dimensions; they produce responses and sensations. They 'seek' owners, they can belong, and their physical existence can be both controlled and altered. Objects can also be divided, shared or destroyed; but they may also be durable.

The language of the object is multi-layered: subtle, universal and at the same time specific. Objects can create links and make connections and the referencing between them fosters intertextuality and 'consumer knowledge' (Partington 1996: 214). They can transgress time and structures, connecting the public and private or past with present, or alternatively they may act to sever such links. Objects are involved in processes of transference, and they are used to operate with. The appropriation of objects into people's lives is part of the cultural process of making meanings with and through things, and the object can be

---

* This discussion does not involve any consideration of whether visual representation of gender should be prioritized in terms of importance (see discussion of visual communication in Riegel 1996). Although a discussion of the difference between the experience and importance of visual communications as opposed to, for instance, verbal ones may be interesting it is nonetheless the case that communication takes various forms and has different ways of being effective. The argument here is therefore that material communication, in its visual and physical form, is critically involved with gender. Its comparative importance is not being considered.

both social and intimate. Objects also provide points of communality as well as of departure, and people construct their identity through object-relations (Kirkham and Attfield 1996: 2, 10). Objects embody temporal relations and social remembering as these occur and are organized in response to a world of things and words (Urry 1996: 50). 'In the very variability of objects, in the ordinariness of their consumption and in the sensory richness of relationships people enjoy through them, they are fitted to be later reframed as material images for reflection and recall' (Radley 1990: 57–8).

The significant role that objects have in the management of social relations is well illustrated by 'the gift'. This interpersonal interaction, mediated through objects, has been studied by various disciplines, giving rise to several seminal volumes such as Mauss's *The Gift* (1954). Its centrality as a practice is well documented. The object of the gift 'establishes or reaffirms symbolic bonds between individuals and objectifies social relationships but, at the same time, carries meanings from the broader cultural context into the domain of the personal and the intimate' (Partington 1996: 215–17). To 'objectify' social relationships literally becomes the role or the effect of the gift. It comes to represent, symbolize and consolidate the relationship. Embodied in a physical form, the relationship is externalized. It becomes tangible; it gains a substance. The relationship also becomes 'measurable'; it becomes embroidered in notions of debt, reciprocity and balance.

The object on its own cannot resist its appropriation, its reinterpretation. Therefore, being embedded within society the object is not neutral. It is never 'pure', unaffected by intentions: it is contaminated (Riegel 1996: 99–100). It is spoken for at many levels, and it becomes imbued with meaning (Sørensen 1999). It becomes the expression of norms, values and traditions, but through this it can also be used to resist or subvert its colonization. Thus, objects can become means of strategic defence and repulse the attempts at their control (Kirkham and Attfield 1996: 2). The object is, therefore, social and it may produce explicit notions of significance and variance. As a consequence, objects are involved with the production of difference; they are partners to the construction of gender, as they provide forceful, partially sublimated, messages about importance, contribution, roles and effect. They influence the ways we see ourselves and the roles and rights we presume access to (Sørensen 1999). Objects, therefore, critically inform and guide our learning about gender difference and their evaluation. This, furthermore, affects both mundane situations, such as the lucky dip at the fair (see figure 5.1), and basic ones with substantial impact on the quality of daily life, such as food allocations.

Figure 5.1 Gendered lucky dip at the Midsummer Fair, Cambridge, UK,
June 1999.

At this point it becomes clear that the project of gender archaeology, in addition to its programme of exploring 'variations in prehistoric gender relations, their generation and maintenance, as well
as their place in social dynamics' (Sørensen 1992: 31), should be expanded to be also concerned with locating where and how gender is
inserted in material discourse and to investigate the consequences of
its presence. In that sense it is useful to think about material culture

as a set of resources (things that are being needed, desired and distrib-uted) involving production and consumption stages. These resources are continuously subject to various kinds of distributions, although the organization of this may differently acknowledge the involvement of gender and other social principles, and where the agreements made about their allocations may range from involving routine practices to discursive strategies or open conflict. The main point to emphasize, therefore, is that the involvement of such resources in the construction of and reaction to gendered differences makes these differences tangible and material and thus gives them a physical reality and real effects upon people's lives and possibilities.

At the same time not all objects and actions are necessarily gendered. Neither are gender associations universal, contrary to the assumptions of many studies inspired by structuralism. For instance, Moore's well-known study of the Endo in Kenya (1986) shows an association be-tween ash:women and dung:men, but that is an association deeply contextualized within the particular society's political and economic relations, and the material dualities constructed there would have lit-tle relevance for most other societies. The example of the Endo also provides us with another important insight into the materiality of gen-der, which is that social prescription and ideals often do not exactly match actual practices (Moore 1987). Thus, from an archaeological point of view, such anthropological studies demonstrate that our ob-servation of, for instance, the Endo society would have revealed a much less rigidly dualistic gender system than their own self-perception por-trays. We are therefore made aware that the material record 'speaks' differently from other media – not necessarily more truthfully, as ob-jects are often used to legitimate and naturalize certain relations, but differently, due to the mechanisms through which it is controlled and acted upon. It is also worth emphasizing that it involves both discur-sive and non-discursive routine practical action, which affects how deliberate and explicit meanings are constructed. This difference means that the archaeological study of gender may be particularly difficult, as gender in practice may often be less explicitly expressed than it appears in its ideological form. This is, however, at the same time also a strong argument for the importance of investigating the practical and physical effects of gender upon people's lives and how essential this is for furthering our analytical insights into how gender is con-structed and lived.

Thus material culture is at the same time active and pliable, mean-ingful but not absolute. Gender, as a basic dynamic of prehistoric so-cieties, would have explored objects as a means of becoming tangible and significant for the people involved. Objects, however, due to their durability and evocative nature, did not simply reflect gender differences but were also discursively involved in the creation and (re)interpretation of difference. In addition, due to their capacity to transgress, interconnect and symbolize (their intertextuality), objects would have been one of the mechanisms through which gender differences could permeate society as a whole and be maintained and recreated through time and between events.

The materiality of gender: communication and practice

It is now relevant to discuss how the character and characteristics of objects bear upon and affect the relationship between gender and material culture. To engage in this discussion it is essential to recollect the arguments made in chapter 4 about gender as a negotiated agreement. Gender exists as it becomes performed through discursive practices and negotiation of norms, and it gains reality, form and consequences only as it becomes associated with the body and other materialities. This point must now be united with an appreciation of the communicative abilities and physical properties of the object. The object is a medium through which gender can operate. It makes gender 'real' and gives it material consequences. Or, in other words, it is through objects and their associated activities that gender becomes enacted. These connections suggest, however, that there are two distinct, albeit related and interwoven, dimensions to gender in which the object is engaged: communication and practice. Thus objects both represent and affect gender. The role of the object in both instances is to embody a code of difference and to provide a means of its recognition and repetition.

To understand gender in terms of communication, the symbolizing ability of the object and the discussion of how it gains its meaning are useful starting points. This is particularly important since the frequent references to the symbolic dimension of gender are rarely supported by any discussion of what 'symbolic' means in its various forms. Symbolic meaning does in fact often use objects as its 'container', exploring how their physicality means that the symbol is materially experienced. Symbolic communication works through repetitive practices of association and uses the ability of objects to be the material expression of norms and ideas – as when an object becomes feminized. Objects used in association with a set of activities can therefore come to 'mean' those activities and the contexts in which they are carried out (Hodder 1989: 259). Thus through repetitive practices an object can become a symbol of an abstract concept, it becomes its reified form as the repeated experience provokes an interpretation of connectedness between elements. This means that a phenomenon of material reality becomes a phenomenon of ideological reality; the thing becomes a sign or symbol. It refers to something that is beyond itself, and its effects reach beyond the physical. As a symbol, the object is imbued with meaning, but the object does not own its meaning, which may be differently understood depending upon the specific contexts of its interpretation. Through objects as symbols, and due to their unique ability to make associations and linkage, such symbolic meaning can be communicated widely, transgressing personal contacts, and survive through time. Moreover, in providing a body for meaning the object also contains and affects meaning. It carries it between contexts and amongst differently constituted groups, making possible interactions and provoking various responses such as confirmation or alterations. Objects and their technologies therefore constitute a way of symbolically (and politically) both maintaining and transforming meaningful cultural environments. These qualities are extremely significant aspects of the object, and I propose that they are of key importance for understanding the duration beyond individual events, contexts and lives of specific gender systems.

The main source of symbolic meaning is the repetitive association between a material form and a particular meaning-context. The creation of symbolic meaning thus involves action, object and interpretation/reading. Symbolic meaning itself derives therefore largely from practice, and is dependent upon repetition. For instance, lace, through its association with particular types of women's clothing and the repetitive reinforcing of this association through a range of imageries, has in the twentieth century become symbolic of femininity. The same material was in the seventeenth century used to represent a certain social group of men within Dutch city bourgeoisie, and was in this context elaborately represented in the formal portraits of these members. The symbolic meaning created from repetitive association between form and context may thus be totally arbitrary. It can, however, also be created by some objects' ability to provide physical embodiment of culturally held views of what constitute feminine and masculine. This refers to the ability objects have of being the material expression of qualities such as fragility or robustness, and accordingly their ability to gender a context. For instance, late nineteenth-century interior design manuals for the middle class in England aimed at the expression of such ideals through, for example, the association between lightness and femininity. For an illustration see figure 5.2.

Figure 5.2   Example of nineteenth-century interior design that aims to embody ideals of femininity (from the showrooms of the Glasgow furnishing firm Wylie & Lochhead c.1900). (Reproduced from Kinchin 1996, fig. 2)

> The character to be always aimed at in a Drawing-room is especial cheerfulness, refinement of elegance, and what is called lightness as opposed to massiveness. Decoration and furniture ought therefore to be comparatively delicate; in short the rule is this – if the expression may be used – to be entirely ladylike. The comparison of Dining-room and Drawing room, therefore, is in almost every way one of contrast. (Kerr 1864: 107 quoted in Kinchin 1996: 14)

Mundane, every-day illustrations of this embodiment of ideological gender characteristics are manifold. Kirkham, for instance, discusses contemporary items such as paper tissues and toilet paper and demonstrates how qualities, such as size (man-size paper tissues) and colour, produce gender associations (Kirkham 1996: 6–8). In addition, certain material forms provide in themselves direct association to gender and therefore have the potential for being symbolic of gender through a different set of associations. These would typically be items or forms that refer directly to sexual differences and people's physical characteristics, such as breast, vulva or penis, or they may be forms that look like these or other parts of the human body. The use of these as symbols brings the meaning of gender and/or sex to their context of use, in contrast to the more widespread production of symbolic association as a result of practice.

Archaeological materials often contain explicit gender or sex symbols and even more frequently can they be inferred from the observation of recurrent practices of association. The latter is, for instance, suggested when a burial rite treats men and women in distinctly different manners, or when different kinds of objects are recurrently partial in their gender association. There are several examples of such differentiations in burial rites. One is the Neolithic Corded Ware culture, which from the mid-third millennium until the mid-second millennium BC is found over a large region of central and northern Europe. In this cultural complex female skeletons are in general buried placed on their left side with the head east, while male ones lie on their right side with the head to the west, making the orientation of male and female bodies opposite (Whittle 1996). The repetition of this formula of distinction over large areas and for some duration would, despite its relatively simple form, nonetheless have produced a very profound association between gender and the orientation of different kinds of bodies in funerary practices. Obviously, this association or similar simple binary oppositions can be pursued as a potential symbolic dimension within other contemporary practices, or alternatively their absence from other contexts can be further explored. In cases such as the Corded Ware culture it is particularly significant that the specific associations were maintained over a considerable duration and within a large area, as this shows how communities without direct contact repeatedly orchestrated and performed their funerals in a manner that reproduced a clear distinction that can be interpreted as being about men versus women. This made them in death different kinds of bodies, but this may have been a difference that exaggerated and regularized a range of less formal practices and the greater messiness of daily life. Such examples point towards the poignant role burials and funerary practices may have played in the performance (and thus in providing visualization) and ideological reproduction of gender systems. The potential variance between such an ideological stage-setting of difference and its existence and effect upon people's daily life is a reality that at present is deeply buried within the archaeological record, and our studies have generally not begun to engage with this complexity. The first step, however, is to recognize the formalization of gendered social life in particular contexts, such as funerals, and to appreciate how this provides insights into 'ideal' symbolic forms that can be contrasted with other types of evidence about how people lived, such as may be suggested by diet or the spatial organization of settlements.

Examples of exclusive association between gender and particular objects, such as dress fittings and ornaments, are also rife in the archaeological record, providing many unused opportunities for investigating how difference was symbolically constructed and communicated within many communities. The many figurines and depictions from different periods and in a variety of contexts could also be more explicitly explored in terms of their symbolizing abilities. These sources have, of course, already been looked at from many angles (e.g. Bailey 1994, E. Hill forthcoming, Knapp and Meskell 1997, Russell 1993). In general, however, the manner in which they provided means of symbolic representation, and thus of reinforcing and stereotyping associations as the material form of ideology, has been little investigated. To explore the insights such objects provide into the construction of gender and the meaning of its difference in various contexts remains a challenging task.

Meanwhile, irrespective of how the symbolic dimension is achieved, it is clear that symbolic communication about gender, its difference, qualities and evaluation, commonly evolves from as well as informs social practices, and that this is a significant means of creating gendered meaning.

A further point about communication and meaning is worth a brief comment, as this relates to the links of signification established through the associative chain of objects–symbols–value. Meaning, this chain suggests, is trans-historical. It is therefore worth clarifying that meaning is only trans-historical in the sense of being transferred through objects from situation to situation and between events – but this is only as the potential ability to mean something, not as an articulated meaning. To turn this passive potential into an active structure it has to be awakened or evoked through reinterpretation or renegotiation. The negotiation of meaning happens within tradition and within memory and it is through these structures, rather than through the object alone, that trans-historical or trans-contextual meaning arises. These points are significant for reconciling contextual analysis with the appreciation of long-term structuring and cohesion.

Gender as part of practice has been little considered apart from the concern with task differentiation and labour organization (e.g. Conkey and Spector 1984). This dimension of the materialization of gender refers to how gender affects action, which returns us to issues of rights, obligations and resources. Obviously, gender archaeology must explore this critical connection between gender and material culture. It must investigate the insertion of meaning in the manipulation and use of objects and in practical action, bearing in mind the active and unique characteristics of material objects. A challenging starting point for consideration of this dimension is Butler's (1993) argument about gender as performance and the possibility of applying this to analysis of material culture. A few archaeologists, such as Joyce in her interesting study of the classic Maya (1996), have already found inspiration in Butler's concept of performative gender, and have attempted to apply this more widely to the analysis of material culture. As a consequence of these influences Joyce argues that the task of gender archaeology is to establish what citational practices of sex and gender were given material form within any specific historical situation (Joyce 1996).

Butler restricts her contemplation to the body as a material corpus, but her central argument and the images of repetition and prescription that the terms conjure up are interesting to explore within different material contexts. Performance may here be usefully considered literally as a staging of events, as the acting out of a script (produced through gender-coding). The employment of objects within such enactments partly acts as a prop directing action at crucial points and partly memorizes stages of such performances. For instance, in the construction of Early Bronze Age graves in Denmark a sequence of construction can be traced as it was enacted and marked by the placing of objects and the involvement of particular actions, such as wrapping the body in a cow hide (Sørensen 1992). Similar sequential staging, which can be traced through the deconstruction of a context into a series of significant events, is now being traced in many case studies in order to understand the performative dimension of, for example, burials (e.g. Last 1998, Mizoguchi 1992, Olivier 1992) and the significance of such sequential constructions within social strategies has become much debated (Barrett 1988, ARC 1992). In Butler's terminology the objects and actions provide citations to the code (1993). Their materiality identifies and memorizes stages in an enactment, and in addition, as an important effect of repetition, they make the code concrete. This ability of objects to function as the identifiers of an event is perhaps most vividly illustrated by the many ethnographic and archaeologically known instances of body mutilation which are often used to visually communicate and to provide permanent social memories and markers of transgression through life stages at both a personal and social scale.

Another dimension of gender as practice is the extent to which such enactments or performances become involved with the distribution of power, including the creation and maintenance of particular gender systems. One of the specific characteristics of objects is their ability to link and transgress contexts. This means that they come to represent tradition, to link past actions, meanings, events and people with the present. This, amongst other qualities, gives objects a potentially important role in the legitimization of power and prestige, as such structures commonly employ and refer to tradition. The ability of the object to construct links through time is well illustrated by Joyce's analysis of gender in classic Maya society (1996). Joyce attempts to identify citational practices through which gender, in the form of a dichotomous heterosexual classification, was maintained and enacted. Based on the iconographic elements of Maya culture she argues that a standardized vocabulary of objects, used for the inscription of bodily practices, were employed to confirm these practices. She also emphasizes how ornaments over a millennium were resistant to change as they were used as media for fixing gender through citational performances (ibid.). This example of long-term stability within an area of material culture, which Joyce interprets as the sedimentation of bodily practices, refers to a common and very important phenomenon in cultural practice: the construction of sameness.

It is interesting here to point out that the understanding of human practice that lies behind citation analysis, despite essential differences in some ways, can be compared with the concept of *chaîne opératoire* as used in archaeology, particularly in lithic studies. This concept focuses upon the sequences of operations which transform a substance from a raw material into a manufactured product.

> Reconstructing such *chaînes opératoires* permits the investigator to come to grips with their *variants*, and thus with both their invariant 'backbones', those *strategic components* which cannot be modified without jeopardizing the entire chain, and with the degrees of freedom and the *choices which the actor can afford themselves*. (van der Leeuw 1993: 240, original emphasis)

It is therefore interesting to note that this approach is now also applied outside lithic studies. It has, for example, been used to understand the construction of funerary space, seeing this as a set of connected practices which produces a deliberate meaningful space, and to compare such construction to a narration (e.g. Olivier 1992: 59–60). In this approach, the production of material culture is seen as a set of interlinked events, and here Butler's argument may be used to add the idea of performance, or citation, and a notion of code or convention, which allows us to identify how gender can be a coherent, affective and affirmative dimension without its necessarily being present in all elements and all decisions.

Any emphasis upon practice and power would easily suggest a Marxist concern with and distinction between ideology and praxis. Current discussions of ideology would, however, take this question to involve more than a concern with the role of ideology in the maintaining of economic groups. The question of 'economic interests' would also in itself be reinterpreted since economy and politics are deeply interwoven. Meanwhile, awareness of ideology and power helps to focus our attention upon how particularly constituted groups or individuals relate to material resources, and the extent to which they can reject, resist or manipulate the meaning of objects. It has often been pointed out that objects may embody various meanings for different people, and that 'tradition' carries meaning through time. I have called this the fluidity of meaning (Sørensen 1992). In addition to this fluidity it is also the case, however, that the presence of power relations and the ability of objects to both symbolize and affect the accrual and control of power mean that the gendered meaning of objects is negotiable through practice. I therefore suggest that the object's pliable nature, its ability to be the instrument of power and difference as well as their symbols, makes the association between gender and material culture both dynamic and crucial for the long-term maintenance, transformation and reinterpretation of gender systems as a part of social and political organization. The (gendered) meaning of objects can therefore be analysed only within their context of action.

Constructing gender through things, making objects gendered

Relationships between objects and gender are formed and take place in ways that are so accepted as 'normal' as to become 'invisible'. Thus we sometimes fail to appreciate the effects that particular notions of femininity and masculinity have on the conception, design, advertising, purchase, giving and uses of objects, as well as on their critical and popular perception. (Kirkham and Attfield 1996: 1)

The unique contribution of (and challenge to) gender archaeology now emerges even more clearly as being its ability to engage with the question of where and how to locate the insertion of gender in various social practices. One of the most central concerns of gender archaeology is then the question of how an object becomes a gendered object. As discussed, an object, either due to its own inherent characteristics or because of repetitive associations, can become gendered. Its gender meaning is, however, merely latent; for it to emerge the object must enter into an interpretative engagement which means the introduction of context and praxis.

Figure 5.3 Girl's dress on a stall at the Midsummer Fair, Cambridge, UK. The particular expression of femininity is connected with the target group being travellers. (Interview June 1999)

The concept of gender as a social construct, maintained and negotiated through material culture, is still, however, extremely abstract, and it gives little indication of 'how it actually happens'. What is the nature of material culture negotiation and how do we recognize the gendered object? It is in fact often argued that, despite its desirability, studying gender in past society is an impossible task. It is therefore worth briefly considering how and where we may identify and locate gender as an effect upon people's actions.

Material culture is a distinct medium with its own 'logic' and potentials of expression. The decoding of the meaning of material objects must therefore be based upon understanding them as participants of contexts, and upon recognizing that meaning is neither absolute nor exclusive. Material culture, at the same time, is an integrated component of social life. Objects are used to express, create and transform rules of meaning. It is due to this integration that post-processual archaeology places material culture in the centre of discourse along with other activities; but, as Moore warns, material discourse is both contextually produced (i.e. the material thing finds its meaning in the context) and refers to an understanding outside the context (Moore 1994: 114).

Meanwhile, gender as a construction has to be created, and this involves context. The nature of such contexts ranges widely, however, and it is of importance that we avoid closure when 'defining' it. Tilley stresses this: 'The evident desire for a non-contextual definition of context is a contradiction in terms, emphasising that our own interpretative actions are included in contexts' (1993: 8–9). The context may therefore be identified as, for instance, a site, a moment, an action or an event, or it could be either an assemblage or a single type, such as 'swords'. Most important, however, is to recognize that they are all formed by us as archaeologists (it is in this enframing that archaeology as a discipline is now in the process of becoming engendered). Gender-coding, furthermore, is part of the processes through which gender is constructed, and our studies must refrain from assuming that contexts or objects by themselves are automatically and statically gendered. Much of the cultural repertoire may in fact have been gender- and sexless until incorporated into particular events and contexts (this may be particularly relevant for the small-scale societies of prehistory which would have involved much collaboration, sharing and interdependency). In view of this, traditional archaeological valuation of different types, such as weapons and ornaments, which assumes them to be similarly gendered in all contexts and throughout time, clearly needs critical reassessment. This does not mean, however, a wholesale rejection of traditional ideas about gendered objects, such as swords being male and ornaments female; rather it is the recognition of their contextual genesis and status that is called for. It is, for example, possible to argue that the sword during the European Bronze Age was conceptualized in a distinct manner, and that its association with male, and in particular with warrior, caused it to become a 'masculine object' (Sørensen 1992). The sword probably gained a special status through a symbolic association between its form and the meaning of the male warrior, and through various cultural uses it might have gained the ability to be the embodiment of masculinity and through this affected its contexts of use and display in very particular ways. This proposition is, however, based on a number of specific observations that demonstrate how Bronze Age communities interacted differently with swords than with any other object. It is, for instance, the case that the production of swords was extremely standardized; they were commonly produced in central workshops, rather than their production being scattered amongst local craft-people, and they were widely distributed, probably through exchange networks that involved some kind of elite. They were also repetitively associated with men in graves. In addition, the emblematic or symbolic dimension of the swords is augmented by, for instance, their depiction on stelae in southwestern Europe (Galan Domingo 1993) or the use of accurate miniature swords as grave goods in northern Europe (Sørensen 1992). Further details could be added to argue for the specific and masculine character of the swords during the Bronze Age; the point, however, is that it is through the practices associated with an object that its explicit inclusion in gender discourse may be identified. Thus, the archaeological analysis of gender involves understanding how different objects are discursively used in its construction.

Archaeology has access to gender relations, their effects and physical consequences in a variety of more or less direct ways. There is, of course, a consistent problem in documenting that patterns observed are due to gender rather than other criteria such as age or social status, but this is a problem common to all gender studies independently of disciplinary context. It is, for example, difficult to establish – even face to face – whether a person does certain things because she is a woman or because she is working class. That does not mean that a useful relationship cannot be established between certain variables and gender, but it does argue that their analysis must become more appropriate to the questions asked and the type of practice being investigated.

Obviously, the more closely evidence is associated with the individual, the more directly statements can be made about how gender may have affected that person. This means that various studies of the human bodies from different cultures provide an important starting point for gender archaeology. Such studies, using isotope analysis, studies of muscle traces on bones, evidence of health, mortality rates, height and build, can trace differences in how individuals lived in the past. A well-known observation is the consistent lower mortality for women than for men, but also that this discrepancy fluctuates through time. But gender affects, informs and is expressed in relationship to more aspects of the person and community than the lived body. Burials, since these are the situations in which many societies most strongly and explicitly reflect upon and renegotiate identities and relationships, necessarily involve a response to gender (even if the burial appears to ignore gender this in itself constitutes a particular interpretation of gender). In many cultures it seems that it was in burials that differences and sameness were most explicitly articulated. Rites of passage, such as death, take place by transforming the deceased and this can be articulated only through statements about his/her/its identity in terms of sameness and difference with regard to relevant social criteria. In the confirmation and reaffirmation of social relations, burials must involve gender both as an effect and as a result, since any shifts within social relations include gender. The statements made about individuals during burials provide us with a rich record of spatial and temporal variation within this cultural practice. For instance, during the Late Neolithic and Early Bronze Age in western and central Europe gender categories were constructed and visualized in burials in a rigid manner that contrasts sharply with the practices in the earlier Neolithic burials in megalithic tombs. Difference was visualized and enacted in death by contrasting the orientation of male and female skeletons, and this distinction also affected many of the accompanying objects which, depending upon area, meant that axes or daggers were buried with men and various types of ornaments with women. In the British Beaker burials, for instance, many objects are clearly differentially associated with men and women, and some objects are exclusively found with either of them. Belt rings, gold buttons and amber buttons are, for instance, exclusively found with men and shale/jet beads are in association with women (Gibbs 1990). The rigid gender categories constructed in burial rites have in several instances been shown to affect even very young children (Sofaer-Derevenski 1997, 1998). This gender categorization is, however, not immediately apparent within other activities from the same period indicating the situational existence or characteristics that gender may have: it exists in some contexts but may be ignored in others. The treatment of the deceased within the grave, their location within the funerary monument and later use of the site may also be affected by gender, and studies have now begun to explore these relationships (e.g Mizoguchi 1992, Sofaer-Derevenski 1998).

There are, of course, many more aspects of life and the reflection upon self and others that are routinely informed by gender. The archaeological record contains an abundance of evidence of the importance given by various societies to this dimension as it found expression in different material forms and consequences. It informed, for instance, self-conscious depictions of people, of categories of people, their gods and deities. The effect ranged further, however, and affected, for instance, also the bodily experience of space and daily maintenance. Some of these traces are easily detectable, others remain more obscure, while many await recognition through more informed investigations into the communication and practice of gender. While analysis must realistically focus upon the traces that can be identified, our interpretations should aim to contemplate the presence and influence of gender more widely, making us increasingly sensitive to its more subtle involvement and impact.

It is now interesting to return briefly to the definitional discussion of sex and gender in chapter 3. The recognition of how in practice the evaluation and recognition of sex/gender is informed by and affects material conditions is an essential addition to the theoretical discussion of the existence of these categories. In its material consequences ideas of gender gain a substantive reality. For instance, during the eighteenth and early nineteenth century European women were thought of as by nature innocent, fragile and childlike, and therefore – it follows – they could not be trusted with the vote or have any financial responsibilities, including rights to inheritance. Thus the constructed notion of femininity had direct economic and political consequences for women's lives. The significance – symbolically as well as materially – of such associations between gender and material resources is further augmented by how alternative notions of gender and/or sexuality are commonly expressed through subversive use of material culture, challenging their restricted association with certain categories of people. Equally, the substantial investment in the suppression of such alternatives and the effort involved in maintaining the material form of particular gender systems testify to the importance these objects gain as the expression and enactment of a code and as they give form to conventions. As objects are made into feminine and masculine items they are also becoming associated with notions of their appropriate use, and breaking these codes, however minute and mundane the items seem to be, commonly produces unease. As a further proof of the strong linkage between gender and objects it has been argued that the most binary-coded items are the ones whose subversive use most disturbs the established order (Kirkham and Attfield 1996: 4, Joyce 1996). Thus, the material expression of gender is not merely its reflection. It is an active element in the construction of differences that affect people's lives, the allocation of rights and responsibilities within communities, and the approbation and prescription of appropriate actions. Gender, one may even argue, is of limited significance unless and until the differences that it contains are associated with evaluations that affect the allocation of resources and thus become influential elements of social and political discourse.

It has been argued here that an essentially post-processual archaeological approach, arguing for the active and discursive nature of material things, is central to the investigation of gender, and that in particular the analysis of the construction, maintenance and transformation of gender needs such a perspective. Thus, the physicality of objects, which gives them the ability to transcend the life of individuals and the limits of events, is seen as providing the material environment for the reproduction of society, including its gender ideologies. This aspect of gender, and the unique potentials of archaeology in this regard, has so far been importantly ignored by the social sciences. The following chapters will therefore focus upon the materiality of gender, exploring this dimension through a set of 'material situations' or 'locales' as the points where particular kinds of material resources are subject to social appropriation. The aim is to show how objects are employed to express and negotiate gender roles and differences. A gendered cultural-historical review of the past will not be attempted. Rather, archaeology will be explored for its ability to shed light upon how gender becomes partner to and is clearly articulated in some situations of social discourse. The chapters will therefore explore a set of specific resources, which each in their way would commonly have become involved in the visual, practical and physical articulation of gender. In the past, as now, they provided a medium for gender to operate within. Furthermore, and of particular importance, these resources, through the mechanisms of their distributions and notions of rights, are frequently implicated in the evaluation of difference. Such material resources can then be used to discuss where and how gender becomes involved within a particular set of practices and concerns. These discussions begin to suggest key aspects of the processes through which communities construct a gendered world in which to live.

These material situations, while all having a clear social dimension, may also be seen in various ways as relating to the practice and construction of self. They must, however, be appreciated as external, as the physical structuring of the activities of the individual – they affect self-construction and regulation, being part of the individual and the communal striving towards compartment and corporeality. These practices 'inscribe' or 'write' upon the body, marking and shaping it in culturally specific ways which are then 'read' or interpreted by others (Lupton 1996: 15). The argument is that while gender is always attempted, inscribed and centralized (ibid.) to become it needs form – and objects and practices can provide this.

Part II

6

Food: the Performance of Feeding and Eating

Mustard, horseradish, vinegar and the like are considered hot things in our household and only the grown-ups eat them. 'Don't like it', Kim Michael says. 'When I am older, I might like it. Maybe when I am seven years', Megan adds.

Nutritious and symbolic: the culture of food

In our discussion of gender it has become obvious that gender discourse and negotiation are constituent of political and economic concerns of society. They are involved in deciding upon resource allocation according to social norms and thus have material effects and inform practice. Food, due to its centrality in life and the obvious possibilities for differentiated allocations, is both such a resource and an important social medium of signification. It is accordingly a well-established area of research within many of the social sciences. It is, for instance, a classic theme within social anthropology, with important discussions by, for example, Bourdieu (1984), Douglas (1975, 1980), Goody (1982) and Lévi-Strauss (1970), and it is an emerging one in sociology partly due to the increased importance given to the body and embodiment in social studies (e.g. Lupton 1996). It is also a topic which has been given much attention in archaeology although, as I shall argue, this has mainly focused upon food as resource, production practices and physiological requirements and largely ignored the analysis of its social and ideological dimensions. The archaeological study of food, with the exception of a few recent studies such as Hastorf (1991, 1998), has therefore generally taken a highly instrumental or functional view of food, which has primarily been analysed as a means to an end, despite the rich and varied evidence of the cultural and symbolic dimension of food in prehistory.

Food involves several stages from its production to its consumption; together with its redistribution, sharing and allocations, this at different levels provides possibilities for the creation of difference. Moreover, while food clearly is essential and is the basis of our existence, it is also a symbolic resource. Studies of our own society, of ethnographic communities and of past activities demonstrate this vividly, showing the range of taboos, significance and special activities associated with food. Through designated practices and associations food becomes permeated with values and normative meaning. Food is also subject to extreme degrees of culturation; it becomes the object of fabrication and alterations and with that follows associated instrumentalization. The manipulation of food, its 'cooking', according to Lupton, is 'a moral process, transferring raw matter from "nature" to the state of "culture", and thereby taming and domesticating it' (Lupton 1996: 2). It is important that archaeologists recognize that food is affected by such processes and how it, therefore, at various levels becomes the object of culture and performance. Both its production and the manner of its circulation and consumption follow rules, regulations and cultured manners of behaviour. Tools and equipment become associated as the necessary instruments of producing, serving and eating food. Furthermore, through its culturation food is often in various ways exaggerated and made highly valuable, and it becomes further objectified as things. Taste, colours and texture and the combination of ingredients are explored beyond any requirements of subsistence or nutrition. Through such practices food is made potentially differentiated, meals become varied and people separated depending upon their access and rights regarding these differences. This investment in the differentiation of food becomes particularly interesting in view of recent arguments that suggest that the earliest plants to be domesticated were probably herbs and spices rather than basic subsistence crops (e.g. Hastorf 1998).

Thus, our food is both necessary and highly cultural. It is produced through transformation of various substances, and in its sustainment of the body it becomes part of the body; hence the common saying that 'one becomes what one eats'. This association with the body, and in particular its orifices, gives food (and its consumption) a potentially psychological dimension as well. It can in various ways be perceived and experienced as an extension of the body, permeating its boundaries and making them ambiguous; 'it forever threatens contamination and bodily impurity, but is necessary for survival and is the source of great pleasure and contentment' (Lupton 1996: 3). By extension, food and its consumption can also be both eroticized and sexualized. These potential associations may be a further reason why food is commonly and rigidly subjected to cultural codification. It is these qualities that lie behind the long tradition of structuralist concern with food classification. Famous and most influential amongst these has been Lévi-Strauss's (1970) discussion of classifications, based on ideas of food practices as part of a cosmological system, such as the oppositions clean:dirty and raw:cooked. Another important approach is that formed by Douglas (1975) who discusses how food categories encode and therefore structure social events, arguing that the predictable structure of each meal creates order out of potential disorder, and that this order is about who people are (Lupton 1996: 9). 'The ordered system which is a meal represents all the ordered systems' (Douglas 1975: 273). The presence of binary oppositions at a certain level of cultural perception or the observation of close association between different classification systems, do not mean, however, that these structures in themselves can provide a sufficiently in-depth analysis of food as cultural practice and material. They show only that societies in their interaction with food respond to some of its properties in a manner that makes this kind of codified linkage obvious. Feminist writers on the sociology of food therefore criticize such approaches for treating the latent meaning of food and eating habits 'as if they were linguistic texts with inherent rules to be exposed' (Lupton 1996: 8), rather than interpreting them in terms of embodiment, agency and change. An analytical engagement with food needs to move beyond observing its associations and begin to investigate how food enables relationships between different meanings and values to be established and how it involves a range of distinct practices. This means that food should be analysed both through the physical and economic procedures that affect its production and processing (including its consumption and associated agreements about allocations) and through its various relationship to the body. Thus, the dual aspect of food as both a physical process of manufacturing, distribution and consumption and an embodied experience should be recognized as affecting how food is a source of both social and economic differentiation and personal identification and subjectivity.

Food has a physical presence, a changeable nature and temporal existence, which can all be variously manipulated. The experience of food is both nonverbal, sensual and physical through touch, smell, taste and seeing as well as a discursive engagement which is about access and fulfilment of needs and desire, and in the latter language enters as a means of deciding, negotiating and agreeing upon its production and circulation. The latter dimension is essential for the meanings we construct around food (Lupton 1996: 13), but the former exists as an undercurrent of sensations that influence that meaning. The personal and the social therefore interact in interesting but extremely complex manners in this medium.

Analysis of food must therefore embrace both of these aspects and at the same time recognize that they relate to rather different dimensions of the individual and society, and that, therefore, their contribution to our concern with gender will differ. Following the arguments of chapters 3 to 5 the focus is here upon the extent to which food, its production, circulation and consumption, provides a central location for the day-to-day enactment of gendered differences between individuals and the effect this has upon the maintenance of such differences and the learning of roles, that is, the focus is upon the materiality of food and its involvement in social discourse about identity and membership, rather than on the embodied experience which is also involved. Such analysis of the social importance of food must look to the processes through which substances are made into certain versions of food and how they become associated with meaning, and furthermore study how such meanings affect social relations. In particular we must aim to locate where difference becomes central or is given new forms and thus may be asserted or negotiated. Moreover, due to its physical properties and the various types of labour and labour divisions that are evoked to produce first the materials and then their processing into meals, power relations are also involved in food production and consumption. This, however, is not just power as a repressive force but also as empowerment and the ability to create and change, and as such it should be recognized as 'a property that runs through and permeates all dimensions of social life' (Lupton 1996: 14).

Food and embodiment

The relationship between food and embodiment has recently become an area of interest within the social sciences. Lupton, for instance, stresses that 'Food and eating are central to our subjectivity, or sense of self, and our experience of embodiment, or the ways that we live in and through our bodies, which itself is inextricably linked with subjectivity' (Lupton 1996: 1). The experience of food is, however, both affected by bodily sensation and informed by tastes, habits and memories; and all of these, while produced and located in the body, are nonetheless also socially generated. The experience of eating, of taking in food, is nonverbal; but the meaning constructed around food – as experience and culture – is discursive and within language. Eating food is an act of bodily incorporation (Lupton 1996: 17): we become the food we eat and the food becomes us. It is also an act through which the body, while it itself incorporates, may become incorporated; having 'partaken of' may also signify partnership. Thus the social and the subjective are often deeply intertwined within this medium.

The dependency and close association between the body, notions of self and subjectivity mean that food also has psychological dimensions, and food metaphors are, for example, ripe in various types of psychoanalysis. These associations seem in particular to focus upon lactation, and thus the relationship to the breast and the mother, as well as other bodily functions. Freud, for instance, argued that the oral phase, involving the infant's initial sensual encounters with the breast and the incorporation of food, is the primary experience in the development of sexuality (Freud 1905, Lupton 1996: 18). The discussion of whether such psychological traits are transferable to earlier societies will not be engaged with here. For the purpose of my argument, which is about how food may be a medium for the expression and performance of gender as socially constructed and experienced identities, it is sufficient to argue that even if the withdrawal from the breast is psychologically experienced as a fragmentation and as part of the process of individualism this does not take place outside context. The responses to and processing of these emotions are also greatly affected by social expectations and the support system within which the individual lives. In addition, even apparently fundamental bodily activities are also bound up with culture. Breastfeeding is, for instance, a practice that varies between cultures (Maher 1992). It is, for example, likely that it involved longer periods of weaning in prehistory than we are used to, as is also witnessed by many ethnographic accounts. This would then place the infant–mother relation in a temporal setting different from the one Freud was familiar with. The infant's 'painful experience of isolation' may thus both have different relevance for and be expressed and responded to in a variety of ways within societies. Some of the aspects of food that are relevant to contemporary sociological and psychological concerns with subjectivity and embodiment may thus not be of importance for archaeology, despite the shared reference to bodily functions and social dependencies. The public absence of starvation, the fashionable aspects of food, the manufacturing of baby-milk substitutes and the concern with diets and bodily appearance are, for instance, obvious characteristics of the Western world of the late twentieth century, and many of these are unlikely to be relevant for prehistory. In response to the current emphasis upon food and subjectivity it is therefore important to emphasize the obvious possibility that there may be fundamentally different food-cultures. This makes studies such as Falk's (1994) important. He argues for a separation between closed bodies and open ones, where the latter are said to be typical of pre-modern societies in which the ritual of eating functions as an integrating mechanism for the whole community rather than as an individual one (Falk 1994: 24–5 quoted in Lupton 1996: 16–17). These are eating communities

(Lupton 1996: 16–17) in which foods are important commodities and significant gifts. In societies of closed bodies, he argues, food is a liminal substance, standing between the inside and outside, that is, it is an individual experience aimed at the maintenance and sustainment of the personal rather than the social body. Therefore, while the bodily incorporation of food and the tangible, sensual experience of its consumption mean that eating food is always also a matter of embodied subjectivity, its varied social and symbolic dimensions will also affect subjectivity. Food is experience, culture and material, and its central effect upon the sense of self therefore has a variety of roots. That is why such distinction between different food-cultures can be a constructive perspective. It is therefore important that we do not automatically assign our own understanding and experience of food to prehistoric people.

Food, life stages and gender

In its close association with the body, as a matter of transformation and sustenance of life, food is an obvious focus for symbolic expression. Food consumption, its rules and regulations, are therefore closely aligned with other central concerns such as the social make-up of the community, and food is often drawn upon to mark gender and age boundaries.

Many ethnographies, as well as rituals in contemporary societies, show how food often is involved in marking rites of passage, changes in seasons and social events. In terms of gender, the important role food plays in the learning and communication of life stages and especially in children's transition into adulthood is particularly important. The marking of these stages is often indicated by prohibitions and prescriptions about food types, their preparation and the manner of their consumption. Rules are made to define boundaries between forbidden and permitted food that relate to, for example, age, places, gender or social status. Food is therefore classified through cultural understanding and norms. Such norms and conventions can be transgressed, but their importance is only further confirmed by this, since transgression in itself gives meaning to the forbidden. Amongst the various types of age-related food the difference between breast milk and other foodstuff is particularly interesting in a gender context. This is because its provision relates to a physiological difference between members of society, it is important for the successful reproduction of the community, and it creates a temporal, intimate link between an infant and the mother or mother-substitute. In addition to these physiologically generated characteristics there are, however, also obvious cultural aspects of this relationship, as breastfeeding and its termination are also distinct cultural practices (Maher 1992). There is therefore an interesting tension between the cultural control over the distribution and consumption of breast milk that may be expressed through cultural norms and expectations, and its production which can only be a little manipulated as only certain persons will be able to produce it. It is, therefore, a food source which in its production is uniquely linked with a particular group of biological women. Its affect upon the social recognition of identity comes, however, particularly from how the early link created between milk provider and infant members of society at some point must be broken or expanded upon. The rupture of the early dependency and intimacy between infant and mother or mother-substitute means that a transgressional threshold exists whereafter the child's relationship to various members of its community can be reinterpreted and transformed.* It is also this relationship that sits behind the idea of maternal objects.† These are objects, which as surrogates for the maternal breast, people associate with this early bond and its emotional significance.

In linking life stages and food, society classifies its members. Children, for instance, are from early on related to socially, and they are commonly made into specific kinds of social persons. This is often done by creating public statements about who they are and become at different stages using, for example, change in dress codes or access to new types of food publicly to mark such transgression. The early dependency of children on their mother or mother-substitute, as discussed above, makes the later construction of other identifications and the importance of other foods culturally significant insofar as they expand the child's social relationships. Initiation practices, such as baptism or food rituals, are social performances where, amongst others, the former blurred boundary between mother and infant disappears through the assertion of their separate identities. The ritual use of food is therefore a central arena for the social construction of identities, and one that needs further archaeological investigation.

---

* It is exactly this physical dependency and closeness between mother and child, as well as the later severing or even denial of the relationship, which so often has been used in psychoanalysis for discussion of the formation of identity (see both Fürst 1995 and Lupton 1996 for a feminist reaction from the point of view of the sociology of food).
† This refers to physical objects external to the body. This should not be confused with extensions of the body such as Lacan's *object a* or Kristeva's *abject*, which are products of the body, being detachables such as blood, hair and skin (Grosz 1994: 81).

Discourse through food

There are numerous transformations and distinct practices involved with food, and in their performances these in various ways affect the idea of gender differences and are themselves informed by them. To appreciate the extent to which negotiation and performance affect our interaction with food, a list indicating some of the things we do to and with food is useful. Food is grown, made, produced, acquired, bought, exchanged, given as gift. It is also cooked, manufactured, changed. It is eaten, tasted, enjoyed, shared, monopolized, digested. It satisfies, nourishes, makes you well or sick. It may be forbidden, prescribed, habitual. All these relations are about action and effects. They indicate situations created and relationships drawn between people and between them and resources, and it is in these various intersections that we can locate practices emanating from the production, circulation and consumption of food. These, furthermore, are practices that will affect social differences, including gendered ones. When food is eaten, it is gone, taken out of circulation. Its existence as a potential resource ceases and none other can now consume it. Its potentials have become invested in the person or persons. Even more central to our interest in how this involves gender is the extent to which food involves sharing and exchanging, how it is produced through labour divisions, and how through the different stages these practices involve power and affect power relations between differently constituted people and communities. Interactions with food are organized according to norms and rules, including those which dictate how gender differences should be evaluated and responded to. This means that differentiation between people is almost unavoidably both articulated and further confirmed through such practices. The society's evaluation of its differently constituted groups becomes associated with its distribution of food, and may be symbolically enforced by food consumption traditions.

In addition to its relationship to the body and its significant symbolic associations, food, because it is needed as a physical substance, also creates different degrees of dependencies between people. Most obvious is the dependency between the infant and mother/carer. Dependency is, however, also characteristic of groups such as the elderly or sick or it may be created through labour division. This, however, adds another significant dimension to the role food may play within various social groups, and it confirms that food, in addition to its importance for the individual, is also an essentially communal concern.

There are thus several dimensions to food. It is both a nutritional necessity and in that sense an unavoidable practical concern, and it is political and ideological, imbued with symbolic importance, surrounded by taboos and prohibitions. It is also a strong metaphor employed to create significance in other spheres of life. In addition, food relates to a range of different resources, which are conceptually unified only through their classification as edible for humans. Its production as well as consumption involve distinct stages, where control and access may change from one type of person to another (whether physical or through knowledge). In its materiality food also makes necessary various physical transactions, such as the processing, cooking and serving of food. These transactions make it possible to further accentuate the 'meaning' of the food by the performance of rituals or the use of items of material culture to create significance. Through these stages food is made cultural and political, but significantly it is a symbolic and political resource that is both partaken of through daily routines and during special occasions. In food, the daily sustenance of life and rituals meet. Food is also extremely malleable, its transformation and alterations are endless, and its control can be silently challenged and subverted. The ways in which resistance or revolt can be expressed through a badly cooked meal is thus often openly acknowledged. Spitting on or otherwise 'revolting' the food prepared for your master or jailer is thus a common image in films to indicate rejection or disgust with persons in power, while, at the other extreme, the sharing of meals and in particular the utensils used, such as spoons or a glass, are intimate, at times even erotic, gestures. Performance theory is therefore extremely relevant, as food is consumed both through daily enactments of difference, dependencies and evaluation and is also used conspicuously, and thus plays significant roles in highly ritualized activities in which membership and status are defined, initiated, confirmed or challenged. Famous ethnographic examples are the pig feast in Papua New Guinea (Rappaport 1984) or the potlatch amongst Northwest Coast Indians (Rosman and Rubel 1971).

Discourses through and about food are practices involved with the project of understanding the production and reproduction of society and its social meaning; they are therefore important aspects of any society, including prehistoric ones. The questions we must ask, as archaeologists, are therefore how such discourses, far back in time, may be identified through strategies for getting food that involve knowledge (in particular the classification edible/inedible) and were expressed through choice, preferences, combination and collaboration around resources. Our history is a history of collecting, sharing and with time also storing and planning for food, and of satisfying both needs and desire associated with its materials.

The social importance of food, and the extent to which access to food and its meaning is culturally constructed and the manner in which it is both affecting and affected by gendered differences between participants in a 'food-culture', is an important field for archaeologists. This has in various ways been directly or indirectly acknowledged in the interests that have determined research focus, such as the so-called economic school with its focus upon subsistence activities and requirements (e.g. Higgs 1972). The explicit awareness of the gendered dimension of these basic activities has, however, until recently been either ignored or merely presented in terms of naturalized stereotypes about labour and role division within different types of society. Thus it has, for instance, been common to assume that within hunter-gatherer societies men hunt and women gather and within agricultural societies women are the agriculturists and men look after animals. Food and its implication in social relationships can, however, be explored far more constructively, including as a means towards gaining insights into a variety of social relations and the ways in which they are maintained at a day-to-day level (see also Hastorf 1991, 1998).

The importance of food in prehistoric societies can be analysed and documented through a range of different sources with attention towards how several processes are involved in transforming raw material into highly cultured objects. There is partly the remains of meals themselves. These are the bones from animals (sometimes with marks of food preparation), and the remains of plants, nuts, shells and much more, which can be used to reconstruct diets and to comment upon this aspect of people's life in terms of requirements, labour investment as well as spatial and temporal differences. The importance and potentials of these data are vast, and several branches of specialism now exist within archaeology which are developing the skills for professional investigations of this evidence. In addition, there is the obvious range of objects and activities used in connection with food. In the following I shall limit myself to briefly considering food practices in terms of production, servicing and consumption, as well as its role in particular events, through a discussion of drinking. These themes are in no way exhaustive of the relevant dimensions of food practices; their aim is to indicate the range of issues that are relevant and how their investigation may respond both to the potentials of our data and the demands from our question about the insertion of gender in discourses around food. They hint at the insights we might gain into the social role of food in various prehistoric societies, confirming this as an area of importance with regard to both gender studies and human history. To explore and locate gender and its discursive engagement in food production and consumption, archaeology needs to look at its many different sources with consistent attention towards how gender is involved in the practices and norms which they reflect. To initiate these inquiries and outline approaches for identifying gender in food we may begin by asking questions about the practices, agreements, habits and decisions that are reflected in its various components; doing this we begin to trace the negotiation and performance of gender through the material dimensions of food.

Producing food

Food is also a commodity. And as a product it is not by itself inherently associated with any particular group within society. This means that the common association between certain types of food, whether during its production or consumption, with particular groups, that are often observed in ethnography or in contemporary society, are culturally created. It is interesting to notice here, how control and organization of the production of different foods may take distinct forms and how this is maintained through local norms and conventions. It is, however, particularly interesting (and revealing) that the production of specific types of food is often divided into different stages involving temporal changes in labour divisions and group associations. Thus within food production labour division is not merely expressed within a particularly contextualized situation but is rather a matter of a choreographed temporal sequence, which, amongst others, creates dependencies and debts. For instance, without even questioning traditional ideas of gender-based division of labour within agricultural societies of temperate Europe one can easily outline a temporal (annual) sequence of its agricultural activities and show how they involve complex collaborations and interdependencies within a community. Figure 6.1 shows one such example based on the annual cycle of a farming community in Jämtland, Sweden, in the seventeenth century (Wichman 1968, Rathje personal communication). It is highly likely that similar, but not the same, temporal sequences would have characterized prehistoric societies.

The point of this example is not to propose this as a model for how prehistoric men and women divided their labours; in fact many ethnohistorical models of farming communities are themselves biased and lacking in insights into women's productive sphere (Rathje personal communication). Rather, the example, by revealing the many separate tasks involved, illustrates how the production of food might have involved different people at different stages, how this affected other ac-

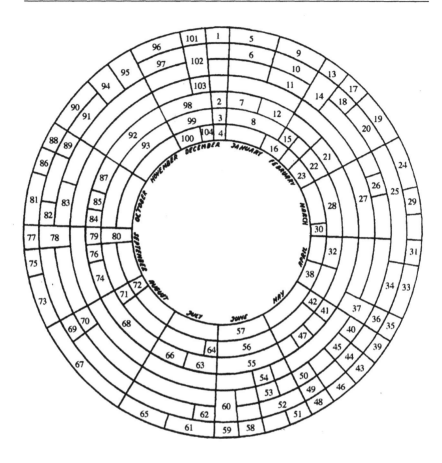

1 transporting hay
2 shearing sheep
3 teasing wool
4 sewing
5 transporting firewood, fodder and spruce twigs
6 cutting spruce twigs
7 spinning wool
8 preparing hemp and spinning
9 threshing
10 driving for the ironworks
11 working on wagons, wooden containers and nets
12 threshing
13 to the annual Candlemas market
14 transport and cutting spruce sprigs and bark
15 spinning
16 weaving cloth
17 bringing home fodder
18 cutting timber

19 threshing (1–2 days per week)
20 transporting iron ore and coal
21 threshing (1–2 days per week)
22 spinning, reeling and winding
23 weaving cloth or frieze
24 travel to Norway*
25 driving for the ironworks
26 hay and wood transporting
27 binding nets and seine
28 hemp spinning
29 travel to the Gregory market
30 flax spinning starts
31 transporting hay and fodder
32 spinning flax
33 end of threshing
34 cutting and transporting firewood
35 transporting manure
36 cutting fence poles
37 sand and ash spread on remaining snow
38 cloth weaving
39 preparing tools for farming

40 grinding grain
41 drying seed grain
42 baking
43 spreading manure
44 ploughing
45 enclosing pastures
46 sowing
47 enclosing pastures
48 weeding the fields
49 enclosing pastures
50 sowing flax and hemp
51 drying and grinding
52 carpentry of hay barns etc.
53 weeding the fields
54 closing the field fence
55 linen weaving and bleaching
56 baking summer bread
57 weaving and sewing of different cloths
58 boat repairing, fishing
59 harrowing the fallow
60 preparing scythes, rakes etc.
61 harvesting the starrbog in the mountains
62 birch bark collecting
63 harvesting the starrbog in the mountains
64 birch bark collecting
65 harvesting horse hay
66 harvesting horse hay
67 harvesting on hårdvalls meadow
68 harvesting on hårdvalls meadow
69 leaves harvest
70 possibly harvesting the starrbog
71 leaves harvest
72 possibly harvesting the starrbog
73 collecting the harvest
74 collecting the harvest

75 leaves harvest
76 leaves harvest
77 bringing home the harvest
78 turnips and Swedish turnips harvesting, roots collecting
79 bringing home the harvest
80 turnips and Swedish turnips harvesting, roots collected
81 ploughing of the fallow and fields with straw on
82 threshing and drying
83 grinding grain
84 shearing sheep
85 baking
86 slaughtering
87 knitting socks and gloves
88 clearing of meadows
89 cutting spruce twigs
90 wood, timber and pole cutting
91 cutting wood for handicrafts
92 teasing and spinning wood
93 winter clothes preparing
94 transporting firewood and spruce twigs
95 transporting timber and building timber
96 bringing home starr fodder
97 handicraft
98 spinning wool
99 baking and making food for Christmas
100 cutting spruce twigs
101 travel to Norway*
102 transporting and cutting firewood
103 threshing
104 threshing
    * travel to market

Figure 6.1 Ethno-historical account of the annual cycle of activities within a seventeenth-century farming community in Jämtland, Sweden. (Based on Wichman 1968 and information supplied by L. Rathje, Umeå University)

tivities, and how such interaction and collaboration must have been organized through agreements, normative conventions and spontaneous responses to immediate demands. Any of the stages indicated in examples, such as the one represented in figure 6.1, could usually physically have been done equally well by any adult person. The particular version created by a society results from how, amongst others, its specific gender ideology is interpreted in its material effects and from how society agrees to arrange its production sequences. Having formed and agreed upon a 'tradition' this in turn, through repetitive performance and the socialization of children into its processes, will serve to concretize a certain view upon the gendered nature of labours; it becomes convention. The variability demonstrated by ethnographic, historical and contemporary accounts of the arrangements of simple production sequences, such as harvesting grain, is therefore vast, and prehistoric societies would probably add to this diversity. Despite the substantial importance of such activities for the social and physical maintenance of society, the way gender ideology would be interwoven with how prehistoric communities arranged their basic subsistence activities has so far been little investigated (but see Hastorf 1998).

Serving food, marking differences

The importance of food is also strongly indicated by the cultural objectification of its consumption and its important role in rituals. The construction of instruments for its presentation and consumption therefore provides interesting insights into both the emphasis given to it and the classifications and elaboration it is subjected to.

As regards the serving of food there are many potentials for revealing changes in attitudes and the manner in which communities were involved in sharing and serving food. It is, for example, interesting to analyse pottery in terms of whether it is a container for food or a platform for its presentation. This simple point illuminates an important aspect of the visibility and display of food in connection with the construction of a meal. For instance, until the Late Bronze Age most pottery in temperate Europe was various versions of containers ranging from large storage vessels to small cups. Then during the Late Bronze Age large flat plates for the serving and visual display of food were introduced in large areas of central Europe. These plates, furthermore, are often beautifully decorated with polychrome patterns painted on the inner surface. With the change in form and decoration it is clearly the inside of the pots that was made visible and meant to be seen rather than, as previously, the outside (see figure 6.2). The role of food was clearly changing at this time. Presumably due to new influences and a socio-political interest in Mediterranean cultures, the food-culture of Late Bronze Age Europe changed and food became served in a manner which emphasized display. The change in pot shapes suggests that this was a change from a previous custom of dishing out from large pots into small bowls or organic plates or alternatively eating directly from the cooking pot. Such changes in the instruments of the meals are suggestive of more changes as well. While soup, broth, porridge and other semi-liquid meals are well suited to bowls and cups, they are less so to the flat plates of the later periods. Changes in the consistency of the meal would, however, also affect the processing involved and while stews and similar meals can be left alone for many hours 'cooking itself' over the fire, other types of meals demand closer attention and interaction. The emphasis upon food display and the specific demands of the meals (in terms of preparation and presentation) that is suggested simply by change in pot shapes (although also shown by other types of evidence) may therefore have involved substantial changes in the organization of food-producing labour. It is also likely to have affected (and potentially to have further formalized) people's interrelationships as roles were established based on people's different involvement with making, giving and receiving food. In particular, an important distinction may have been drawn between the ones serving and the ones being served. As a result gender relations shaped by previous practices surrounding the production and partaking of meals would have been challenged and new relationships (rights and responsibilities) negotiated. Such evidence of changes in the cultural construction of meals are frequently suggested, but are usually rather superficially considered. The changes during the Late Bronze Age and Early Iron Age outlined above have thus primarily been investigated in the context of the elite and their explicit adoption and construction of local versions of the rituals of the Greco-Etruscan banquet

Figure 6.2   Examples of Central European Hallstatt B plates with interior decoration. (Redrawn after Brun and Mordant 1988)

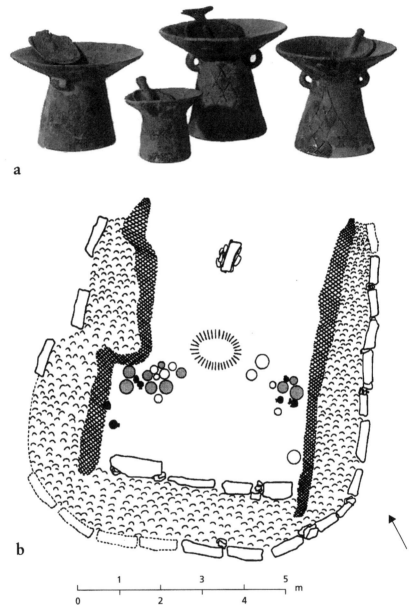

Figure 6.3a Middle Neolithic pedestal bowls and clay spoons from the Tustrup 'temple', Denmark. (Courtesy P. Kjærum and Forhistorisk Museum, Moesgård, Århus)
b The location of Middle Neolithic pedestal bowls (grey circles), clay spoons (black circles) and other vessels (open circles) within the Tustrup 'temple', Denmark. (Redrawn after Kjærum 1955)

(Bouloumié 1988, Oliver 1992: 57), although Dietler recently has emphasized the importance of analysing different local effects of such colonization (1996). The impact these changes have upon the social meaning of the meal, upon labour division and in particular upon eating-groups as a consolidation and confirmation of the in-group are questions largely ignored. The extent to which these changes, albeit in this case probably initially mainly adopted by the elite, permeated society more widely through various mechanisms of acculturation and imitation is also neglected a question. As a result the life of the elite is seen isolated from the society at large, although the data show that at the very basic level of ideals, productive labour and labour divisions, such imitations may have resulted in sweeping changes that affected roles and social expectations widely.

There are also distinct examples of pottery that are used to display rather than contain food before the Bronze Age. It is the case, however, that their appearance and find contexts suggest that these are special objects used in rituals where food was an offering or gift and its visual presence therefore emphasized. One extremely interesting case is the ceramic pedestal vessels with associated clay spoons known from the Middle Neolithic in southern Scandinavia. These pots, which look like highly decorated plates placed upon a decorated conical trunk (see figure 6.3a), are distinctly different from the contemporary pottery both in form and idea, and while common in burial monuments they are rare in settlements (Kjærum 1955). It is therefore feasible to argue that they were used for the presentation of food as part of the practice of display and performance acted out at Neolithic burial monuments and ritual sites (ibid.: 20).

Simple observations, such as the difference between pottery for displaying or containing food, may therefore help to identify some of the distinctions that were drawn by prehistoric communities and to trace how they shift in importance, distinctiveness and context. Locating the construction of practices and material forms that affect how identity is experienced and related to within communities is also made possible by such observation of apparently simple technological or cultural choices.

Consumption: incorporating body and food

Methods for the analysis of the effect of differential access to different kinds of food upon the members of a community have also been developed and increasingly sophisticated. In a few instances unique preservation has allowed us to study the physical remains of a single meal through the preserved stomach content of an individual. This is, for instance, the case with the so-called ice man from the Italian Alps (Spindler 1994), and with many bog bodies. Two of the latter, the Iron Age men from Grauballe and Tollund, both in Denmark, were found to have had meals composed of a range of different domestic grains with wild seeds partly accidentally included with it and partly deliberately collected from other habitats (Helbæk 1958: 107). The range of grains and seeds collected from different fields and environments shows that both regular harvesting and selective gathering of wild seeds were involved in accumulating the resources used to cook the meal. Thus, the 'frozen events' that these bodies provide indicate how in such Iron Age communities a range of activities and possibly different types of labour, which must have been organized according to agreements and understanding of roles, were involved in the production of a simple porridge.

New techniques, such as isotopic analysis of bones, also make it possible to compare a community in terms of the main components of the diets of its members. This method has, for instance, been used, in combination with other arguments, by Hastorf (1991). She argues that the expansion of the Inca empire, due to its differential effect upon the public life of men and women living in the countryside, had consequences for their daily life and resource allocation within local communities. This interpretation is informed by stable isotopic analysis of sexed skeletons from just before the Inca and during Inca control (1991: 148ff). The analysis suggests an increase in male consumption of maize during the latter period (ibid.: 150–1). Hastorf argues that since maize was used for beer this may be explained in terms of men beginning to participate in a range of public political gatherings during which beer was consumed, and that these meetings related to the politicization of the rural area. The comparative changes in the diet of men and women during this time therefore show how apparently minor changes in food allocation may be part of more significant changes in socio-politics that affected the cultural evaluation and the practical potentials of women. Rega has used a similar method in combination with dental caries rates and attrition in a study of an Early Bronze Age cemetery in the former Yugoslavia (1997). The dental characteristics are used as an indirect indication of dietary carbohydrate consumption, while the chemical analysis aims to establish the proportion of meat and plant food in the diet. In her case, both methods showed that males and females had similar diets, while, on the other hand, differences in food consumption were observed between groups within the cemetery that are interpreted as representing family or residence-groups (Rega 1997: 238–9). The Early Bronze Age is a period of considerable change in material culture due in part to the rapid development and elaboration of bronze metallurgy and extensive exchange systems. So far it has been common to suggest that the social impact of these changes resulted in growing asymmetries between men and women, as men became the metalworkers and were the ones engaged in and controlling exchange (Shennan 1993). Rega's analysis, although as yet only based on one cemetery, may suggest that social responses to these changes were more complex and less divided along gender lines than we have assumed.

Another example of dietary variance, which is interpreted as resulting from social differences, comes from Early Iron Age temperate Europe. Here skeletal differences have been used to argue that the person buried at Hochdorf, Germany, in contrast to the rest of the population 'came from a privileged background on several generations of good food' (Olivier 1992: 57). Certainly, more studies of this kind would be an invaluable contribution to the further analysis of how differences within communities affect resource allocations. It could also help towards analysing what impact major technological and sociopolitical changes have upon local communities, and how gender and other social principles are affected by this. Increased sensitivity towards how differently constituted people lived their life is an area where much more attention is needed, and one which could add essential data to current understanding of the relationship between people and communities. Such analysis would also contribute much-needed insights into social conditions such as hunger, malnutrition, privations and various types of diseases and how they relate to variously constituted groups within a community.

Drinking as social performance

The focus upon the production, service and consumption of food helps to consolidate daily life and routines as a central arena for the construction of gender. This does not mean, however, that gender is not also involved in other dimensions of food, such as its status as commodity or gift and its use in rituals or as part of conspicuous display and consumption. The interest in daily life should not mean that we automatically make the importance of food and of eating domestic only; rather it should be recognized as being involved with different levels of practices. One of the central roles of food, is, for example, its involvement in rites of passage and the marking of changes in seasons and social events (Barrett 1989) and thus in helping to give meaning and structure to life. This theme is interestingly illustrated by food in the form of drink and drinking activities.

Within archaeology the topic of drink has mainly focused upon the luxury or ceremonious aspect of drinking (for discussion see Vencl 1994), being concerned with the creation of social elites, with evidence of trade and gift exchange, and with processes of acculturation. Less attention has been given to the role of drinking in the creation of solidarities and thus its potentially important role in social dynamic (but see Vencl 1994).

Drinking is known from ethnography, historical and classical sources as well as contemporary societies as a practice commonly used to celebrate and mark important political, social and economic events, as well as being a practice through which social relations are confirmed. Through drinking, contractual relations are expressed and confirmed, and as a social practice it facilitates and moderates interaction. Drinking plays a central role in, and at times is the central means of, the expression and experience of hospitality, and thus of creating links, obligations and debts beyond the immediate group. It is an important gift, and it is used to construct networks of reciprocal obligations (Vencl 1994: 312). The potential ceremonial quality of drinking together and its obvious social implications (the construction of solidarities and the experience of the we-group) mean that drinking is often used to mobilize groups (Hastorf 1991:139). Ethno-historical evidence suggests, for example, that drinking in farming communities, which need to mobilize the community for collective work, often has a ceremonial aspect (Vencl 1994: 313).

Another interesting aspect of drink is that many types of liquids (such as milk or various kinds of fermented drinks) are both non-durable and time-consuming to produce. They are therefore often either transformed into another kind of food, such as cheese and butter, or made for a particular planned event. This makes it likely that food such as fermented drinks had particular strategies for its production and consumption, being an occasional product, planned and partaken of as a group activity and event (Vencl 1994: 310), and that participation bestowed social significance, including the confirmation of in- and out-groups. It also means that drinking often become formalized in various ways which may affect its archaeological visibility.

Milk, it is believed, was drunk from the Neolithic onwards, and mead is know at least from the Bronze Age, when wine also appears in some parts of Europe (for references see Vencl 1994). In addition, cups, goblets, jugs and other vessels for holding liquids appear in most parts of southern and central Europe from early in the Neolithic (ibid.: 316) and from other parts of Europe during the Neolithic. This hints at the classification of food into different types that should be differently stored, served and consumed. Behind these classifications are the practical reality of different substances and the specific labour that was involved. We are again confronting situations where differences exist that affected people and their interactions and social recognition.

It is therefore interesting that some materials and finds from prehistory may hint at collective drinking ceremonies. It is often suggested that during the Neolithic feasting and drinking were a motivating force behind monument-building (e.g. Evans 1988b, Dietler 1996), and drinking feasts seem indicated by pottery hoards of small cups known, for example, from the Neolithic Baden culture in Bohemia (Vencl 1994: 316). The importance of drinking, especially in ritual contexts and as a means of defining and bounding the in-group, has also been argued for the Late Neolithic and Early Bronze Age with special attention towards the phenomenon of the Bell Beaker culture, with its distinct beakers. The latter has been extensively discussed by Sherratt (1997), who has emphasized the link between these ceramic forms and drinking as a socio-political event. This interpretation often has gender implications. Thus, it has been common to emphasize the occurrence of beakers with weapons in male graves and to see this as testifying to the connection of drinking with the formation of a warrior elite (e.g. Treherne 1995). The spread of drinking rituals across the European Eneolithic cultures is then seen as a manifestation of new norms and modes of social relationships amongst men (e.g. Shennan 1993, Sherratt 1997, Vencl 1994: 317). It is clear that these implications need critical reconsideration.

Communal drinking is also suggested by materials from the Bronze Age, where many Central European hoards contain large numbers of small vessels, sometimes even made of gold. The special ceremonial character of the drinking may be suggested by their incorporation in hoarding practices, although this has not yet been thoroughly studied. Some finds are, however, so obviously special in their character that the drinking can be firmly placed as part of a particular event. One of these is the Middle Bronze Age hoard from Raddusch, Germany.* Here over fifty cups together with a few containers and service vessels were buried in two pits (see figure 6.4). This suggests organized events in which drinking was important, and where ritual deposition or withdrawal of the drinking vessels of the group was also of significance (Hänsel, A. and B. 1997: 177). The importance of such events is further confirmed by the occurrence of similar cups made of gold (e.g. ibid.: 136–7). It is also significant that such deposits of drinking utensils are found at several locations (A. Hänsel 1997: 84–6), since this

---

* I am grateful to Dr Alix Hänsel for drawing my attention to this example.

Figure 6.4 More than fifty cups and vessels from two pit deposits at Raddusch, Germany. (After Hänsel, A. and B. 1997: 176–7)

suggests it was a practice held in common by many communities. While it is not possible to determine who participated in such ceremonies, it is clear that they were part of the community's life and would have participated in constituting its members in terms of distinct categories.

The profusion of cauldrons and various other types of vessels during the first millennium BC and the European-wide distribution of such items of southern and Central European origin attest to the importance given during this time to the equipment used for holding drinks and thus presumably to its social significance. During this period the consumption of wine became increasingly popular amongst certain sectors of society and it became associated with the use of special drinking sets composed of drinking-horns, cauldrons, amphorae and flagons. These were objects of prestige, commonly imported, and they were often reinvested into local socio-political competition. The degree of imitation and acculturation that is expressed in food, and in particular in drinking activities and utensils, continues as an obvious element in the further development of Europe. For example, in the borrowing of Roman drinking ceremony into various parts of Europe (even outside the Roman empire), their wine-serving utensils became symbols of a certain lifestyle and of political connectedness. Drinking is also a theme recurrent in Norse mythology and early medieval Germanic cultural institutions, where the concept of *Männerbund* invoked drinking rituals to maintain the institution of a warrior elite (Treherne 1995: 109). The involvement of and the effect upon gender of such drinking activities remain another underexplored theme in archaeology, and several simplistic assumptions can be found in their interpretations.

It is, for example, common to discuss such drinking ceremonies in terms only of how feasting was focused upon males – their identities, solidarities and positions. The focus of any individual event cannot, however, be understood isolated from how that event is situated within a larger social web of relationship and meaning. Bevan, introducing this point to archaeological discussions of feasts, argues 'even when feasting is an important manifestation of male social competition other members of society and probably in particular female play a pivotal role in the preparation and organisation of the feast' (1997: 85). From a gender-critical perspective there are therefore two obvious points to make concerning drinking rituals. The one is that drinking communities are not just stable, well-founded institutions, but are also locations of change and contestation. The other point is that discussions present only those seen as members of the drinking communities as having their identity affected through these rituals and their emblematic objects. Such performances are, however, simultaneously both affected by and commenting upon inclusivity and exclusivity, and the intersection of age, gender and social differences would have affected individuals within the community in a far more complex manner than suggested by these discussions. Rather than detaching the drinking-solidarities from the community at large, they can be understood as constituted by the community and as a forum in which the identity of its members is being confirmed rather than first now constituted. This then means, as Bevan argues (1997), and as shown also by Hastorf's Peruvian case study (1991), that drinking and feasting involve more people than their apparent participants, and they bestow and affect the socially perceived identity of the many rather than the few. Therefore, as the archaeological record is rich in potential evidence of such practices, it is important that we learn to use them for more than identifying and isolating one particular kind of social membership.

Archaeology, food and gender

Gender, I have argued, can be located as a difference created and negotiated in the allocation of resources. In practice this is expressed through actions and norms which allocate to certain kinds of people specific rights and expectations over food. The processes through which food is made into a cultural and symbolic medium with permissions and prohibitions attached to it is therefore a central research area for archaeology. The means through which these relationships are formed, and therefore the potentials for studying them, have a wide scope. They range from productive activities to consumption of food and the involvement of different kinds of people, practices and skills. This means that the interaction between food and social identities can be expressed at many different points and may shift content between different stages. The varied practices and resources involved and the often fluid borders between them make it fortuitously obvious that we should not attempt to *fix* the construction of gender within this medium. The medium itself and the many ways it is being explored push us towards thinking about food and eating both as economic practices and resources and as a kind of theatrical event, as a performance of difference and a simultaneous incorporation (bodily and social). Food is about actions and relationships: it is about giving and receiving and about making and unmaking (Fürst 1995). Rather than providing a fixed point for gender construction, it gives us insights into its maintenance and negotiation as it affects it, providing as it does a means for its material recognition and the learning of it as a difference. The evidence of food helps us to understand and recognize the necessary and critical involvement of both women and men in its production and social evaluation, the inclusion of different life stages and the central role such activities have in confirming social relations. The study of food also confirms the discursive nature of these relationships as it shows labour division as something that is made, not given, and food allocations, likewise, not given but something agreed upon and performed.

This chapter has argued for the importance of food – not just as subsistence but also in cultural life and how this knowledge should inform our investigations of prehistory. It has, furthermore, outlined how it is possible to identify characteristics in our interaction with food and in particular certain situations, such as food allocation, which show how it can become actively involved with the construction and maintenance of identities, including gender. While the examples referred to give neither an exhaustive account of the possibilities of investigating such issues through the archaeological record nor a representative view of the complex relations involved, they nonetheless begin to demonstrate how and where these central concerns and their material manifestations and consequences may be identified. Such analysis, moreover, would give us access to situations where gender differences informed practical performances and in turn were reproduced through their repetition and negotiation.

7
Dressing Gender: Identity through Appearance

When Megan, my daughter, had her first pair of shoes, we could choose between dark blue boys' shoes with trains on, or red girls' shoes with bunnies – there was nothing in between!

Megan, now six years old, said to me 'It's kind of funny boys usually have dark clothes and girls have light ones.'.

The point of clothes

I have argued so far that a useful archaeological concept of gender must relate to how society creates particular groups of people and how these are related to bodies and their assigned activities and use of objects. Gender policies are therefore dependent upon the recognition of and agreements (however discursively) on who are members of particular groups. Gender is about identity and difference. Material objects are central in this communication, and amongst objects those used to fabricate people's appearances are particularly interesting.

Dress is a central medium for both the acquiring of socially ascribed identities and the communication of them. This is most clearly illustrated through 'uniforms', which are standardized appearances that are socially acknowledged to represent certain positions and the duties and rights which come with them. Gaining the right to wear a specific uniform furthermore becomes an expression of having become part of the group represented by the uniform. Wearing the uniform visually communicates this membership. The example of the uniform also emphasizes other visual and material characteristics of this medium. For those who are knowledgeable, in possession of the code, the membership is communicated visually and without involving direct contact. It is the material elements of the uniform: the hat, the shiny buttons, the belt, the cut of the coat etc., together with the particular way they are combined, that signal who is represented. We recognize visually and identify accurately the groups as being, for example, the police, the navy or the Salvation Army. We do this because we are meant to recognize them and tell them apart; see, for example, figures 7.1 and 7.2. When we are not meant to identify membership, unless part of the group ourselves, the code is not so widely shared and in the reception of the visual message we are meant to be divided into the initiated and the rest. This is, for example, the role of club ties. The extent to which we use appearance to identify people is also well illustrated by the theatre, where costumes are central to the identification of the characters in terms of variables such as gender, age, wealth and occupation (Roach and Eicher 1979: 11). Stories such as Shakespeare's play *Twelfth Night* or films like *Tootsie* explore these associations as their ploys are based on confusions arising from characters dressing as the 'wrong sex'. The social assumption about gender identity that is based upon how the person dresses is therefore presented as in conflict with the emotional/sexual attractions felt. Such ploys work and are understood by the audience according to their intentions due to the common assumption that appearance reveals identity. Thus the stories play upon the possible confusion of sex and gender. Another example of the explicit communication provided by appearance is evident in the cardboard photographic stands at fairgrounds, where the entertainment is

Figure 7.1 Florence Nightingale nurses in uniform. The hierarchy amongst them is signalled by details of their uniform. (Reproduced courtesy of the Florence Nightingale Museum Trust, London)

Figure 7.2 Formal photograph of the farm workers from a middle-sized farm in northern Denmark, late nineteenth century. The variations in dress indicate differences in terms of gender, age and rank (i.e. work). (Reproduced courtesy of Vendsyssel Historiske Museum, Denmark)

provided by the momentary obliteration of real-life identity (Sørensen 1997).

The medium of dress is extremely varied and exceedingly malleable in how it can communicate. Throughout history and prehistory people have dressed themselves and others, and in doing so they have used the social surface of the body, its second skin, for many purposes. A recurrent theme within these differences is the construction of identities, of membership or exclusion. Another theme is how changes in dress map many of the changes in the life of an individual as she or he progresses though different life stages. This is well known from ethnography and is often expressed through rites of passage that involve a ritualized change in appearance. This is, for instance, the case with the Kalabans in Nigeria. The way changes in dress map life stages amongst them is particularly interesting in that they show that these processes can take different forms for men and women. For the Kalabans, the dress of the former expresses their achievement of power and responsibilities while that of the latter indicates moral (i.e. knowledge of the world and behavioural expectations) and physical development (Michelman and Erekosima 1992: 179). Dress therefore can be critically involved with both the communication and construction of identities, including the learning and socialization of them. Dress in its materiality, which involves fabrication and allows manipulation, is therefore central in the communication of social differences in many societies. There are two additional reasons why gender archaeology should explore dress. One is that various types of evidence of dress are well known in the archaeological record. The other is that archaeology's concern with the active role of objects will bring a new dimension to the study of dress, moving it beyond fashion to a more explicit concern with its role in social discourse.

Dress and archaeology: a brief outline

Although appearance is so clearly of social importance, it has been relatively little studied and has mainly been relegated to a specialist field of textile and costume research carried out by women (as a kind of continuation of women's role as dressmakers in recent historic periods). Alternatively, it has been part of descriptive reconstructions of the material culture of particular periods, as seen in many museum exhibitions, such as those by the costume department at the Victoria and Albert Museum in London.

Clothes and costumes are traditionally embedded in our expectations of civilization and they play a role in the origin myth of many societies. For instance, within Christianity much emphasis is put upon the stage when our 'ancestors' discovered their own nakedness and hid themselves. In an extension of these views, clothing has often on a general level been emphasized as part of our uniqueness as a species, as when Carlyle in *Sartor Resartus* defined man as 'a clothed animal' (quoted in Eicher and Roach-Higgins 1992: 9). It is also referred to by, for example, both Darwin and Spencer (ibid.). There is therefore a small area of research, often early in date, which has considered costumes in terms of (social) evolutionary accounts of the past and which has particularly focused upon the origin of dress. An aptly named volume *From Nudity to Raiment* represents this view well: 'Dogmatic nobody can be about the beginnings of human life on the globe; but marking those beginnings was the adoption of dress. . . . the chief distinction between the savage and the beast is that the savage is adorned' (foreword by Sisley Huddleston in Hiler 1929). In such works anthropologists or psychologists have often argued that feeling of modesty or shame, the desire for sexual attractiveness or functional needs were the reasons for the origin of clothes (Hiler 1929, Fischer in Polhemus 1978: 181–2). Archaeology often produced the data used in such works, but it is interesting that the discipline itself rarely engaged with these largely functionalistic discussions of clothing. As a result our discipline has taken costumes for granted. This means that the obvious potentials provided by this important feature of human behaviour have been largely ignored.

Sol Tax has argued that the reasons why the non-functional aspects of clothing were not considered earlier by anthropologists are that it had to await the development of the theory of cultures as systems of symbols as well as a cross-cultural comparative perspective which was not evolutionary (1979: v). Whatever the reasons, the social effect and significance of appearance have only resurfaced as an important research topic within recent years, and interest in this field is now dramatically increasing (e.g. Barnard 1996, Barnes and Eicher 1992, Craik 1994, David 1992, Eicher 1995). The field of theoretically informed investigations of costumes is therefore both patchy and relatively recent (for a review of the anthropological literature see Eicher and Roach-Higgins 1992). For instance, although Barthes used clothing as one of his examples in *Elements of Semiology* (1967), and despite communication usually being recognized as a central element of appearance, the obvious application of semiotics to costumes, treating them as signs, has been little explored. It seems that it was first extensively used in a study of the function of folk costumes in Moravian Slovakia in 1971 by Bogatyrev, who argued that costumes usually are simultaneously an object and a sign (Bogatyrev 1971). Otherwise this obvious dimension has been little explored. Generally it was first during the late 1970s that an appreciation of the social significance of costumes developed within behavioural psychology, anthropology and sociology – but not in archaeology. The latter subject never gave any specific attention to the communicative aspect of costumes and their involvement with identity, although substantial energy has gone into their reconstruction and conservation. Traditionally archaeology has thus seen costume in a rather passive and empiricist manner.

Recently, however, the ways in which we construct our appearance have become recognized as a central element of social and individual identity formation. It is being acknowledged that appearance is a significant element of social communication. It is recognized that through specific acts and in- and exclusive appearances different types of social personae and categories are signalized and thus effectively involved with the construction, maintenance and negotiation of these differences. These signals are a significant aspect of social learning, which means that social roles are partly implemented and learned from dress: appearance (and the means of appearances) play a role in how one acquires gender identity for instance. One can also argue that children acquire notions of their own gender identities by comparing the ways they are dressed with the dress of others. The daughter recognizes the similarity between her clothing and that of her mother and she notices that her father and brother dress differently. One acquires knowledge about gender-appropriate dress and this 'extends to learning rights and responsibilities to act "as one looks." Accordingly, gendered dress encourages each individual to internalise as gendered roles a complex set of social expectations for behaviour' (Eicher and Roach-Higgins 1992: 19). This engendering aspect of clothing is furthered by mechanisms of social (re)enforcement as people comment upon and in extreme cases will ostracize those who do not conform. In response, phenomena like 'cross-dressing' become both possible (as there is 'something' to cross over) and socially suspect and repressed.

The meaning of dress, furthermore, is a social knowledge which becomes naturalized in appearance codes (Kaiser 1983–4). Appearance provides a means of social communication concerning relationships between individuals or groups. I would further argue that the association between a person and his or her dress at the same time is distinct (particularly when worn), and that costumes in principle also have a degree of self-determination and self-expression. Appearance might therefore also occasionally provide insight into people as persons (Sørensen 1997). 'Clothes are activated by the wearing of them just as bodies are actualised by the clothes they wear' (Craik 1994:16). The tension between the articulation of self and the social construction of particular groups of people can therefore find expression, for example, through the construction of subversive appearances. This suggests that the construction of appearance is a field in which negotiation of difference and sameness will often take place or become expressed.

In our own society the appearances which are created are significantly gendered. Clothing is very much a social artefact (Joseph 1986), and while learning about gender-appropriate dress one also learns about the rights and responsibilities to act appropriately (Eicher and Roach-Higgins 1992: 19). Differences between, on the one hand, women, girls and female babies and, on the other hand, men, boys and male babies are from the first moment in the delivery ward created by differential assignment of variables such as colour. Looking at apparently 'neutral' items of clothing like socks, vests or shoes, their gendered nature is obvious to anyone familiar with the particular cultural code. In northern and western Europe, for example, boys have dark colours, robust edges, no frills or bows, clear geometrical patterns, wild animals and trains. For girls the colours are red or pale, they have frills and little bows, softness and curves are emphasized, and their objects are decorated with flowery, soft patterns and soft animals. These differences, having no relationship to labour division or individuality, assign socially accepted personalities to these young members of society. Such associations, apparently silent and yet so articulate about how our differences should be understood and evaluated, are found in many items of clothing. Even apparently entirely functional objects, such as spectacles or bicycles, are designed and consumed as ladies and gents. The gender-coding contained in clothing is also well illustrated through some of its historical changes. During the 1960s challenges to social norms and in particular the so-called 'sexual revolution' were often expressed by radicalizing clothing. It is, for example, well known that women during this period conquered or took over many items of men's clothing and in particular trousers, but it is interesting to notice also the detailed elements of distinction that were involved and often differently negotiated. For instance, differences between women's and men's clothing were for a while still signalled by the placing of women's zips on the hip (or back) but not at the front of the trousers and women's clothes are still buttoned right over left, in contrast to men's clothes.

> This [the same way of buttoning] remained until the mid-nineteenth century when front-buttoning dresses and coats became more popular and the convention appeared to develop of women's clothes being fastened in the opposite direction. . . . However, the explanation may simply be the Victorians' greater concern to denote rather strictly male and female clothing. Whatever the cause, by 1900 virtually all women's clothes fastened right over left and men's left over right. (Tarrant 1994: 24)

In hindsight, such distinctions are bemusing but they were at the time significant codes, which were deeply rooted and almost taboo-like. Such associations between people and their clothing are profoundly affected by and in turns maintain a specific gender ideology concerned with establishing feminine and masculine characteristics and qualities. Dress, however, does more than merely translate these categories; it also gives them a distinct physical reality and their transmitted information cannot easily be expressed in words. The communicative ability of dress is in fact striking, and it is clearly one of the most effective means of indicating a person's gender (Eicher and Roach-Higgins 1992: 17). We routinely receive and respond in appropriate ways to its signals. Dress therefore provides us with a means of investigating the construction and symbolic reflection of social categories. Gender archaeology would benefit greatly from recognizing appearance as central to its investigation of social identities and especially gender.

Methodology and analysis

There will be many ways of approaching the medium of clothing, but common to all current ones seems to be the recognition of costumes as part of a system of communication (Schwarz 1979). This involves communicating differences, categories and events (e.g. initiation), but it also provides a means of transformation, coercion, concealment, pretence and taking on a role. The last is, for example, relevant for the common discussions within archaeology of the differences between achieved and ascribed status (e.g. Shennan 1975). In addition things can be done to and are done with clothes through the processes through which they are transformed into costumes. This means that variables such as weaving types, dyes, painting, embroidery, and cuts and their 'architectural assembly' (Schneider and Weiner 1989: 1) create potentials and nuances of communication. Worn or displayed in an emblematic way, cloth can denote variations in age, sex, rank, status and group affiliation (ibid.: 1). The rights to particular costumes are therefore often subject to social control and prohibition. In the medieval period the use of various colours was, for instance, sometimes made into the exclusive right of certain social groups, and in England sumptuary laws which aimed 'to define exactly what fabrics, furs and trimmings could be worn by each rank of society' (Ashelford 1996: 289–90) were passed during the reigns of Richard II, Henry IV and Elizabeth I. The manner in which the use of such clothing would simultaneously have reinforced the ability to identify these different groups is obvious. Another example is the regulations during the late seventeenth century in Nuremberg, Germany, which dictated the amount the four ranks of society could spend on clothes (Roach and Eicher 1979: 12). Examples of such regulations abound, demonstrating how costumes and the rights to wear them can play a central role in social discourse upon difference.

Within archaeology, Meskell has criticized the analysis of the externalized, uninhabited body, which focuses upon clothing, adornment, posture and gestures, for not acknowledging the recursive role of the individualized body (1996: 8). The intimate relationship between clothing, adornment and the human body has often been emphasized, and it appears as a central theme in traditional ethnography (see comments in Polhemus 1978: 176). Meanwhile, the fact that these dressed bodies were inhabited, embodied, is not ignored by approaches that do not incorporate the body, rather this is considered less central to the particular type of analysis than the emphasis on social conventions. People dress themselves, they activate clothing feeling the texture against their skin, notice the colours and have personal preferences such as liking red and disliking green or finding the daisy pattern more pleasing than the rose. Social norms and fashion (the difference and dependence between them is in itself a fascinating study) do, however, also exist, and they force these choices about personal adornment within more or less clearly established limits where even the challenge to these rules, such as the dress of punks during the 1970s, uses codes of dress accepted and formulated within their own 'peer-culture'. The personal, individual experiences of choice and textile sensations while at a certain level central is nonetheless of little significance for how the material culture of dress is formulated. We can therefore argue that while dress is self-composed and experienced and in that sense embodied, it is also extremely susceptible and aware of social responses. This is well demonstrated by (young) people's sensitivity towards their own and other people's clothing and the importance they assign to the reaction of their peers. The manner in which fashion explores this insecurity and the desire for conformity illustrates how easily this dependence can be identified. Individuals do not invent their dress, rather their sense of dress is learned from others, and their personal choices, embellishments and elaboration do not constitute a unique language (Roach and Eicher 1979: 7). It is through appearance that our membership of social groups is symbolized and expressed. Therefore, although this is expressed through individual bodies they, in this context, are in many ways not primarily individual but rather social bodies, symbolizing socialization processes and the collectivity of existence (Polhemus 1978: 151).

These points are particularly relevant to archaeology since it is the material qualities of appearance that provide us with a means of its investigation. For archaeology, appearance is interesting and extremely important insofar as it provides a medium/material objects through which we can analyse how different individuals are constructed and distinctions be made in the way they looked. It can also investigate temporal, spatial and social variations regarding how such differences are articulated, how they relate to other identities such as age and social standing, and what importance they may have had. In addition, these investigations can be carried out without a priori deciding upon the relationship between sexual differences and gender. For instance, if within a particular society swords are a masculine and masculating item, then the contexts in which swords were deposited can be interpreted as related to or commenting upon masculinity independently of the sex (and sexuality) of the person with whom the object was associated and also irrespective of whether the remains of a person are in fact present. When such categories have been established it would also be possible to investigate how such gendered categories overlap or differ from the categories established on the basis of physical sex characteristics. This approach has recently been outlined by, for example, Hodder (1997). In addition, independently of how we understand the relationship between sex and gender, it is useful to be able to engage with the archaeological record through different combinations of these constructions.

Now that we have recognized the potentials of costumes for gender archaeology, the practical realization of how such data may be analysed is urgently needed. Primarily this involves a change in the way we think about appearance. So far it has mainly been approached as a state of being, rather than realizing that a process of becoming is also involved. The analyses have therefore focused upon reconstruction and categorizations of types of dress. A similar approach is also still found in anthropology (probably influenced by the routine inclusion of dress in descriptive ethnographies), despite the call for 'a method for summarizing how dress is both a repository of meaning regarding gender roles and a vehicle for perpetuating or rendering changes in gender roles' (Eicher and Roach-Higgins 1992: 12–15). The method put forward by Eicher and Roach-Higgins, for example, aims at grouping types of dress by a classification of all the elements that may make up a dress and of their properties. As a method this is similar to standard archaeological use of combination tables. For instance, in their schema a 'body enclosure' may be classified as wrapped, suspended, pre-shaped or a combination of these and it would have various properties in terms of colour, shape, surface, odour etc. Such methods will, however, provide only a descriptive account of various combinations and possibly show clusters within them. Archaeology has routinely classified elements of costumes according to such methods for a long time, and various patterns and clusters are known to exist within some of the large assemblages such as dress fittings in Anglo-Saxon graves or Viking Age cemeteries. Such methods provide little help, however, in understanding what significant differences are created within these costumes and how this is achieved. This, I believe, is due partly to such methods treating all elements as equal, which neglects how significance can be affected by relationships between elements, and partly to these methods reducing costumes to a number of single elements, ignoring the range of activities and relationships through which effects were designed. Basically, these methods are limited in their effectiveness for social analysis because they limit themselves to the appearance of dress as a static creation and ignore the construction of that dress. In such approaches the medium of dress is recognized only as an object of discourse, while its own active involvement in discourse is not appreciated or at least not made available for analysis.

In response to such limitation I have proposed that costumes should be appreciated as being composed of single elements that are combined at different levels which may each involve distinct concerns and principles (Sørensen 1991, 1997). At each juncture, where items are associated or composition created, an opportunity for altering, adding or transforming the message that is communicated is created and responded to. It is these processes that archaeologists must engage with in their analysis of items of dress, because it was through them that differences were constructed, agreed upon and challenged. Our analysis, rather than being about either the single objects or the total costume can constructively employ the former and deconstruct the latter in terms of the distinct manners in which objects interact with each other and the body (Sørensen 1997). Each element, furthermore, may be gendered or have the ability to engender a context. This means that action, context and objects must be united in the analysis of the costume. It is also significant to appreciate that there is often a temporal element in the creation of appearance and its meaning.

Various routes to meaning can be detected within these processes, and different analytical procedures could be developed for their analysis as soon as we recognize how the medium is constituted. For example, in order to consider the creation of differences through the use of costumes during the European Bronze Age, I have suggested three principles of analysis (Sørensen 1997). One is concerned with the distinction between and separate existence of cloth, pieces of clothing and the full costume, calling for attention to how these constitute separate spheres, each with meaning and practices associated. Furthermore, for one to become the next, interference is needed, transforming the material from one stage of being to another. Thus, each of these stages provides us with a special situation from which different costumes could have resulted. A piece of cloth could be made into a skirt or a blouse or a gown, and in deciding what it becomes potentials are being negotiated. This also means that gender identification and ideologies may be differently recognized at the various levels of construction.

The second principle is concerned with how the objects are used. It suggests that differences can be created through the individual object especially due to its biography and physical attributes and quality, through its combination with other objects and also through how objects are physically composed upon the body or attached to pieces of clothing. For instance, the simple gold band of a wedding ring usually tells little apart from the married status of an individual, although if it is an heirloom it might have personal meaning as well. In combination with several elaborate rings the wedding ring may be seen as part of a woman's possessions revealing gender, marital status and wealth.

Finally, two wedding rings on the same finger in some countries indicates that the person is a widow(er). Thus the object can be exposed as a participant in different communications. This method can be usefully explored for many situations in prehistory where, for example, figurative depictions or funerary arrangements reveal the object situated and as a participant in a specific context. Many of these contexts have already been investigated in order to reconstruct dress from different periods; attempting to engender these appearances we can now focus upon how and where appearance was involved in constructing sameness and difference.

My third principle is therefore directly concerned with the articulation between objects and the body, recognizing that this relationship is culturally constructed in different ways, which again provides us with a location for negotiation and differentiation. The relationship can be fleeting, continuously open for difference and change, as is the case of removable objects like pins and necklaces. The use of these objects is deliberate and controllable. The relationship can also be fixed and yet movable, as is the case for objects that are parts of garments such as buttons, belt-rings or adornments upon hats. The use of these objects does not in each instance involve their negotiation as in use they are part of another context. Finally, the relationship between the object and the body can be made permanent, as in the case with necklaces or arm- and ankle-rings with a diameter which means they cannot be taken off. Such objects, which are well documented in both the ethnographic and archaeological record, become parts of the social body. From ethnography we know that permanent markers on the body, such as specific ornaments or tattoos, are often employed to indicate transitional stages in a person's life. This is, for example, the case amongst the people of the Andaman Islands, where scarification is used to mark the passage from childhood to adulthood (Roach and Eicher 1979: 12). Such marks become the visual expression of membership. The significance of recognizing the potential relationship between objects and the body is that the manner in which such 'embodied' objects can comment upon the individual is quite distinct, and that therefore how this may be challenged or negotiated at both a personal and group level is also distinct. In particular, the static relationship which can be made between body and objects means that at times these are not transient statements; on the contrary, they are fixed, irreversible and permanent markers similar in effect to the phenomena of tattooing and scarification. The importance of analytical principles like these for the further progression of gender archaeology is that they demonstrate strategies of differentiation that express themselves through objects. Due to their material expressions such strategies can often be traced in archaeological assemblages, opening new venues for analysing the emphasis upon and creation of difference within pre-historic society.

In any investigation of costumes it will appear that certain elements show clear gender categorization, some give a more ambiguous message about difference and others appear non-gendered. Probably the categorization of gender did not permeate all aspects of costumes, nor was it always present and all the time used discursively. The engendering of the costume comes through two processes. One is the inclusion of gendered objects, which refer to some but not necessarily all items. For instance, during the Bronze Age the sword was probably a gendered object, as was also likely the case for several forms of ornaments especially those designed for the hair, neck or waist, or specific types of garments such as hats. The other process takes place through the 'manipulation' of items, when they become combined and composed in ways that create differences. This confirms the central role of material culture since the adding of a single element to an assemblage can entirely change its message. It also suggests that negotiation and change will be located at the juncture of objects and actions.

Dress and identity in prehistory

In prehistory the appearance of the dressed person was a medium through which social roles were both learned and expressed. Their meanings were formed and made natural in appearance codes communicating relationships between individuals or groups. Such meaning was, of course, neither simple nor static; but it was nonetheless part of the cultural fabric of societies and can now provide important insights about them. So far I have argued that appearance is socially important and that the manner in which it is used to construct differences can be analysed. Now I shall briefly consider the archaeological record, and the range of evidence that may be available for investigations aimed at understanding this aspect of material culture and its employment in the construction of gendered persons.

Fragmentary evidence about the dressed person is abundant in the archaeological record and can be used to trace and analyse the manner in which this medium is used in the construction of social difference. It is also possible to foresee that future research could become engaged with questions about the ways in which such meanings (and therefore also their expressions) may be transformed over time. This relates both to changes within individual life cycles, as the person undergoes different stages that may be celebrated and visually commu-

Figure 7.3 The Palaeolithic figurine from Willendorf, Austria. The decoration suggests the use of ornaments and distinct hairstyle. (Reproduced courtesy of Naturhistorisches Museum Wien)

nicated, and to social time. It is also obviously the case that meanings are created at different levels, and that these may be superimposed upon each other, interrelating different identities such as age and gender.

As already mentioned, early interest in evolution often emphasized clothing and our desire to cover our bodies as a sign of our difference from animals. Although not always expressed as crudely there has been a consistent interest in evidence of dress from the earliest periods. While rejecting the simplistic evolutionary emphasis upon clothing as a stage representing the transition to civilization, there are nonetheless good reasons for studying early evidence of clothing. As will be discussed in chapter 10, obsessional interests in origins for their own sake are of little value. If, however, we ignore these phenomena as something distinct and as social products and practices which came into being at certain times, then we also ignore how they constituted important influences upon social interactions and communication. Early evidence of clothing provokes questions about group identities and self-awareness; clothing, as an extension of the body and a means of fabricating its appearance, is part of our cultural history. The coming into being and continuous transformation of clothing, and clothes' existence as cultural expression, must be explored. If this is not recognized we risk them being taken for granted, seeing them as an automatic, natural extension of the body. This will return us to thinking about clothing as a necessity rather than a cultural language.

The topic of analysis for the early periods is what the adornment of the body becomes concerned with, and, therefore, how people relate to the bodies of society. Adornment of the body is known from the Upper Palaeolithic with evidence of pendants and necklaces relatively frequently found (see further in chapter 10). These items are further augmented by figurines, who are decorated in manners suggesting pieces of clothing similar to loin-cloths together with necklaces, armrings and distinct hairstyles (see figure 7.3). Despite the sparse evidence we can detect certain concerns in this behaviour. The evidence reveals the body as an object of decoration. Such traces upon the body create differences of many kinds within a group, and they make distinctions easy to perceive. The emphasis upon the head and hair suggested by elaborate hairstyles on figurines is especially interesting, as it is a recurrent theme throughout (pre)history and also known from ethnography. Hair is clearly often of symbolic importance (Polhemus 1978: 123–33, Treherne 1995). It is often prominent in rites denoting change in social-sexual status, and it may in various ways represent an extension of the person. Dressing the hair or cutting it, as a ceremony of ordering, transforming or controlling it, can therefore be an important act. Hallpike (1978), for instance, shows how in some societies such acts are associated with a symbolic re-entering of society performed as part of a rite of passage. Widows covering or cutting their hair or the many examples of rules dictating that adult or married women cover their hair also emphasize both the association between sexuality and hair, and the linked themes of control and seclusion: the widow cutting her hair erases herself as a woman.

For a more detailed example of the importance of clothing in prehistory the Bronze Age is useful.* During this period pieces of clothing and associated objects were both distinct categories which in composition constituted costumes. The reconstruction of the costumes from the Bronze Age is still debated, with the evidence from northern Europe being particularly influential as many full costumes have been recovered there from oak-coffin graves (Bender Jørgensen 1991). Reconstructions based on evidence from well-preserved burials in Denmark show that three basic costumes were in use, one associated with swords and male skeletons, and the other two used together with various ornaments and found on female skeletons. The recognition that differences in women's costumes divide them into two distinct groups is highly significant. The data strongly argue that this was not due to the time of the year of the death/burial (i.e. a winter and a summer costume), nor is it directly related to the age or wealth of the women. It is therefore probably the case that the costume of the north European Bronze Age shows that women were differentiated visually on the basis of categorical identities or special group status within Bronze Age society. It is highly likely that this involved differentiation based upon their gender identities such as distinctions made due to physical or 'moral' development, reproduction or 'marriage'-like contracts. The north European material is extraordinarily rich in its details but as the sample is small it could be questioned whether the costumes that we know were unique rather than the norm. It is therefore extremely interesting that a division within the female costumes can also be demonstrated in the Middle Bronze Age of southern Germany (Sørensen 1997, Wels-Weyrauch 1989). This division is created through differences in the composition of objects, as one costume has the ornaments organized on the chest and the other has them arranged around the waist. This division, furthermore, cross-cuts differences in wealth, the types used and regional traits. This suggests that these societies were socially and conceptually seeing women in terms of differences within themselves. Moreover, within this large area the construction of two appearances amongst women was by each regional group made by exploring the same basic principles of differentiation, although physically it was expressed through different local types of ornaments and dress fittings. This suggests that at this point in time the distinction

---

* The Bronze Age is used as the main example here. It should therefore be stressed that although the material from this period is very rich, the possibility of investigating the construction of appearance within other periods is equally obvious.

was maintained at an interregional level, that went far beyond local communities. I have, therefore, proposed that the construction of these costumes was not solely concerned with gender asymmetry, and that the differences within women's appearance may be interpreted as relatively independent of men as it was concerned with the maintenance and expression of differences within (Sørensen 1997). The difference was between women and not, it seems, directly about their distinction from men. In fact, this interpretation of the meaning of gender differences in the Middle Bronze Age of central and northern Europe is congruent with other aspects of that society where male and female often appear as distinct and separate categories rather than relational ones. Research into Bronze Age dress which moves the analysis beyond reconstruction of costumes and begins to investigate social significance of appearance is a relatively recent development. The potential of this field and especially the ability to draw connections between appearance and the construction and communication of identities is, however, by now obvious.

Much rich and varied evidence of costumes and the construction and emphasis upon appearance exists for later periods, including textual descriptions. There are therefore already many studies of these materials, and large data analyses have been carried out for Roman and later periods, often demonstrating the intersection of social status, age, gender and sex as well as showing the patterns and the regional boundedness of these discourses. Although the specific implications in terms of gender ideologies have not been routinely addressed, a few studies have begun to explore these constructed in terms of a more concise understanding of the involvement of gender in these practices and the insights this may bring to social relations (e.g. Lucy 1997).

The importance of gender within such data is obvious, but it is equally clear that the articulation of gender through the medium of appearance takes many different forms, exploring its various potentials and elements. For instance, in the northwest province of the Roman empire the 'Gallic' coat was the basic element of dress. It was used by both men and women, and in that sense the type of dress was uni-sex. It appears, however, that men's coats were knee-length while women's were worn down to the ankles or calves (Allason-Jones 1989: 109). It was thus first when worn that the coats appeared gender specific. The more obvious articulation of difference was, therefore, made through the use of further pieces of clothing and objects, such as shawls, dress fittings and ornaments. Such further elaboration often seems to relate primarily to status, which may have dominated the construction of appearance at this time. The Romans also provide an important example of what may be called 'the technology of self' (e.g. Treherne 1995) with their lavish attention to the beautification and care of the body (Carr, personal communication, Hill 1997). This change in body culture is indicated by the introduction of various types of toiletries, substances such as perfumes and the common use of mirrors (Allason-Jones 1989). The potential of these rich data for analysis of the inter-section between gender and other social concerns, in particular different aspects of power, is obvious. It would, for example, be extremely in-teresting to compare the creation of appearance amongst natives and foreigners during the Roman expansion, and how this reveals the in-volvement of gender in the politics of colonization and acculturation, as discussed in chapter 10. The relatively modest but nonetheless ob-vious regional differences in appearance throughout the Roman em-pire would also provide an opportunity for analysing the coercive nature of appearance, and the manner in which gender intersects with other solidarities such as ethnicity or regionalism. This material also pro-vides examples of life stage variations in the costume of women within certain regions (Allason-Jones 1989: 114). Similar explicit patterns exist for other periods as well, such as the Bronze Age (e.g. Schumacher-Matthäus 1985, Shennan 1975), the Iron Age (Lorenz 1978) and later periods such as the Anglo-Saxon or the Viking Age (Brush 1988, Hägg 1983, Jesch 1991: 14–18), while as yet this is an under-explored con-cern regarding the Neolithic. The importance of recognizing life stages rather than a simple gender–age correlation is that this begins to pro-vide a means of understanding how gender differences are perceived and readjusted as people's bodies change, and in particular how men and women are evaluated as they undergo change, and whether they are valued and ranked through the same or different variables. For instance, one community may think about all its members on the basis of their contribution to production, while another may evaluate women though notions of reproduction but divide men according to their po-litical power. The Kalabans in Nigeria, as mentioned earlier, are an example of the latter, and they provide us with an important case study that illuminates the complexities which can exist and which chal-lenge simple notions of gender dualities or symmetries. It shows, for instance, how in their case men and women in addition to being thought about through different variables are also subject to discrete hierarchi-cal orders that are differently bound up with life stages. This differ-ence is due to all women in principle progressing through all the life stages accessible to women, while only some men will achieve the higher positions of power (Michelman and Erekosima 1992: 179–80). In this case there are therefore asymmetries developing at several levels: be-tween men and women and within both men and women. But in addition the asymmetries within men have a different basis from those within women. The social recognition and cultural marking of life stages through, for example, rites of passage including changes in appearance, might in fact be one of the main cultural means through which gender differences are constructed out of individual lives as they express a recognition of the potential of the human being (for a fuller discussion of the importance of age see Sofaer-Derevenski 1997, 1998).

A fabric for discourse

Reconstructivist histories of dress are clearly of little use for the understanding of what dress enables and does within society. They do, however, make one important point: despite enormous variations, the complexity of the media used, the changes through people's lives and the intersection with other concerns, the dressed people of the past were generally made to look as *particular kinds* of persons. Their difference, moreover, on the most basic level was commonly about separating people visually in terms of gender categories. These gender categories were often further elaborated, articulating other socially constructed differences between people, but this does not erase or undermine the commonality of male(s) and female(s) categories being expressed and constructed through appearance. The fact that these categories may not have corresponded to, or had an ambiguous relationship with, people's own sense of self and their sexual identification is another matter.

There are, of course, many other aspects of these materials that would have affected gender organization as well, and they should also be the subject of studies. For instance, the production of the items of the costumes, which involves a multiplicity of stages in the fabrication of their various elements, and where men and women may be differently integrated in these processes, is an obvious area of interest. Another is the importance of cloth as a symbolic medium in its own right. It is also often a valued commodity and it may have had particular significance and affected gender politics due to its role in organized exchange systems, an aspect already suggested for a few areas such as the Inca empire (Dransart 1992: 145), Ur III Mesopotamia (Wright 1996b) and Aztec Mexico (Brumfield 1991), or it is clearly indicated by well-known archaeological sources such as the Linear B scripts for the Aegean (Barber 1994, Killen and Olivier 1989).

Amongst the many dimensions of clothing, I have in this chapter focused upon the construction of appearance as an aid to and expression of difference within society and its role in communicating social and moral conventions and traditions. I have furthermore been concerned with considering this medium through its physical properties, as these are the necessary starting points for an archaeological engagement with the constructions. Variation in appearance must, of course, be appreciated as a communication about categories; it is about sameness and difference. Gender archaeology can therefore explore the evidence of dress, the manner in which it is constructed, including its temporal transformations, to investigate how a given society reflects, maintains and negotiates its perception of these differences and to trace how these material resources may also be explored in short-term strategies through which such differences may be challenged and changed.

8

The Engendering of Space

As a child I often visited my maternal grandparents. In their home the men would congregate in the study, which was my grandfather's room, and the women would be in the kitchen. I remember the two places very differently. The kitchen was bright, big, buzzing with life. I remember light streaming through the windows and the noise of the women talking. The study was dark, smelling of books and dust but cosy and quiet, withdrawn in waiting.

Gendered space

Space is another physical source for gender construction as it profoundly affects our embodied experience of where and who we are. An ultimate example of gendered space is provided by Kirkham, who describes how a hotel in Bilbao had introduced rooms and bathrooms specifically decorated for the female executive (1996: xiv). Reading her example made me recall numerous 'ladies' rooms' in up-market public places with salmon-coloured walls, the odd pastel watercolour or print and the single bouquet of dried flowers: the public notion of a feminine place?

Space and the manner in which it is organized affects perceptions and action, and in turn it gains meaning which, if subject to routine practice, sediments as convention. Its organization becomes the spatial embodiment of codes of behaviour dictating where practices should or could happen. It therefore also affects the creation of difference and provides a medium for the articulation of prohibitions and permission. Space thus both affects the sense of individual subjective embodiment and helps to confirm people as members of society and as belonging to particularly constituted groups. Space is individual as well as social, and it affects the acquisition of gendered identity and the negotiation of its content at both of these levels. Through these qualities it provides an arena for the performance of gender. In addition, spatial structures 'exist' at different levels, including their outer form, their potential meaning and the ways they affect physical action providing embodied subjectivities. The distinction as well as the relationships between such levels mean that the social understanding of space can be negotiated in diverse manners. In particular, social space is affected and affective through both its cognitive resonance and physical impact. Moreover, while the understanding of space is commonly articulated around boundaries and thresholds, neither their form nor meanings are fixed, and space, while largely meaningful through its physical manifestations, is discursively understood and brought into being as a social stage. These properties, in particular the lack of fixed relationships, mean that while space produces and enables both the understanding and performance of gender, its classification, content and meaning are brought into being only as gender is enacted in space and through the insistence on its distinction from other potentialities. As in many other cases of materialization of gender the association between material and social divisions is maintained by prohibitions, rules, laws or taboos – since without strong, and routinely maintained, social conventions, these distinctions have no basis of existence and will easily disappear. The organization of space is therefore a medium through which social differences are made and learned, but nonetheless also an area through which these may be transformed, distinction subverted and conventions challenged. In addition, space provides a physical medium that may be differently interpreted depending upon the situation. It is, therefore, an area of practice where distinctions may be dormant and evoked only in particular situations, so that, for example, within the same spatial setting daily practice and routine behaviour may contrast sharply with ritualized or ideological versions of the social order. For instance, contemporary European seating arrangements during certain church ceremonies are commonly based on a binary notion of gender, although many other activities have become much more multi-faceted in their relationship to gender. Similarly, within the family it is still common that some of its practices, such as seating arrangements for Sunday dinner or at major family events, is clearly gender-based, but that same order is not necessarily maintained during other meals or family activities.

It is therefore important to appreciate that materialities, such as spatial structures, are useful media for both the maintenance of and challenge to social relations. Both attempts at fixture and at revolt need material means to show themselves. Even transformation and gradual change in social relations use such forms as their reference. Spatial structures are not, therefore, reflections of gender relations. Rather, gender relations are embodied in the way space is understood and responded to, and space provides a medium for its performance.

The control of spatial access is therefore also an act of in- and exclusion with its associated messages of difference and value. Access to and right over space is therefore a political act. This has often been expressed in political movements and claims. The symbolic importance of access has recently been interestingly illustrated by the importance that some feminist groups give to claiming/gaining access for women to Mount Athos. This Greek peninsula is settled by monks belonging to Eastern Christian monasticism, and it is a most famous monastic 'republic'. The emphasis upon contemplation and a women-exclusive philosophy is a central element in its self-aware history and sense of purpose – its creation of a distinctive self. Many communities and architectural spaces exist that give access to men or women only, but in presenting and emphasizing itself in the politics of space as a male-only republic Mount Athos has become a gender-political provocation. Challenging their right to make such a declaration can therefore become a political act of symbolic importance for women's groups.

The study of spatial organization is a traditional topic within archaeology, where it has been used both to define various kinds of boundedness and to interpret a range of activities; as a physical framework it has routinely been employed to make meaningful both behaviour within a given location and interactions between communities. It has also consistently been explored at different scales from the single feature to territories or large-scale landscapes. Within all these dimensions gender is an instrumental variable. A thorough discussion of the varied relationships between space, as recognized by archaeologists, and gender is beyond the scope of this chapter. The following reflections, apart from briefly considering some of the issues brought out by the application of phenomenology to landscape studies, are therefore primarily based upon the built place that may relate to the daily life of a community. This choice is dictated largely by the fact that we frequently encounter prehistoric communities through this type of remains, which archaeologists routinely investigate and give meaning to.

Archaeologists, when investigating the spatial organization of different communities, come in contact with how and at which levels these communities reflected upon and attempted to codify themselves and their differently constituted members. In addition, changes within these structures, as well as contrast between form and practice, can be observed, showing how through time communities transform or reinvent themselves in some areas while other elements remain intact.

Archaeology and space

An awareness and use of space are found early in professional archaeology as many of its basic terms, such as location, site or culture, are based upon assumptions about space. More particular spatial models were later developed, some of them clearly influenced by human geography. The more specific concern with how social relations and spatial organization interlink is, however, a more recent development rooted in social anthropological and sociological debates, together with a continuous strong influence from human geography, especially the discussion around time–space geography and spatial logic, syntax and semantics (for a discussion of these influences in archaeology see Parker-Pearson and Richards 1994c: 29ff). These developments have, however, in general not been specifically concerned with the intersection of space and gender.

An explicit interest in gender relations was therefore probably first introduced to spatial archaeology through the influence of structuralism. Its emphasis upon binary opposition has continued to dominate much of the work on gendered space, and now includes studies of the construction of cosmologies as a bounded space or the projection of the body onto space (Parker-Pearson and Richards 1994c: 10ff). This approach has also provided an important background for work more generally concerned with the social meaning of space such as Hingley (1990), Hodder (1990), and Parker-Pearson (1996) (for discussion see Brück 1997: 69–75, Gilchrist 1997). As regards gender, the important critique of such studies is that in their ordering of differences and a range of activities into opposites or binary structures they tend to assume universal values and behaviours. Gender categories are accordingly treated as fixed and their relationship to spatial organization as static. Gender as a difference that is brought into being through values and practices and in need of maintenance is ignored. The processes through which differences are created and the easy ways they can become fragmented and challenged are not considered. The continuum of space – the fact that any division may be imposed upon it, and that therefore it has a potential for meaning rather than its meaning and divisions pre-existing – is disregarded, and instead space is presented as if it has absolute borders and 'real' divisions. Despite such obvious weaknesses structuralism has been extensively used, which is probably due to its providing an apparent guide to what to look for: divisions into right:left, out:in, dark:light, public:private etc. (see figure 8.1). For an archaeology insecure about its ability to 'observe' gender such an option is obviously attractive. Increasingly, however, we have come to accept that if such divisions are merely abstract, timeless structures that have little or nothing to do with how people built and perceived their constructed places then they only aid us in assigning a universal world order to these communities and they will prevent us from exploring how people structured and lived within these spaces.

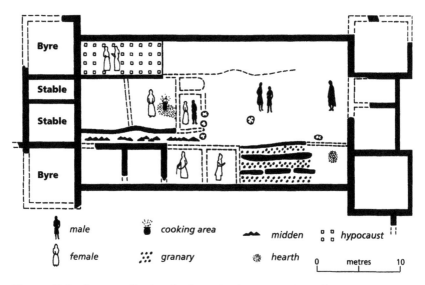

Figure 8.1 Structuralist-inspired gender interpretation of a Romano-British aisled hall at Warnborough, Hants., UK. (Redrawn after Hingley 1990; reproduced with permission of the author and Edinburgh University Press)

The increased debate surrounding the opposition domestic:public (or private:public) illustrates the progress of such critique. In terms of the past it has, for instance, been pointed out that these concepts may be relatively modern ones and therefore potentially inapplicable (e.g. Arwill-Nordbladh 1998). It has also been argued that there is no clear division between such apparent oppositions as they are always contextually constructed, so that, for instance, formerly public spaces can become private ones and vice versa (Parker-Pearson and Richards 1994c: 9). The significant point that arises from such objections is that spatial structures and categories are not stable and fixed but emerge from practice.

Related to this approach, but nonetheless significantly different due to his critical stand against structuralism and because of his empathic emphasis upon practice, is the influence of Bourdieu. In particular, his concept of 'habitus' (Bourdieu 1977: 72ff) has been important. He describes it as 'a system of lasting, transposable dispositions which, integrating past experiences, functions at every moment as a *matrix of perceptions, appreciations and actions* and makes possible the achievement of infinitely diversified tasks' (ibid.: 82–3, original emphasis), and he outlines its effect in terms such as the following:

The habitus, the durably installed generative principle of regulated im-
provisations, produces practices which tend to reproduce the regulari-
ties immanent in the objective conditions of the production of their
generative principle, while adjusting to the demands inscribed as objective potentialities in the situation, as defined by the cognitive and motivating structures making up the habitus. (Bourdieu 1977: 78)

For archaeology, one may suggest, it has been particularly important
that while habitus comprises structuralist principles these are understood as

principles of the generation and structuring of practices and representations which can be objectively 'regulated' and 'regular' without in any
way being the product of obedience to rules, objectively adapted to
their goals without presupposing a conscious aiming at ends or an express mastery of the operations necessary to attain them. (Bourdieu 1977:
72)

This means that both agency and the interaction between individuals
and their society become central themes. For archaeology his work,
therefore, adds a dimension which at one and the same time seems to
provide us with the fixity of structures and the fluidity of action and
individuals. 'It is just as true and just as untrue to say that collective
actions produce the event or that they are its product' (ibid.: 82).
Bourdieu's emphasis upon how the ordering of space and the lived
experience of it enable the 'inculcation of the habitus', that is the reproduction of sets of beliefs, values and social relationships including
gender, has therefore been significant for the development of post-
processual spatial studies. This influence has in particular been expressed in approaches that see space both as the medium and the
outcome of social practice and more particularly as a medium through
which social relations are produced and reproduced (Barrett 1994,
Brück 1997, Gilchrist 1994, Parker-Pearson and Richards 1994c: 3).
    Another major influence has been Moore's study of the spatial mean-
ing of the structuring of activities within compounds amongst the Endo
people in Kenya (1986, 1987). For archaeology two points made by
this study have been particularly important. The one relates to how
the spatial construction of meaning affects both architecture and practice as well as products/debris such as dung and ash; this emphasizes
the wide range of material remains that may be partners to social and
political structuration rather than merely being meaningless residues
of life. The other (less referred to) point is the clear difference between
the ideal, as expressed through rules and regulation, as well as people's self-representations, and the reality of what actually happens as

ideals become compromised by the practice of 'coping' (Moore 1987). This important theme, which may be expressed as the difference and tension between gender as an ideational system and as practices will be returned to in chapter 9 where I discuss how various forms of contact, as they affect practice, can undermine and erode existing gender systems, making discrepancies between ideal systems and real ones obvious and challenging.

More recent developments, while continuing the influences from Bourdieu and Moore, have also seen increased concern with the uniqueness of people and the fuzziness and accidental nature of much of their action. Brück in her analysis of Early and Middle Bronze Age sites from southern England emphasizes, for example, spatial organization in terms of the values and understanding which enable people to get on in the world. In her, and many other archaeologists', use of Bourdieu it is the emphasis upon practice that is being particularly explored rather than any structuralist principle. To Brück the interpretative impact of 'habitus' is that

> The fuzzy logic of the *habitus* produces a number of possible choices for strategic action; the agent is disposed to behave in a particular way but is not constrained to do so. Like a grammar, the *habitus* works as a set of generative principles which enable people to deal with an infinite number of different situations. It is therefore essentially innovative rather than constraining, although only those strategies that are thinkable ... will be followed. (Brück 1997: 74–5)

There has also been extensive interest in how the physicality of space, and in particular architecture, may be used as a means of structuring social relations (Barrett 1994, Gilchrist 1994, Thomas 1993). The categorization of space, its segmentation and division, is recognized as having the potential to participate in the construction of different social personae. Social groups can be created through prohibitions of access to certain spatial structures or locales. Thus categorization of space also make the categorization and ordering of people possible, and distinct social identities may be constructed by people's relationships to this order (e.g. Barrett 1994: 14–17). These effects have, however, particularly been studied in terms of somewhat abstract ideas of social roles and power structures, and little attention has been given to the specificity of how gender is negotiated through spatial structures. The roles physical structures and the architectural ordering of objects play in directing people's movements, interpretation and use of space may in time prove extremely useful also for the study of gender.

In terms of gender the important point about spatial organization is, therefore, that the physicality of architecture may be used as a means of experiencing as well as structuring social relations. Space provides a physical opportunity for segmentation and exclusion. This means it also has the potential to be both strategically and routinely a tool for differentiating people. For example, access to certain types of space may be held exclusively by particularly defined people. The sacristy in the church is a good contemporary example, and one where additional importance is added by the lack also of visual access. An obvious prehistoric parallel is how access to megaliths and participation in the activities which took place within them may be understood as a practice of exclusion and control (e.g. Thomas 1993). Other types of distinction may be founded in social expectation. This is exemplified by the slightly elevated 'High Table', set at right angles to the other tables, in a traditional Cambridge college which places the fellowship as a collective above the rest of the college community.

Thus, recent theoretical discussions suggest that through physical and perceptional responses and the need to materially frame and anchor action and meaning, space is reacted to and made into a meaningful cultural place. The constructed space, its meaning-laden elements, in turn provide direction for appropriate action – which includes also a notion of appropriate actors. The organization of space thus enforces notions of social identities as well as providing margins where identities defined through rights may be subverted. The interesting influence from Bourdieu is that we are made aware of how the vagueness of the relationship between rules or norms and actions in itself creates new locales and opportunities for action. It is from the 'space' between conventions that new meanings emerge most easily. Social distinction and differentiation is therefore maintained and recreated through the control of who can move through or have access to particular spaces (see also Brück 1997: 59). This means that certain social roles and power structures are being reproduced by spatial arrangements, but we are also learning that the dynamic, changeable nature of these categories and the ability to challenge their accepted meanings are of substantial importance for how they 'work'. The categories of differences that are created exist only to the extent that people recognize and respect them, which means that the elements most open to change may also be those most significant in the negotiation of gender.

Another major issue that has arisen is how space affects and is articulated through the body. It is argued that the 'environment exists in terms of our action and meaning; it is an existential space which is neither external object nor internal experience' (Parker-Pearson and Richard 1994c: 3–4). It follows, the argument goes on, that architectural space is a concretization of existential space (ibid.: 4). It is obvious, however, that while existential space implies nothing about routine or physical action architectural space is dependent upon it. Practice and repetition, the performance of spatial meaning, must intersect for the existential to materialize as form. Concretization therefore implies the invoking of form through physical practices and the construction of meaning through recurrent use (ibid.: 5). Another area of increased interest is how the structuring of space constrains, directs or affects interpretations of what a locale is about and shapes the social relations played out in it (e.g. Brück 1997: 69, Barrett 1994: 13–32). This emphasis upon the physicality of architecture refers to how through repetition, performance and practice architectural space is made meaningful *and* creates meanings. Despite the shared reference to embodied experience the implied concern with routine practice and social understanding suggested by these debates is subtly but significantly different from a more distinct phenomenological approach.

Phenomenology and the landscape's space

As part of recent developments one can also see a distinct interest in cognition and phenomenological meaning, particularly in terms of the bodily experience of space. The development is best illustrated by Tilley's influential argument, based on Heidegger and Merleau-Ponty, about individual subjective embodied experience as a basis for meaning and understanding through Being-in-the-world (1994). Tilley has discussed this with particular reference to cognitive space and in relationship to landscape and large, standing, non-domestic monuments (ibid.: 17). The argument, however, is, of course, also relevant to discussion of the built environment in general. Phenomenology aims to provide a universally applicable interpretation of the nature of Being. It argues that the material world is constitutive of existence, and that the body is the centre of spatial experience, so that the ordering of experience shapes the experience. This means that landscapes should be approached in terms of the embodied experience they provide rather than as resource and environment. In archaeology, this indicates a shift from land or space to landscape and with it a change of concern with land as an independent variable to its becoming constituted through the relationship established between human subjects and the place they act within. Thus the interest has turned towards the cultural acts and perceptions that transform physical space into cultural landscapes as people map meaning upon their surroundings. Or in other words 'space is created by social relations, natural and cultural objects' (ibid.: 17).

This has replaced an earlier dominant view of the environment as a physical resource-area. Such approaches have been characterized by Tilley as concentrating on variables like relief, climate, soils, water supply and the seasonable variability of resources and as being related to factors such as demography, technologies, transhumance systems, territoriality, control over exchange networks and the social organization of economic exploitation (1994: 1). At a rather coarse level it is correct, as Tilley states, that 'space has generally been considered as an abstract dimension or container in which human activities took place' (ibid.: 9). The approaches contrasted may not, however, be quite that polarized.* In particular the importance given by earlier approaches to the physical properties of the land, and especially their interpretation in terms of resources, need not imply that space, as place, is conceptualized merely as a passive stage for action and understanding. For example, when interpreted in terms of subsistence exploitation space has often been presented as fragmented into a number of separate spheres that affected and involved people practically and cognitively in different ways. Furthermore, recognizing that an emphasis upon resources can result in fundamentally different understandings of the relationship between individuals, society and their environments, like the differences between environmental determinism and Marxism, should warn us against seeing former approaches only in terms of their essential sameness. It is correct, however, that earlier spatial studies decentred space from agency and meaning (ibid.: 9), but it does not follow that space in these approaches was nothingness, as Tilley has argued (ibid.: 11). The recent interest in perception and experience, does not, of course, deny that land was a resource out of which was created, for example, food; but it gives hardly any importance to subsistence activities. Even if subsistence practices are considered to have been instrumental in the location of a site, then the practice of living there, it would be argued, transforms that landscape from being a set of resources to being a culturally and emotionally meaningful experience. In the other camp, for example amongst different versions of Marxism, many would acknowledge the importance of ideology, of the culturally constructed ties to a place etc., but the land as a means of production and the ways it is being explored would nonetheless take a much more central place in the description and understanding

* Tilley (1994: 2) states that 'I do not wish to set up a polar divide between a supposed economic rationality and a cultural or symbolic logic but rather to suggest that each helps to constitute the other'. His account of different approaches to space does, however, tend to present them as opposites (e.g. Tilley 1994: 8). Together with the downplaying of economic and subsistence concerns in his landscape studies this produces an obvious impression of polarity.

of that society. Thus the suggested shift from land to landscape in fact involves several layers of change relating to our perception of the nature of society and the importance of different types of practices. It also affects what are considered primary or even important structures of society, and it centralizes the individual as the experiencing subject who constitutes meaning. This changes (and that is why this debate is of substantial importance) how we understand society. Responding to current tendencies towards polarized approaches to the landscape it is worth considering whether understanding (which is not necessarily the same as explaining), for instance, the choice of a site location is dependent neither upon any single factor nor upon its potential bodily experience. Rather, such understanding rests upon appreciating how a range of individual and group-based motivations, including perception, social memory and reasons that are by us associated with economic rationality, help to constitute each other. This is not in conflict with a phenomenological approach, as interpreted by Tilley, but as the approach focuses upon Being its application tends to leave the multiplicity of meanings and the interaction between self and communities under-explored. This would be detrimental to a fuller understanding of prehistoric landscapes, which are constituted by people doing things together, in response to each other and former generations as well as through interactions with natural and cultural objects and material possibilities.

The role of perception – through the centrality of the experiencing subject and the production of meaning through bodily transitions or movements – is an enormously interesting question. One may, however, argue that as the *bodily* experience becomes *the meaning* there is an obvious tendency for other meanings to become irrelevant or part of a bland reference to polysemous meanings. There is, therefore, a tension here between a focus upon individual experience as the source of all meaning and the appreciation of spatial structures as instruments of difference. The interaction and mutually enforcing impact between individual and social understanding is still largely missing from these debates. Amongst the questions that should concern us now is therefore, for instance, whether social meaning as pre-meaning (a meaning brought to experience due to previous (contextualized) experiences, an emphasis that one may relate to Ricoeur's arguments about pre-understanding; for an archaeological application see Arwill-Nordbladh 1998: 244–6, also Moore 1990)), affects all meaning. Until such issues are further explored the contribution from phenomenological approaches to the analysis of the construction and maintenance of gender seems severely restricted, since gender is both about Being and its social recognition and contextualization.

Archaeology, despite the considerable general influence from human geography, shows little awareness of more recent developments of feminist and gender interests in that discipline. This means that the symbolic construction of gender in different dimensions of space, which has been a concern within geography since the mid-1970s (albeit for a long time marginalized within the discipline), has remained unexplored by archaeologists working with similar questions. One of the concerns of feminist geographers seems to be, as in archaeology, the relationship between place/location and identity and gender as social performance (e.g. McDowell and Sharp 1997). The interest within architecture in the politics of space has also been ignored (e.g. Colomina 1992). Further exploration of these debates would probably prove to be of interest to gender archaeology although beyond the scope of this chapter.

Current theoretical discussion of the social dimension of space has greatly enhanced our understanding of how practice is implicated in how people come to understand their surroundings and themselves. One can, however, discern two different emphases within these debates which, although probably interconnected and entwined, nonetheless provide us with separate foci for further analysis. They arise from the difference between stressing practice as experience or as performance. The critical point in terms of connecting this to the intersection of space and gender is that the former focuses upon the individual while the emphasis on performance brings us into a collective communal domain in which performance places the individual within dialogues about identity and membership. Gender archaeology in its concern with an identity beyond individual experience clearly needs the latter focus. This does not constitute a rejection of phenomenological approaches to the spatial encounter (that would have to take quite a different form), rather this is about recognizing what different approaches help us to understand. While phenomenology may appear significant due to its clarification of how individuals experience and make sense of and with the material work around them, it is less helpful in providing analytical guidance to how that experience and interaction become part of the construction of differently constituted groups. In the following discussion I shall therefore try to pursue this relationship further and in particular to consider how difference may be connected to material possibilities. I strongly believe that this is where the gender impact (and therefore also the analytical possibilities) are to be found within archaeological spatial evidence.

Therefore, in its routine encounter with spatial constructions and their effects, archaeology, exploring its own tradition, the archaeological evidence and theories about spatial practice and performance, can constructively engage with questions about how gender affects and are affected by spatial organization. The task is to investigate how space is already inscribed in the question of/construction of gender. To address some of this I shall briefly discuss spatial constructions in terms of houses.

House and home

Archaeologists routinely differentiate material from settlements on the basis of features, materials, boundaries and other structures found in association with them. Such differences are interpreted in terms of, for example, activity areas caused by the spatial ordering of what takes place within the settlement. Or, alternatively, they are interpreted in social terms like households (e.g. Clarke 1972), kinship (e.g. Ellison 1981), gender (e.g. Parker-Pearson 1996) or status and hierarchy (e.g. Fletcher 1995). As it has become increasingly recognized that space is an area where negotiation of rights and access can take place, the question of how such practices may be identified and analysed on the basis of archaeological data has become ever more relevant. It is therefore important to appreciate the implications of current arguments.

The first point to emphasize is that many of these arguments suggest that the organization of space is a contextual articulation, a materialization of relations between elements and concepts. Secondly, it is important to recognize that the argument that social relations are metaphorically mapped out in spatial organization implies that spatial divisions embody social ones or become their extension or transformation (Gilchrist 1994, 1997, Moore 1986: 88), and that they may inform about or provide a model for other concerns within the community, such as cosmology, belief systems or attitudes towards death (e.g. Hugh-Jones 1979, Parker-Pearson and Richards 1994b, 1994c).

Examples of the latter are found throughout prehistory as connections are drawn between the house and death. The house, as a model of the world and the 'home', a place of belonging, is frequently imitated by the space containing the dead. In European prehistory there are, for instance, many examples of burials using either models or metaphorical presentation of houses. There are, for example, communities who make funerary containers in the form of a symbolic house, like the house urns of the Late Bronze Age in northern Germany (see figure 8.2) and the Lusatian culture in Poland, or instances where the deceased is 'laid to rest' in a chamber or room made up in imitation of an interior architectural space affected by ideas about gender and status. The latter is well illustrated by many of the rich Iron Age burials

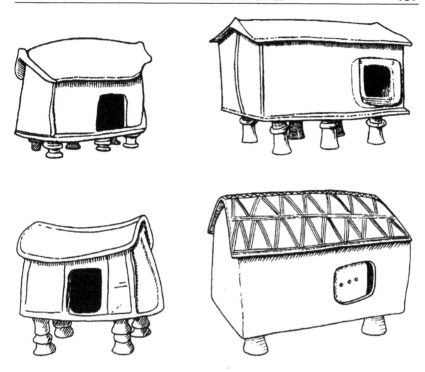

Figure 8.2   Examples of Late Bronze Age house urns from northern Germany. (Redrawn after Oelmann 1959)

from central Europe such as the one from Hochdorf, in southern Germany (Biel 1985). Here the burial chamber appears as a hall-like room, its walls draped in textile and the floor covered by a rug and with various groups of materials – a huge cauldron, drinking sets and a four-wheeled vehicle – 'furnishing' the floor and walls. The deceased was lying, fully dressed, on a bronze couch (see figure 8.3). The effect is scenographic space (Olivier 1992: 58), and the links made between grave chamber and house are quite obvious. Alternatively, the relationship between death and life is stressed through a physical link to the house, as when deceased members of the community are buried under house floors. This is, for example, known from the Chalcolithic in southeastern Iberia (Chapman 1990) and from roughly the same period in the Balkans (Coles and Harding 1979).

The house, and its various metaphoric qualities of home, head and heart, has long been recognized by many disciplines as a central focus for the construction of social relations. It is also one of the few areas of materiality where gender has become well established as a research

Figure 8.3   The rich burial chamber of Hochdorf, an Early Iron Age grave from southern Germany. The parallels with house architecture and interior space are obvious. (After Biel 1985)

focus within archaeology. This line of gender archaeology was developed by Gilchrist (1988, 1994), who used it to interpret the influence of social order upon the architectural form of medieval nunneries and monasteries respectively. The central point made by her work, that gender is also mapped out in space, has been further pursued by prehistorians.

The house, with its presumed domestic* activities, has various obvious associations with gender, which have been approached in a number of ways. They have been particularly extensively analysed through structuralist ideas of oppositions between, for instance, inside:outside or private:public, with different degrees of permeability and transparency between the two spheres being argued. The house is, however,

---

* Much debate has focused on the term 'domestic activities/spheres' and its association with both women and lower status or value and need not be added to here. (For archaeology see, for example, Arwill-Nordbladh 1998, Brück 1997, Picazo 1997: 60, Tringham 1991; for anthropology see, for example, Moore 1994, Strathern 1984.) I use 'domestic' to refer loosely to activities that take place in connection with spaces, such as houses (*domus* = house), where people routinely interact as well as sleep, eat and partake in a number of subsistence, craft and leisure activities. Neither value nor gender association is intended, although in a variety of ways both were probably read into that particular space throughout prehistory.

primarily an important spatial construct due to its central involvement with the production of specific kinds of socialized people. This aspect of the house/household may furthermore have been even more essential for earlier small-scale societies organized around family-like units, where the socialization and 'education' of new members of society were presumably centrally located and based within a core community. It is important here to re-emphasize that socially established differences, such as gender, 'draw on normative understandings and practices which are linked to accepted power differences and ideologies' (Moore 1994: 91). The house/home has obvious possibilities and means (food-sharing, socialization of children, seating and sleeping arrangements, access etc.) of acting as a primary (i.e. at the level of the smallest social unit) location for the exercising of both gender and power differences based on such understandings. This has led some scholars to develop the notion of 'contractual relations between household members' (Moore 1994: 91 with references). These contracts can be characterized by, for example, a sense of agreed understanding of the form the relationship takes, of rights and obligations, as well as awareness of options and the possibility of breakdowns. This means that the household is constituted and maintained through discussion and agreements and their performance. The obvious parallels between contractual relations and the concept of negotiation, as both refer to the act of reaching agreements, should be noted here, as this may help us to understand the gender negotiations that take place within domestic space.

Moore has proposed that social anthropology should focus upon and work out how to examine precisely how bargaining power in the household is significantly affected by questions of power and ideology (1994: 87–8). Archaeologists, in contrast, are in a position to investigate how the bargaining and negotiation taking place within the household affect and explore its material form. This does not mean, as Moore warns against (ibid.: 87–9), that the household is necessarily thought of as bounded, but rather that in addition to its other dimensions it is recognized that the physical locale in which the household is acted out provides an additional medium of differentiation, and also that this physicality produces thresholds and points of transgression that are of relevance to the maintenance of differences and their negotiation. Men opening doors for women in Western culture and the rejection of this 'custom' after the 1960s illustrate this well. The door was used as a spatial focus for the performance of gender difference: waiting for the door to be opened and passing through it the woman became passive, weak and demure, placed under male protection and guardianship. The man opening the door became differently constituted: active, strong, full of will and direction, the protector. Challenging this (apparently merely courteous) performance was therefore part of a wider negotiation of gender roles and values.

Within households, differently gendered individuals coexist, overlap and interact, and the maintenance of their difference therefore has to be articulated through its continuous performance and associated materialities. For example, by assigning differently shaped chairs to different members of an eating community, such as the family, or by seating and serving them in a distinct order, their distinctions are reproduced. Therefore, rather than presenting houses as, for instance, women's domain, we must approach them as spatial constructions that have the potentiality of being perceived as, for instance, women's space if that is how different participants agree to understand them, but also as places that may change their meaning as different things happen in association with them.

The ideas of dispersal or (re-)inscription of meaning may be helpful for understanding how such meanings are made, agreed upon and challenged. This refers to how architecture halts the dispersal of meaning, constraining its possible interpretations, and it has been variously explored by, in particular, Barrett (1994), Thomas (1993) and Tilley (1994). The presence of particular architectural elements that may be used to make connections, visualize transgressions or suggest change is particularly useful as their ability to affect meaning, by providing a focal point for its articulation and performance, is obvious. Such elements are, for instance, buildings, enclosures, fences and hearths, which define and structure space and constrain what activities may be done at particular parts of a locale, but in addition such foci are also provided by partitions, corridors, openings and entrances that connect or separate specific locations. Architecture therefore provides a physical form to which categories and meanings can be attached and later challenged.

A further point that I find relevant here is that the blurring between ideal and actual practice does not only relate to the social meaning assumed to be represented in architecture but also affects spatial structures and elements themselves as space is never so rigidly defined and maintained that it does not include areas that are ambiguous and negotiable in terms of meaning and category. Space, in addition to its potential objectification of social relations, also involves movements and points where these relations stop, are not yet brought into being or become ambiguous. Spatial relations always also involve the confinement of these relations and that which is outside or excluded. Reaction to conventions may thus potentially manifest itself at several levels within spatial relations: in the dependency upon their continuous reconfirmation, in its re-enactment and bodily performance and in the areas not controlled or identified by such conventions. The latter point can be conceptualized as connections; they participate in the bringing of people into spatial experience but they are culturally invisible as they are not categorized. They make possibly the segregation of difference while their lack of formal recognition suggests that their future inclusion is a possibility. This confirms the existence of ambiguity within spatial relations: does a room begin outside the door, on the doorstep, inside the door, and where is inside the door?

Wondering about how a house may affect gender construction and experience we may then usefully consider properties of space that have obvious potentials for discontinuities, shifts and negotiation or are ambiguous. Such locales are, for example, physical spaces where different actions and perceptions may interconnect. This may relate, for example, to access, permeability, foci, borders and connections, and they may, as mentioned, take the form of hearths, walls, doorways, entrances, thresholds, fences, fittings, divisions or corridors. Houses are composed of such elements, and singly or in various compositions they provide us with locations that may be used for negotiating rights and obligations.

Amongst such possible features, the hearth is particularly interesting as it fixes in space a range of on-going primary activities associated with the sustenance of the community. It is reasonable to assume that it 'acted as an important material and symbolic focus in the life of the group' (Picazo 1997: 59), and its central role is often also suggested both by its location and the ways in which it affected other activities. As a centre for maintenance activities hearths would also be involved in continuous and interactive processes of sustenance and socialization (ibid.: 60, see also argument in chapter 5 about the relationship between food and socialization). It is therefore worth noticing that houses throughout prehistory, while relatively undifferentiated in terms of internal spatial structures, commonly had hearths and that these often are centrally located, providing an obvious focus for activities (see figures 8.4 and 8.5). The forms of the hearths vary widely. They range from permanent decorated furniture-like platforms in some of the Neolithic and Early Bronze Age tell sites in southeastern Europe, such as those from Toszeg, Hungary (Gimbutas 1965), or the architecturally embedded and decorative oven/hearths in the Late Neolithic/Early Eneolithic Vinca culture in the Balkans (Hodder 1990: 60f, Whittle 1996: 116), to much simpler structures composed mainly of the remains of the fire itself. In some areas hearths are associated with various apparent symbolic activities or objects. This is, for example, the case in Switzerland in the Bronze Age where 'fire-dogs' with curvedup corners, commonly interpreted as representing bulls' horns and fertility, are found in large numbers in settlements and often in close association with hearths (Wyss 1971). Within the lake site of Cortaillod-Est, for example, some ninety-six of these objects were found amongst the houses (Arnold 1986). The social importance of hearths as places is also hinted at by numerous sites where they are constructed in physical relationship to each other. This is observed even at very early sites, like the Upper Palaeolithic site of Abri Pataud (Champion et al. 1984: 70–3) and may even be suggested for some Middle Palaeolithic sites (Mellars 1996: 295–301) in the Dordogne, France, or Mesolithic (Maglemosian) sites in northern Europe (Grøn 1991). Another indication of the hearth's central role is provided by the tendency for their

a

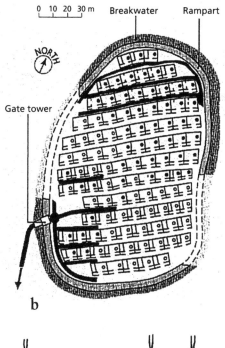

0 10 20 30 m   Breakwater   Rampart

NORTH

Gate tower

b

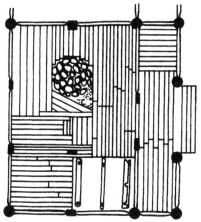

c

Figure 8.4
a Reconstruction of Iron Age house with oven/hearth structure at Bohuslän, Sweden. The physical dominance of this structure within the interior space of the house suggests that it would have affected the planning and execution of many activities as well as the movement within the house. **b** Plan of the Early Iron Age settlement at Biskupin, Poland. The circles indicate the standardized location of hearths within the houses (black circles show excavated hearths, open circles unexcavated ones). (Redrawn after Rajewski 1959 and Scarre 1998) **c** Plan of one of the houses from the settlement of Biskupin, Poland, showing the central location of the stone hearth. (Redrawn after Rajewski 1959)

location to remain unchanged through several phases of rebuilding even when this involved the rebuilding of the entire settlement and took place over several hundred years. This is observed at many well-stratified sites, such as tell sites from southeastern Europe. Hearths and their location within settlement units were also often highly standardized as shown by uniquely preserved sites such as the Early Iron

Figure 8.5 Reconstruction of a Late Iron Age long house from Rogaland, Norway, showing the dominant position and effect of the hearth. (Reproduced courtesy of Stavanger Museum, Norway)

Age settlement of Biskupin in Poland (see figure 8.4b and c) (Scarre 1998).

This diversity shows both how very differently a basic activity such as cooking may be organized and architecturally embedded within different kinds of domestic space, and, at the same time, how most often it would have been experienced as central to the house (see for example figure 8.5). It also shows great variation in how associated activities, such as the preparing, serving and eating of food, are organized, controlled and experienced. The ways in which practices such as cooking are materially anchored within social space is therefore extremely varied as is also the ways in which it integrates with and affects other domains and concerns within a community. Obviously, the engendering of such locales and their associated activities would also be specific. In line with this, Picazo argues for the importance of incorporating into their analysis the fundamental roles their associated activities played in society. She also points out that maintenance activities should not necessarily be assumed to be gendered activities as this depends upon their social and temporal contexts and articulation (1997: 66). This point usefully pushes us towards analysing such activities and locales in terms of how they affected and involved gender rather than aiming at classifying them in such terms. To illustrate this Picazo refers to Halstead's analysis of the spatial arrangements of cooking facilities in early and later Neolithic Thessalian villages in Greece. He shows that cooking facilities were first located in open yards between houses and then later were located either indoors or within closed yards. This he interprets as a change from some degree of communal sharing of cooked food to preparation and consumption of food being done for and within the household (Halstead 1989 quoted in Picazo 1997: 66). Her point – and this is where gender becomes involved – is that 'While this shift is dependent on other economic variables and is related to other production domains, it must be analysed in terms of the social and temporal consequences within which maintenance activities are embedded' (ibid.: 66).

Houses and their various elements, fixed or fluid, are, as architectural spaces, places for learning who one is, including confirmation of one's gender identity. They are the locales where one's primary relationship with core units of society is established and worked out. It is important that this understanding of houses informs the archaeological investigation of their remains.

Archaeology, gender and space

Seeing the organization of space as a product of on-going social negotiation (Bourdieu 1977, Moore 1986), as on-going communal projects
(Brück 1997, Evans 1988a), and understanding the extent to which it
communicates social categories and identities make it quite obvious
how space and gender intersect. The point is to recognize how spatial
structure provides a locale in which gender relations, as an on-going
performance, can take place, and to recognize that different forms of
spatial architecture provide a more or less open interpretation and
will focus renegotiation, performance, as well as the evaluation of difference upon specific practices and invest them in particular material
forms. With the increased attention towards gender as a process, as a
difference maintained through practice and as negotiated contracts
about rights and obligations, the intersection between space and gender cannot any more be approached in terms of how the former corresponds to or reflects the latter. Engendering spatial architecture is not
just about how artefact distributions or spatial division correspond to
gendered activities; it is also always about how through the participation in and performance of agreed meanings people are confirmed in
their gendered identities and how these may be changed. Temporal
changes and transformations reveal how communities reinterpret these
identities and their correlates, and transitional points and ambiguous
locations provide us with pointers towards space not easily dominated
by gender contracts or vulnerable to challenge.

Spatial knowledge and experience is social; it is learned through
processes of interaction with variously constituted we-collectives which
direct and interpret subjective experiences. Individuals are made profoundly social – physically and mentally – through the effect of space
upon the experience of self. As part of this project individuals also
learn and experience themselves as gendered members of communities, which in turn affects their interpretation and understanding of
their physical and social space.

The argument of this chapter has been concerned with showing that
the relationship between gender and space is not just about spatial
gender divisions. Gender is implicated in spatial constructions and is
in turn experienced through them. Both the nunnery with its spatial
concern with seclusion and the apparently undifferentiated long houses
from much of prehistory are informed by gender. Our analysis needs
to evolve towards investigating how gender is experienced, learned
and performed within different types of spatial constructions. We must
also learn to explore how the dynamics within such spaces (whether

areas of seclusion or undifferentiated space) are always threatened by transgression and the temporal imposition of meaning. Investigating the relationship between space and gender as an interaction we will begin to comprehend and trace facets of gendered life in prehistory that move us beyond merely its representation.

9
Contact: the Short-lived Triangle

When Megan met her new brother for the first time, she brought him a present, and he had one for her also. One of the stories they sometimes tell each other is about the gifts they gave on that very first meeting.

Adultery – changing partner

It is by now clear that understanding gender as a social construction means understanding it as changeable and responding to its context. The notion of negotiation, as contractual arrangements of rights and obligations, therefore becomes central as gender is understood as an outcome of on-going agreements that take the form of convention. The discussion that we began in chapter 8 on contractual relations – whether within the household, in terms of labour organization or as part of sexual behaviour or marital expectations – becomes relevant again here. Contractual relations are set within a context that defines the people and practices covered by that contract. This means that challenges to that context or the inclusion of persons or things not covered by it are open to interpretation and that their potential meaning or positions are yet to be agreed upon. For instance, marital contracts – as a normative understanding of marital relations (Moore 1994: 91) – 'change according to the location of the household in the wider economy' (ibid.: 91). Whitehead further emphasizes that 'certain gender ideologies, such as the construction of motherhood, mean that individuals are constrained as to the kinds of strategies they can employ in the processes of bargaining and renegotiation, and that this becomes particularly crucial at moments of rapid social and economic change' (Whitehead quoted in Moore 1994: 91). The point I want to extract here is that gender relations as contractual and agreed arrangements, while always under discussion and negotiation, are especially vulnerable in situations of change and therefore become particularly volatile in such contexts.

Contact, in the form of new interaction between people or groups and thus as an interference in social relations, then emerges as an important mechanism of change and transformation of gender contracts as they affect these agreements. The consequential shifts in alliance, loyalty and behaviour are well illustrated by the classic case of the 'triangle' caused by adultery. Some may find this comparison offensive, but I make it to stress that the changes we are concerned with are about people's relationship to each other rather than an abstract concept of society. Relationships, like that constituted by marriage, are based on a number of expectations about behaviour involving exactly such notions of rights and obligations as we have been concerned with in the previous chapters. The marriage vow, in its different forms, constitutes a pledge or promise from both partners to behave towards each other in specified ways; they give away certain rights in return for certain promises (all of these are primarily concerned with the body and extensions thereof – 'honour you' – or the products of its labour). This pledge, furthermore, while personal is commonly performed as a public act. Those committing adultery challenge these promises, and rights are given to a third party. As a result, established agreements are fragmented and the gender relations and politics embedded within them are disrupted. The new partner challenges existing links, and this is the point I want to stress here in making an analogy between adultery and contact. The break-up of agreed contracts and disruption to assumed relationships is what I aim to emphasize through this example of a common but nonetheless specific type of social interaction, as one may see this as causing radical renegotiation of social relationships and as introducing discontinuity in a social system whether on the scale of a marriage or 'culture'. This does not imply that gender is not also being negotiated within apparently harmonious and continuous situations (as I have argued in the previous chapters). It is the case, however, that in situations where social relations become fragmented gender relations will often become substantially involved and therefore subject to reformulation. We may therefore be able to identify situations or periods within prehistoric societies where gender relations become particularly critically involved in social transformation. Attention towards such situations may in turn further clarify the relationship between gender and both political and cultural formations.

Contact and innovation

Using adultery as analogy, and as our starting point, we may identify such situations of fragmentation as when either new partners engage with each other – they come into contact – or even situations when new materials and ideas are being introduced to a context. The former may have been most starkly experienced during the centuries following Columbus's arrival in the Americas and the succeeding colonization of various parts of the world. Significant contact periods can, however, also be identified throughout our more distant past, including possibly even such remote 'situations' as the 'arrival of modern humans' in Europe. In such situations, of short or long duration, existing social relationships must – voluntarily or not – accommodate the presence of new partners. The introduction of new forms, materials or ideas represents a less drastic confrontation, but we may nonetheless see them as similarly involving a fragmentation of society since the new elements demand a response even if it takes the form of rejection. Continuing our analogy with adultery, we can usefully compare things or ideas that are not yet part of how a community lives with the arrival of a new partner: they challenge and may rupture existing relationships. This means that technological innovations, such as the development of metallurgy, or foreign things, like exotic imports, may be potential agents of change, despite being in themselves inert objects (for a thorough discussion of the value of things from afar see Helms 1988). As there are no pre-established roles (rights and obligations) for either such new people or things they float freely within society and may interfere with established relationships until they are incorporated and given their 'place' in society. The ways things are done within that society and the relationships between the people doing the things therefore have to be readjusted – and thus renegotiated – to accommodate them. Gender relations will be part of such negotiation.

The impact of contact (people) and the social importance of innovations (new technologies, unfamiliar or exotic objects, and ideas) are well known ethnographically. Famous case studies include the introduction of steel axes for stone ones in Australia (Sharp 1952) or the range of activities observed in Melanesia and neighbouring regions and traditionally discussed in terms of 'cargo cult'.

> The typical prophetic message holds that if people establish social harmony and consensus, setting aside disputes and disruptive practices such as sorcery, then cargo will arrive. . . . Prophets typically prescribed more specific courses of action to induce cargo's arrival, including mass gatherings on appointed days, the construction of airfields, docks, warehouses and new villages, the raising of flag-poles and short-wave radio masts, burial or washing of money, sexual licence or abstinence, graveyard offerings of money and flowers, military-style marching and drilling and especially dancing. (Lindstrom 1996: 85)

More recently, the impact of missionary activities and of development agencies has become recognized as another type of problematic contact due to their 'interferences' with the cultures they interact with (e.g. Moore 1994:102–4).

The various case studies demonstrate in different ways how contact constitutes a challenge to social relationships and social organization. The result is always change, and often it becomes a matter of acculturation. This means fragmentation, collapse or change to local networks of power and control, loss of identity and independence. It also, however, provides new opportunities for alliances and gives particularly constituted groups (through their bodies, social identities or roles in production) the ability to circumvent traditional practices and routes of interaction. The study of the introduction of steel axes to the Yir Yoront group on the west coast of tropical Cape York peninsula in Australia illustrates this particularly well as it shows how the new objects challenged the values and power relations which were embedded within the trade in stone axes (Sharp 1952). Amongst other effects it highlights the disruption of both age and gender hierarchies, as adult men controlled the production and use of stone axes. Women, who used such axes extensively in their daily routines, were therefore dependent upon men for access to these tools. The borrowing of axes was part of confirmation of kin relations and of structures of power and dominance. The axes became a means through which gender, age and kin relations were generalized and standardized (ibid.). The introduction of steel axes, brought by the missionaries and available to all gender, age and kin groups, broke the monopoly of adult males and made women less dependent upon them for their productive activities. The effects upon the cultural and political life of the local groups, including their gender arrangements, were profound.

The archaeology of contact

The history of the world is a story of different levels of contact between people. The impact of this upon the construction and experience of gender is, however, under-explored. In archaeology, the importance of contact has either been discussed in terms of the mechanisms and reasons behind the movement of objects (e.g. trade and exchange), the motivation for movement of people (e.g. invasion and migration) or more general references to the cultural impact of asymmetrical cultural relationships and dependencies (e.g. the centre–periphery model). The gender dimension of such interactions has largely been ignored, however. Attempts at archaeological investigation of the impact of contact upon gender relations are therefore primarily found within the archaeology of the 'contact period' in the Americas and the parallel phenomenon in Australia. There are several obvious reasons why the socio-political aspects of contact have been recognized as a concern in these parts of the world while it has remained understudied in the 'Old World'. Obviously, these regions are themselves shaped by the relatively recent experience of contact in very drastic forms. There are, however, also specific disciplinary reasons involved. Gender archaeology in both America and Australia is more closely aligned with anthropology and ethnography than it is in Europe, and this means that analysis of the effect of social and recent historical changes on gender relations is more easily identified as an area of research. Often, however, it has been the period of transition rather than the process of change that has been studied, and it is only recently that attention has moved also towards how gender was affected and could even be strategically employed in the response to contact.

The point of the various studies conducted is that they contribute to our general understanding of contact and disruption while at the same time pointing towards an aspect of human interaction where gender becomes highly motivated, strategically explored and vulnerable to change and disruption. Within the early phase of gender and feminist research, colonization was mainly interpreted as a catalyst of change, including profound effects on the relations between men and women. For instance, Etienne and Leacock in their early study of colonization argued that the resulting shift in gender relations causes loss of status, power and rights of women (Etienne and Leacock 1980). 'Matrilineal societies are pushed towards patrilineality for inheritance purposes; women's production activities are shifted to men; political power is vested solely in men; women are marginalized in economic production; and women are subject to sexual abuse' (Trocolli 1992: 99 commenting upon Etienne and Leacock 1980). The effect upon and involvement of gender in these processes are, however, probably both more discursive and more varied than such a generalized interpretation suggests. Etienne and Leacock tried to acknowledge this by stating that women are not passive victims but are also able to utilize the situations in which they found themselves (Etienne and Leacock 1980: 17 in Trocolli 1992: 99). This does not, however, fully take into account the variety of responses and transformed gender relations that may be observed in connection with such contacts nor does it begin to explain why such differences are possible. As our understanding of gender has developed since the early 1980s we can now identify 'contact periods' as cultural situations ripe for further investigation of the construction and maintenance of gender. In particular, the shift from understanding gender in terms of roles to an emphasis upon its construction through negotiation and practice means that the impact of contact can be approached in terms of processes through which differently constituted people change their alliances and have their rights and obligations altered.

Recent studies have made it clear that contact affects people differently depending upon their perceived sexual identity, locations within pre-existing divisions of labour and their productive potentials (skills and knowledge). Furthermore, the people who interact enter into contact as already differently constituted and they are responding and being responded to in terms of such differences. This, moreover, applies both to the colonizers (or other types of contact person) and the ones subject to colonization. Whether the colonizer comes in the form of a missionary, a fur trapper or a soldier greatly affects, for instance, how that person relates to native women: is she a potential convert and labourer, wife, concubine, slave, part of social exchanges and political alliances, a fleeting unwilling sex partner or an object of abuse and degradation?

For instance, the changes in various local cultures in Mesoamerica and southern parts of North America as an immediate result of Spanish interference and influence during the sixteenth and seventeenth centuries and the slightly later changes throughout large parts of northern America in the wake of missionaries, soldiers and economic enterprises are well documented. Such case studies help to pin down the effect of contact on local communities' cultural and economic behaviour, including what we may call their gender contracts. The studies show that native men and women, due to their internally established differences in terms of productive activities and traditional skills as well as their sexed bodies, are typically affected in different ways. In particular, how their spheres of action become altered varies greatly. It is also clear that the changes are not everywhere of the same magnitude nor concerned with the same aspects of social interaction.

Historic records and archaeological studies combine to show that women in some instances, such as amongst the Inca in South America and the Aztec in Mesoamerica, clearly were victims during Spanish colonization as it resulted both in them losing political and economic power and involved substantial sexual abuse (Levy and Claassen 1992: 121–2). In other areas, the impact is more subtle, producing a socially more complex web of changes. In some instances it is, for example, proposed that women used sexual contact as a means of improving their status and of getting access to resources and exchange systems (ibid.: 121). For instance, amongst the Timucuan people in Florida, Spanish men and native women often cohabited and children from such unions were placed higher in the emerging local rank system than the native ones were (Trocolli 1992: 95). In their case it was only through women that native people could get access to higher social positions in the society which was evolving. 'The establishment of bicultural households, through the marriage, concubinage, and servitude of Timucuan women (and women from other tribes as well), served to incorporate native knowledge and production directly into the Spanish domestic sphere' (ibid.: 99).

It is also common that contact, particularly in the form of colonization, affects both the relations of production and its products. This change is often presented in terms such as 'colonization altered the relations of production that were based on the complementary nature of women's and men's productive roles' (Trocolli 1992: 96). If, however, we accept that such pre-contact complementary roles are not naturally given but are themselves already part of agreements, albeit between partners who are all from within a common culture, then both the ability and possible willingness to change become easier to recognize. If, furthermore, we assume that these women typically were involved with food and craft production (as many contemporary documents seem to suggest) then it is also obvious that these are products that may be desired and needed by the colonizers. Women, who previously exchanged their products with or through various men, including their husbands, may in such situations have gained access to a wider exchange system which made them less dependent upon their local hierarchy of obligations. Such situations as the one illustrated by the Timucua people of Florida, suggest, therefore, that the impact upon women's lives, upon traditional dependencies and partnerships and upon society generally is probably more complex and more varied than the early feminist arguments about the resulting degradation of women's role propose. In fact, in some contact situations women did – at least for a while – enhance their position and in particular they gained more from the contact than native men did. For the Timucua it is suggested that 'Eventually, a hybrid, creole culture was the result of these interactions; the domestic/subsistence sphere was dominated by native ways (female), and the public sector was dominated by Spanish (male) traditions' (ibid.: 99).

A picture emerges then of differently gendered groups having specific potentials regarding strategies for dealing with cultural upheaval. Devens in describing the Cree and Ojibwa people of western Canada provides a vivid case study of such differences. The pre-contact communities there are described as ones in which gender roles were prominent and 'permeated all aspects of daily life – authority, productive and reproductive activities, spatial arrangements, and food distribution. . . . Each sex was an integral yet autonomous part of the social

and productive unit' (Devens 1991: 510). The missions and the introduction of the fur trade disrupted this balance and in some cases even
caused gender-based antagonism as native men and women had different potential gains from their involvement with them (ibid.: 511).
In New France, for instance, missions often became a divisive force,
with men wanting to adopt Catholicism and a sedentary lifestyle, but
women resisting the imposition of Christian values and gender roles
(ibid.: 511). The impact of missions (which in this context may be
thought of primarily in terms of ideological and commercial contact)
and how it furthered or undermined gender-based interests was not
everywhere the same, however. It has, for example, been suggested
that amongst the North Atlantic Inuit women were attracted more
quickly to the missions than men were (Levy and Claassen 1992: 125),
and a similar pattern has also been argued for Australia (Sharp 1952).
This may at least in part be due to how pre-existing arrangements
between men and women meant that they might differently lose or
gain by becoming assimilated; gender-based differences in response
may therefore be part of processes of maintaining status and identity
(see also Devens 1991: 512).

Devens also points towards contact as having many different dimensions and how therefore differently constituted groups can engage
with distinct aspects of the interaction. The Canadian northwest is
again an illuminative example as the missionary activities were not the
only form of contact in so far as they were complemented by economic ones in the form of the fur trade. This furthered both disruption
of pre-existing social relations and contributed to women losing economic status. In this process it was particularly significant that the
Indians' growing dependence on European goods reoriented male hunting towards fur for trade, which meant that many female productive
activities, such as processing skin and making garments, were altered
or eliminated. 'As a result, the significance of women's direct contribution to the community's welfare diminished as their relationship to
the dispersal of fur changed' (Devens 1991: 512).

Such variations in the effect upon differently constituted people
would have many reasons. One of these would relate to whether the
colonizers included both men and women, or whether they were men
only or mainly. The former was, for example, the case with the Norse
settlement on Greenland, where there is little evidence of interaction
between settlers and the native people (McGovern 1985). This has
also been suggested to be the case for the Vikings in Russia, where
Stalsberg, on the basis of grave assemblages, has argued that women
constituted a considerable proportion of the Scandinavian population
(Stalsberg 1987: 95). In contrast, the Spanish conquest of Mesoamerica

involved in many instances only or mainly men. Another major factor relates to how the production of both subsistence commodities and prestige items was organized locally and the degree of separation between the products and skills of various people prior to contact. Thus, in many areas of the Americas it seems that native women's manufactures often experienced a prolonged market value while men's manufactures were replaced by European goods (Levy and Claassen 1992: 111). The same potentials may not, however, have existed amongst, for instance, the Inuits or Australian Aboriginals due to their specific food-cultures, where the potential for conversion through a new market may have been more limited. While contact causes mutation of indigenous gender arrangements the specific effect it has upon local communities is dependent upon the particular contexts in which it is played out.

Contact period archaeology, despite the need for applying source criticism and recognizing biases, is privileged in the multi-faceted records available about the range and rate of changes and responses. They can therefore also be used to identify concerns relevant for other times and places where these processes are not as obviously available for analysis. Relevant and pertinent examples from Europe range from our speculations about contact between different early human populations, such as the potential meetings between Neanderthals and anatomically modern humans, the interaction between early agriculturists and Mesolithic hunter-gatherers and various colonizing and expansionist movements within Europe, such as those documented in connection with the Roman empire or the evidence of Viking raids and settlements. These and many other events, while not all similar to colonization in the sense of conquest and acculturation, are all about the meeting of people who are differently constituted and in possession of different technological skills and themselves formed by and within distinct ideological and cultural contexts.

To take the spread of the Roman empire as our example, it is immediately obvious that the so-called Romanization process is about interaction. It is about natives and foreigners and the ways in which they affected each other in a particular time and space. It is also obvious that gender relations were part of these interactions, as the Roman army, and later settled Romans of various ranks, needed and desired different things from and relationships with local men and women. This difference would, furthermore, be in terms both of sexual and social interactions as well as access to the producers of various commodities. In turn, the various interacting groups were themselves transformed and must be understood and perceived in terms of their new relationships. The effect of contact is therefore not just the apparent passivity of acculturation and decline but also takes the active form of emulation and selection. New ways of being are formulated and the sense of self and social identities are affected. With the expansion of the Roman empire into its western provinces of France, the Low Countries and Britain this is seen, for instance, in the adoption of new styles of dress and a changing concern with the body and appearance. New items, such as specific toilet instruments (nail-cleaner, ear-scoop and tweezer) and perfume, appear, and some of the well-established objects, such as ornaments, change their form. A few specific objects, such as razors, have a renaissance in their importance as they become part of new attitudes towards the body and the expression of social identity. The ways in which this both involves a fracturing of existing gender relations and the articulation of new ones have so far been little studied. It is therefore only recently that the importance of these aspects of 'Romanization' are being emphasized, causing its analysis to be increasingly framed in terms of intense changes in interpersonal contacts (Hill 1997, Meadows 1994). The involvement of and effect upon gender relations in these processes are obvious.

Technology and the danger of the new

If we take the impact of contact also potentially to apply to other disruptive elements or phenomena, such as newness itself, ideological movements or exotic or foreign objects, these other situations may also be analysed in terms of their impact upon gender arrangements as social contract.

Okley has pointed out that gypsy women use their special relationship with outsiders to resolve the problem they have of formal subordination to men (Okley in Ardener 1975). 'Therefore the disjunction between the outsider's stereotype and the insider's ideal, expressed in pollution taboos, is to some extent bridged by an exchange of fantasies between the women and men of opposing groups' (Ardener 1975: 55). The idea that the third partner, the outsider, or that which is new or from far away, can be an object of imagination and desire (see also Helms 1988) provides us with a venue of analysis other than merely searching for suppression and force, as suggested by the earlier contact studies. Contact – interpreted widely and metaphorically, as suggested above – may also be explored in an entrepreneurial and voluntary manner. It can be a force within, used for redefinition of position and to challenge established values. The traditional danger-association where foreigner and young woman are coupled (e.g. 'Beware of the tall, dark stranger') is clearly related to the potential challenges to rights as perceived from within. It is therefore of interest that foreign objects and foreign contacts are also prestige-associated, and that therefore through such items and contacts relationships between communities can be potentially highly charged and ambiguous.

The challenge to social relations that may arise from technological changes illustrates this well. For example, the introduction of both bronze and iron into prehistoric Europe were complex processes which, on one hand, involved the availability of physical resources, the knowledge and skill to recognize and manipulate these and the organization of labour needed for the manufacturing and distribution of the new objects and, on the other hand, the construction of meanings and values for a range of both new activities and products. Different aspects of these innovation phenomena have been analysed but the overall complexity and the interconnectedness of various factors remain obscure. It is, however, obvious that the introduction of bronze and iron would each in their way disrupt local communities and the way labour was organized and products exchanged. It is therefore interesting that Shennan in his discussion of the social context of Early Bronze Age metallurgy in central Europe proposes that within the primary production area 'copper provided a basis for the emancipation of junior from elders through the increased prosperity it generated' (Shennan 1993: 67). It is significant to stress here that reformulation of social relationships based on age almost inevitably also affects gender relations as age groups are informed by gender (for an archaeological discussion of the interconnection between age and gender see, for example, Sofaer-Derevenski 1997, 1998). If we agree with Shennan's interpretation there are therefore various possible gender implications. For example, the emancipation of juniors must have affected their incorporation within other productive activities and in many instances their labour had to be replaced by that of others. Therefore, while junior men might have gained independence from their elders, women may have increased their importance within the productive spheres vacated by junior men. It is also likely that such changes within age hierarchies and labour would affect not only the age of 'marriage' but also the arrangements of such relationships. This in turn may have changed girl's and young women's position within the group and given them greater independence within these arrangements as these were not solely agreed between elders. Despite such obvious possibilities, social relations in Early Bronze Age central Europe, even when gender relations are clearly acknowledged, are still largely interpreted through an assumption of technological change benefiting males and an equation between this and a decline in women's position (e.g. Robb 1994, Shennan 1993: 148–50).

Such interpretations pay no attention to whether women, individually and as social groups, may also exploit the disruption of social relations and the challenge to conventions and norms to their own benefit in terms of status and rights. It is therefore worth noting that many of the cemeteries from the Early Bronze Age contain both rich female and male graves, and that during the Middle Bronze Age female graves become even richer and more varied in their assemblages (e.g. Sørensen 1997). There are also apparent discrepancies that demand further exploration, such as some extremely rich female grave assemblages. Such characteristics of the burial rites contemporary with the proposed changes in social relations do not appear to support the view that the impact of the new technology caused increased subordination of women, nor do they sustain the suggestion that internal distinction amongst women was entirely due to the success of the group into which they married (e.g. Shennan 1993: 151). Clearly, while a concern with the fracturing of gender relations during this period already has been expressed, more detailed investigations of the social implication of such disruptions are needed. It is, in particular, important to acknowledge that differently gendered groups may all respond strategically to technological innovations in order to enhance their identity and status, and that gendered identity is not necessarily defined within a male–female hierarchy.

One of the essential factors that must have affected how copper and later bronze could be explored in social strategies is the physical scarcity of the raw materials which means that attempts at its control are feasible. In contrast to this, the introduction of iron probably challenged such monopolies and controls as iron in various forms is available in most parts of Europe. The social impact of this technological innovation was therefore probably different and may have become involved with processes of social fragmentation and regionalism. As iron technology is more complicated than bronze, it probably also resulted in the development of specialists and more rigid labour divisions. The impact of these changes upon gender relations has not yet been considered, although the parallels with the impact of contact should now challenge us to explore how these technological changes affected negotiation and transformation of gender relations as new ways of living together came into being.

Finally, while considering innovations and strange and unfamiliar objects, the impact of ideas and ideologies should also be recognized as an important cause of change. The spread of cremation rite during the Late Bronze Age in many parts of Europe is an important and interesting example of this. The variability observed in different local versions of cremation burials provides significant insight into how

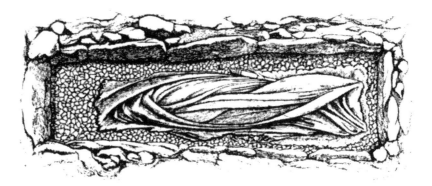

Figure 9.1   Example of cremated bones 'dressed' in cloth and buried as an inhumation grave in a stone cist. (Brøndsted 1966 based on Herbst)

different communities responded to such innovations. In Denmark, for example, during the first few hundred years of this tradition, various forms of combinations of elements from the former inhumation rite and the new cremation practices exist, such as cremated bones buried in large cists or 'dressed' in cloth or objects being placed in their 'correct' position on the cremated bones (see figure 9.1). This illuminates both how different local communities comprehend and, in turn, translate and give form to innovative ideas and forms of behaviour, and it may also indicate who within a local community are first affected by these changes. It is, therefore, interesting to note that, although as yet not systematically investigated, there appears to be – at least in some areas – an aspect of gender politics involved in the adoption of cremation rites. In the Netherlands, for example, all the earliest cremations are of females (Lohof 1994).

Gender and contact, gender as contact

Gender arises as a result of contact between people. Through forced, necessary or voluntary interactions between differently constituted groups, people change their alliance and self-perception. In such meeting, as in the contact between different value systems, people and things change their positions within various internal systems of valuation and obligations. Contact will, therefore, often result in basic changes in areas such as subsistence production; it may stimulate the development of new commodities and the adoption of new types of food and new manners of their consumption, and it affects and alters local modes of dress.

To help us understand these confrontations and their influence upon agreements about gender in terms of rights and obligations, various instances of contact provide us with case studies in which social relations are being redefined and therefore open both to their own strategic defences and our scrutiny. Contact archaeology, in particular the developing concern with gender as an active ingredient in changing social circumstances, helps us to recognize

> the necessity of focusing seriously upon the role of agency by indigenous peoples in the process . . . consumption of alien cultural elements is an active, motivated, creative process. . . . both parties – natives and colonists – were linked in complex networks of interaction driven by different logic of social action and interest that produced continual transformations in the regional structures of power. (Dietler 1995: 90–1)

This does not mean that women were always strategically improving their social status, or that contact always benefited them. On the contrary, the range of case studies referred to above demonstrates that the impact upon local gender arrangements varied enormously. They do argue, however, that gender relations will always be affected. The presence of new partners, as well as the introduction of alien cultural values or of unfamiliar material objects, alters existing social relationships and in particular those between the sexes (Devens 1991: 512). Past communities lived through and responded to such interruptions of their lives and in their response, through the intersection of technologies, objects, practices and people, we can explore further how within differently organized societies the gender contract become affected and renegotiated when its basic assumptions and material basis was being challenged.

10
The Beginning: on Becoming Gendered

We had a goldfish. She was called Scarlet!

A gendered world, or looking back to the beginning

It seems so natural that the world is gendered. The notion of difference that this generates permeates our thinking, it colours our labelling of the world around us, and it affects both discursive and practical actions. Gender is a strong metaphor: some nations are spoken about as women, peaks in the mountains may be personalized as male or female, ships are feminine, and many innate objects are gendered. We live in a gendered world, and while theoretically its discursive nature has become increasingly recognized, as a normative practice gender continues to be performed and experienced. Human societies, despite their tremendous variability, seem familiar as gendered communities. But is that necessarily the case? The time depth of archaeology puts the discipline in contact with humans so deep down in our past that they are beyond the reach of any of our experiences. These people are at the beginning of human history. The previous four chapters have engaged with particular types of human practices through which material culture both communicates gender and involves it with and affects it through practical action. Throughout these chapters, as in gender literature generally, the cultural construction of gender is assumed to exist as a possibility within any society. This chapter, in contrast, considers how studies of the earliest history of humans question the existence and recognition of gender. It recognizes that archaeology is uniquely placed for considering the origin or coming into being of gender as an affect of human interaction, and it argues that these questions, despite the problems that immediately attach themselves to such concerns, cannot be ignored. The aim of this chapter will not be, however, to engender the Palaeolithic period but rather to contemplate the central issues that are raised by such attempts.

It is common, at both a popular and a discursive level, to assume that humans are distinct from other species, and that their production of 'culture' is one of the distinguishing traits. But assuming this uniqueness immediately gives rise to questions about when and how such distinctiveness arose and how it – the beginning of humans or cultural behaviour – can be identified. Gender research, in its continuous reference to gender as a cultural and social phenomenon and in its rejection of biological essentialism, assumes this distinctiveness. Thus, the existence of culture is taken for granted by the study of gender (and to some extent also in current discussions of sex) and as an assumption this is non-discursively embedded within our theoretical foundation. It follows that if the status of culture is questioned then the assumption of the existence (or at least the nature) of gender must also be challenged. This point was strikingly brought to my attention through a paper at the 'Archaeology of Gender' Chacmool Conference in Calgary in 1989. Referring to 'Lucy', a human fossil from Hadar, Ethiopia, which at the time was one of the oldest known hominids (Hager 1997a: 10), the speaker turned around the question about whether this was a woman by asking whether Lucy knew she was a woman, and thus challenged the whole notion of gender. This question stresses at the level of the individual that knowing that one is a woman is a cultural knowledge.

The search for origin is in many ways simplistic as well as ideologically corrupt. The critique raised in response (see for example Conkey 1997, Dobres 1988, Hager 1997b, Nelson 1997) shows how such research ultimately serves presentist purposes and in particular how it invests current or recent gender systems with roots, and thus legitimacy, by presenting them as permanent and essentially static. These are serious flaws and consequences. Despite these problems the coming into being of that which we recognize as a cultural response to difference between people is a central concern due to the dependence of gender on culture itself. As archaeologists we have to accept that the time depth we cover makes it our responsibility to engage with the question of where and how gender enters society as a distinct practice and concerns that are given material form. Recognizing the limitation of this question and the almost unavoidable tendency of our analyses being affected by notions of progress, uniqueness and evolutionism, I nonetheless suggest that this is an important field that may substantiate our understanding of gender as invested in and invented through cultural practice.

Partly in recognition of this, gender concerns have been more clearly articulated and more widely recognized within Palaeolithic research than in other periods of prehistory. In addition, during the 1970s the man-the-hunter model, which had become increasingly dominant in interpretations of early human societies, provided a well-defined point of gender debate. With the new awareness of the cultural embeddedness of gender relations one could now turn to this seminal period with new questions and critiques of previous assumptions. One obvious line of concern was 'has there always been gender? when and under what conditions and in which contexts does gender come into existence?' (Conkey 1991: 87, n. 4). Another approach, and one now seen within all periods, was to investigate gender relations as expressed through the production, use and discard of material objects. This approach often became preoccupied with demonstrating the presence and active contribution of women and re-evaluating their importance (for instance to subsistence production) against that of men. As a result much attention was given to the production and the dietary value of various resources. Alternatively, the focus was upon assigning tool kits to each gender. The obvious importance of these studies was their attention to women's contributions and how they gave value to hitherto invisible activities. They were also, however, limited by their simplistic equation between importance and contribution in terms of calorie intake or by proposing rather static gender divisions of labour. Clearly much of the early gender research regarding the Palaeolithic arose out of the desire to include women in the past, to demonstrate their presence in the archaeological record and thus to locate them as part of our ancestry and roots and to argue for their contribution to our history. Zihlman, who played an important role in these early discussions, has stated that the models were developed in response to the data rather than due to feminist influences (Hager 1997a: 6). They were, however, in essence, similar to the discipline's general responses to contemporary influences. The further development from this early challenge also follows the same trends as the discipline in general as the two fields of feminist critique and reinterpretation have been the focus. The latter has in particular aimed at engendering part of Palaeolithic assemblages and especially reinterpretations of early 'art'.

Feminist critique

To arrive at an engendered interpretation of the Palaeolithic it was first necessary to 'weed out' blatantly sexist assumptions and to develop a critical and reflexive understanding of how the existing interpretative framework had been constructed: which were its empirical foundations, what was its theoretical underpinning and were some of its assertions merely assumptions? Increasingly other biases, such as Euro- or ethnocentric ones, have also been recognized as deeply entrenched both in how we organize data and how we reach interpretations (e.g. Conkey 1997). The general feminist critique of science has also extended to Palaeolithic research, often with the result that apparent facts are revealed as contingent upon a set of gender assumptions, forcing us to recognize the inferential basis of much knowledge about early humans, their behaviour and their societies (Hager 1997a: 3–4, Wylie 1997: 44ff). As a result, the epistemological basis as well as the ontological framework of Palaeolithic research has been substantially challenged. This has in particular increased awareness of the contemporary and political assumptions used, and, more rarely, it has even assailed our basic notions of gender and identity as well as questioning the relationship we establish with past people, turning them into an object subjected to our gaze (Conkey 1997).

Reinterpretation: Labour division and task-differentiation

One response to the invisibility or assigned insignificance of women in the Palaeolithic has been to focus upon developing methods, such as the task-differentiation approach, in order to generate new insights into gender relations through the study of roles and in particular labour division. As employed within Palaeolithic studies, the task-differentiation approach (which became influential through the emphasis given to it by Conkey and Spector (1984)) uses universal assumptions about task-differentiation in hunter-gatherer societies especially, but also male and female task associations more generally, to argue logically for the importance and contributions of women in Palaeolithic societies. This focus is strongly affected by the central role that labour division by gender, in combination with a pair-bonding mating system, has played in many models of hominid evolutionary adaptation. Such models are usually based on the assumption that gender is a basis for labour division both practically and symbolically (Zihlman 1991: 64) and that this is a universal phenomenon (Binford 1992, Willoughby 1991: 284).

Such approaches are well illustrated by Conkey's study of the Magdalenian (Late Upper Palaeolithic) rock shelter at Cuerto de la Mina in Spain (1991). Rather than demonstrating the presence of women, her concern was to explore how the material culture revealed a range of different activities and contexts which were likely to have involved gender. The interpretation builds upon a set of propositions such as accepting that the rock shelter was a seasonal aggregation site of otherwise dispersed hunter-gatherers and assuming that such sites are likely to be locales where a larger than usual number of people came together, and therefore constitute a context in which gender concepts and relations were brought into play (Conkey 1991: 72). The study is one of the clearest advocates of an approach where 'engendering' is not dependent upon the physical identification of women. A more detailed account of the interpretation is therefore worth outlining to identify how gender can be introduced to a typical and apparently genderless Palaeolithic assemblage.

Conkey looked at the site in terms of a group of people who engaged in diverse productive activities and amongst whom socially meaningful differentiation along the lines of sex and age is likely (1991: 73). The sample of worked bone and antler from the site shows that extensive bone- and antler-working took place; harpoons were manufactured and their perforations suggest the making and use of cord, string, line and by extension perhaps even weaving (ibid.: 76), a technology also indicated by the many needles. Incomplete needles suggest that they were produced within the site. Other bone and antler implements may have been for the making of nets and cordage. Activities on the site included lithic working, shaft-straightening (batons), hideworking (scrapers), vegetation-processing (scrapers), bone- and antlerengraving (burins) and the use of compound tools (microliths, antler tools). Other activities were carried out outside the site: perforating shells and teeth, obtaining pigments, antler and bone, hunting and gathering from a variety of ecosystems, butchering and processing and so forth. It is unlikely that these activities were all monopolized by any one group or individual. Conkey, therefore, proposed that social differentiations had to be 'at work' (ibid.: 77f). Using ethnographic analogies she suggested that women were involved with productive activities involving string lines, cords and weaving. She also proposed that one may assume that those who use certain tools and facilities are likely also to be those who are primarily engaged in their manufacture and maintenance. This simple assumption (with which one may not agree, but which certainly is possible) broadens the whole area of women's involvement, despite the original conservative assumption about women being associated with cord and string. She summarized the picture of women's active engagement with several levels of productive activities as follows:

> First let's assume that adult women with young children were primarily the makers of cordage, nets, and 'lines', and were primarily engaged in the activities associated with the use of these products: making of 'clothing', storage bags or sacs, sewing sections of hide together for 'tents'; collecting and transport of shellfish with nets; use of cords in harpoons for fishing; collecting plant resources for cordage; setting 'net' fences

and traps. Thus, these females would be making their own scrapers for hide-working, their own needles, and their own harpoons for fishing. This implies that they had to work at least some blanks of antler and flint or quartzite for such implements. From their involvement in shell fishing, these women would be associated with the perforating of shells for wearing, attaching to 'clothing' and/or exchange of shells that extend over great distances. (Conkey 1991: 78)

Conkey furthermore suggested that these technologies are simultaneously partitioned by the occupants and generating such partitioning, and that such division gives rise to both social order and tension inasmuch as the different tasks have to be scheduled and may be dependent on each other.

The interpretation suggested is not surprising; but it is satisfying and stimulating because it does not make imaginary jumps, it relies on conventional assumptions about labour divisions, and it even manages to make sense of material from an old excavation (the site was excavated in 1914) and yet it presents women as much more actively and fundamentally engaged in the maintenance of their communities than is common. It also suggests that there were areas of tension through which gender ideologies may be transformed. As a case study, it is also important for demonstrating that the engendering of the past is not dependent on new excavation techniques or other methodological developments; it is contingent upon sensitivity towards the issues and an ability to ask questions differently.

Gender research and the origin of humans

Much research has been invested in the question of the origin of humans and in the separation of different stages of human evolution and thus the degree of humanness. Such stages may be indicated by, for instance, activities such as hunting, tool use, bipedalism or 'significant' morphological changes such as increase in brain size, as when $873c^3$ is used as the transitional size between *Homo habilis* and *Homo erectus* (Lewin 1989: 128). From the time when bipedal hominids walked over the lava flow at Laetoli in Tanzania (Champion et al. 1984: 26) some 3.8 million years ago and until so-called 'modern humans' appeared in Europe (and other parts of the world) the human fossil record and a limited range of simple objects are the only data available for study. Research, concerned with locating the origin of specific defining aspects of our humanness therefore commonly uses evolutionary theory and comparative primate biology to reach conclusions (Marchant 1991: 50, Zihlman 1991). The nature and aims of this research cause it to be typically concerned with morphological differences (degrees of sexual dimorphism, for instance) that are interpreted also in terms of behavioural differences such as sexual division of labour. The central role given by such studies to sexual behavioural variation means that the origin and evolution of sex differences has become a distinct area of research. Therefore, although the remains from this early phase of human history provide neither direct evidence for social differences between people nor contain clear and repetitive cultural expressions, gender has become an issue in the interpretations proposed.

Some of the earliest and most prominent feminist contributions to Palaeolithic archaeology can be directly connected to this debate and took, as mentioned, the form of a critique during the 1970s of the man-the-hunter model (for a feminist discussion of this debate see, for example, Balme and Beck 1993, Hager 1997a). This interpretation, while having roots back in the nineteenth century, developed into a distinct evolutionary model during the 1960s (for detailed discussion of this development see Hager 1997a, Nelson 1997: 71ff, Zihlman 1997). Seeing hunting (and meat-eating) as a behaviour that set humans apart from other primates, research focused upon evidence of hunting and its resulting development in hunting technology and social organization, and these changes were interpreted as evolutionary adaptation (Washburn and Lancaster 1968). As hunting, for various reasons, but often including references to women's role in reproduction and child rearing, was firmly associated with men, such cultural and social developments were similarly associated with them. The first wave of reaction focused upon arguing that woman-the-gatherer provided a major part of the diet, formed the core social unit (the mother–child relationship) and were inventors (Hager 1997a: 6). Influential in this development were the works by, amongst others, Dahlberg (1981), Zihlman and Tanner (1978) and, for archaeology in particular, Slocum (1975). The reasons for these responses were dissatisfaction with how women's contribution to society was assigned and in particular how it was evaluated, and their aim was to demonstrate the vital role women had as procurers and inventors, rather than merely being nurturing members of their communities. Their underlying importance within the Palaeolithic debate was both substantial and specific inasmuch as the man-the-hunter model had come to imply that hunting was an evolutionarily significant activity resulting in morphological, technological and social innovations (e.g. Washburn and DeVore 1961, Washburn and Lancaster 1968; for a discussion of the development of this model see Zihlman 1997). Hunting by men was, the models argued, directly responsible for the sexual division of labour, food-sharing, co-operation amongst males, planning and developing technical skills associated with human societies (Willoughby 1991: 285). Men were evolutionary adaptive, while females were made peripheral to evolutionary history (Hager 1997a: 5). These works, both the original ones and their critiques, are now generally held to be too simplistic in their assertion of women's roles and significance. It was an important debate, however, as it resulted in a substantial challenge to androcentric thinking and gradually brought more aspects of social life into the debates by focusing, for example, upon sharing and more complex forms of labour division (Hager 1997a: 7–8).

That these discussions are affected by notions of gender is clearly not due to the character of the cultural material associated with early human history, rather it is caused by the observation and expectation of morphological sexual differences and by the way these render themselves open to political interpretations (i.e. interpretations in terms of social meaning and impact). Responding to the interpretative challenge of sexual differences amongst early humans, recent feminist studies try to reinvest these relationships with different meanings. This includes more detailed attention to how the special role assigned to women, by virtue of their reproductive abilities and associated behaviour (such as the mother–infant relationship (Marchant 1991: 50)), is not necessarily static and may be affected by life-stage changes. Another line of research uses morphological comparisons between primates and early humans to reconsider the notion of labour division by sex on the basis of more recent studies that provide accounts of far more complex behaviour, including food-procuring and sexual activities, amongst primates, than was previously assumed (Hager 1997a, Marchant 1991). Such studies may begin to question the taken-for-granted assumption of labour division by sex that underlies models of early human evolution. Concern with how separate tasks may have different but not therefore necessarily unequal status is also likely to be of relevance, renewing debates about the foundation and reasons for asymmetries.

In addition to these debates, recent feminist critique has added political awareness to these studies as they are concerned with how origin research has aimed either to show our distinctiveness as humans or our progress and how in doing so we link the most remote past and the present. This means that the past is used to lend legitimization and permanence to present gender arrangements (Conkey 1997) and furthermore that these easily take on the form – through their distribution by mass media (Conkey 1997, Moser 1998) – of sublimated messages about what is right and natural (Nelson 1997: 65). Conkey, for example, criticizes origin research for looking for the origin of categories that are defined at the onset (1997). Similarly there is a growing concern with the ways in which this research is couched in terms of a specific identity dominated by a concept of women as secondary or supplementary (e.g. Dorse 1997: 3). Feminist involvement in origin research has therefore been particularly active and articulate in pushing for a solid critique of how ideas about the remote past are influenced by modern assumptions about human nature (Willoughby 1991: 284) and modern organizations of social relations (Zihlman 1991). The impact of such contemporary assumptions ranges widely. Hager, for instance, argues that bias may enter when sexual dimorphism in modern human skeletons is assumed to mirror that of the earliest hominids, which means that we are consistently assigning our own differences to people in the past even to the earliest ones (1997a). The influence of contemporary assumptions also means that sexual relations amongst early hominids are often interpreted in terms of pair-bonding in such a manner that this is often a euphemism for 'marriage', thus assigning a very specific social institution to the past (Zihlman 1991).

Gendered cultural expression and practice during the Upper Palaeolithic

Within the debates about the earliest humans the appearance of anatomically modern humans is often seen as a particularly important threshold in our early history: at this stage humans became recognizably human beings and cultured. It is therefore upon this part of the Palaeolithic that I shall particularly focus in the following discussion.*

The creation during the Palaeolithic of images that represent something distinct, and in particular representations of human beings, has for a long time been given special attention both professionally and amongst the general public. Such expressions have been used as an undeniable proof of the cognitive abilities of modern humans and in turn emphasized as our opportunity to gain insights into the Palaeolithic mind (e.g. Leroi-Gourhan 1968). Their reasons, content and messages have been intensely disputed, and their production and material qualities analysed (for general overviews see Bahn 1998, Bahn and Vertut 1988). Recently, various groups of feminists have added their voices, and many gendered interpretations of the material exist.

---

* In this chapter alternative claims about the earliest modern humans are not considered. This is because the points made are not dependent upon origin and earliest in that sense but rather rest upon the observation of early recurrent practices that associate people and material signs resulting in a materialization and machination of gender as one kind of difference. That this happened at different times and in various places is entirely possible.

Painted and engraved surfaces and movable objects are found from certain periods of the Palaeolithic and in different parts of the world (Bahn 1998, Conkey 1997). One of the earliest and most distinct concentrations is the paintings from caves and decorated portable objects from the Upper Palaeolithic (40.000–10.000 BP) in Europe and Eurasia. The cave paintings and engravings (parietal art) are concentrated in France and northern Iberia with fewer examples along the Mediterranean and in Russia. Decorated ornaments and objects (portable art) are found more widely, with several distinct concentrations in western and eastern Europe and Eurasia (Bahn 1998, Bahn and Vertut 1988). At a general level all these different expressions reveal cognitive abilities amongst Palaeolithic people. They are, however, also more specific, and there is much variety both between categories of expressions, such as cave art* versus portable art, and within each category in terms of their production, depositional context and the elements used in their compositions. The cave paintings, for instance, are mainly composed of more or less naturalized images of animals, geometric designs and outlines of hands. The engraved objects often combine a three-dimensional form, both figurative and non-figurative, with geometric designs, indistinct patterns or imitations of physical things such as hair. Ornaments, understood here as objects that could be used by humans to wear, are often decorated in geometric designs, are made in imitation of physical objects such as canine teeth or are without any obvious pattern beyond perforation or other means of attachment.**

Conkey has very succinctly warned against interpreting these various data detached from their contexts of use and against understanding them as isolated pieces of art, as this would give their reasons and meanings an essential sameness that is probably inappropriate. She and others (e.g. Dorse 1997) have also emphasized the diversity within the data as it is neither temporally nor geographically either a bounded or a unified phenomenon (Conkey 1997). The known objects are clearly varied, in particular they must be recognized as belonging to a very long time period and as being found over a vast area. They are not distinct phenomena defined within a concentration of time and space; neither, however, are such objects just individual, single pieces either evenly or randomly distributed throughout the Upper Palaeolithic in

---

* While the term 'art', with its connotation of a Western sense of intentionality, sensitivity and the singular artist is misleading (Conkey 1997), it is nonetheless used here as a shorthand reference to the kind of archaeological data that is commonly placed within this rubric.

** This is not meant as a list of all types of portable and parietal art from the Palaeolithic; rather it refers to the objects in terms of categories that may usefully inform us about the presence and cultural articulation of gender awareness and relations during this time.

Figure 10.1 Reconstruction of one of the costumes from the Sungir graves, showing the use of beads as attachments on clothing. (Redrawn after Ladier and Welté 1995)

Europe and Eurasia. In fact, they cluster in certain areas and are at times found in large numbers on specific sites, such as Kostenki in Russia, or in individual graves, such as some of the Sungir burials, Russia. In the latter, for example, some graves have several thousand beads, and in some the arrangements indicate that beads were sewn onto individual pieces of clothing (e.g. Bahn and Vertut 1988: 72) (see figure 10.1). This suggests that while we acknowledge their diversity we should nonetheless also recognize how at some locations such objects – through particular practices and repetitions of forms – became part of a repertoire. They were often not a singular spontaneous creation, as may be suggested by the emphasis upon their diversity, but were part of a certain practice and a specified material form. Therefore, while agreeing with Conkey's objections to standardizing the objects through our interpretative engagement, such objects nonetheless seem to provide an important opportunity for questioning the social recognition of self and responses to differences between people early in human history. It, therefore, seems to me that these material remains must play a role in our attempts at understanding what gender is, how it constitutes itself and how it is enacted through material objects at this early time. Furthermore, following the argument of chapter 5, which proposes that a central aspect of gender is how people materialize themselves – whether as an individual or as a social person is not essential here – the appearance of objects for personal adornment and of figurines is an enormously interesting and intriguing cultural expression that for the first time is consistently given form during the Upper Palaeolithic.

Ornaments: technology of the self

In many of these later Palaeolithic societies people used beads and similar apparently decorative objects. Such objects, their perforations suggesting they were pendants or attachments upon clothing (see figure 10.1), can reasonably be interpreted as personal adornments, that is, they were worn by a person and added to that person's appearance.* This suggests attitudes of care and attention towards the body and thus a culturation of the self. This is further supported by the indication of elaborate hairstyles on some of the figurines, such as the famous one from Willendorf, Austria (see figure 7.3) or the head from Grotte du Pape, France (see figure 10.2). As the evidence is sparse and spread over time and space the exact interpretation of such adornment is not agreed upon and should, probably, not be attempted; nonetheless ornaments do provide significant pointers towards perceptions/fabrications of the person in these early communities.

These ornaments are commonly interpreted as part of the Upper Palaeolithic 'package' of cultural innovations and developments. White, who has worked extensively with beads from the Palaeolithic, for example, states that 'the invention of material forms of representation went hand in hand with a major social transformation across the Middle/Upper Palaeolithic transition in Europe' (1992: 537). Some scholars (e.g. Bahn and Vertut 1988: 71f) argue, however, that the use of beads and other personal ornaments may go further back in time, although it is clearly first with the Upper Palaeolithic that they become common and regularly used within some communities. Its significant importance during this time is therefore not necessarily as an innovation in material culture (contra LaBouff 1997, White 1982), but is rather due to the ways in which the practices associated with such objects within some communities become normalized and part of routines. It is through its extended social usage and recognition, rather than merely through its existence, that the Upper Palaeolithic ornament may have articulated new concerns and certainly confirmed and

---

* This does not exclude possible functions, such as magic or initiation. The object adds to the appearance, but the meaning assigned to the addition is culturally specific.

Figure 10.2   The human head from Grotte du Pape, France. The pattern on the head suggests that some Palaeolithic communities gave attention to dressing the hair. (Reproduced courtesy of Musée des antiquités nationales, Saint-Germain-en-Laye, France)

expanded its forms. It is therefore probably useful to acknowledge that this is a blurred threshold in terms of whether particular objects and practices may be found earlier and to maintain nonetheless that we, at this time, see a qualitative departure in terms of changes in how objects are made and *what is made of the existence of objects*. Thus it may be possible to reconcile the various attempts to reject the Upper Palaeolithic phenomenon as a sudden appearance (Bahn 1995/96) with a strong argument for marked changes at this time in terms of how people expressed themselves and the concerns and practices of communities (Mellars 1989, 1996). This coexistence of gradual change and temporal intensification of certain practices may be helpful for a discussion of gender and personhood in the Upper Palaeolithic.

From around 40,000 BP pierced or perforated animal teeth, ivory and bone fragments, stones and shells were used as beads widely in Europe with early appearances particularly concentrated in Aurignacian (40,000–28,000 BP) assemblages in France, Belgium and Germany (White 1992, 1993). The beads and pendants have been discussed in terms of raw material use and manufacturing techniques, demonstrating the long-distance exchange involved (White 1989). For example, at the site of Kostenki on the Don River in Russia there were shells from the Black Sea, while at Les Eyzies, southern France, shells were found that came from Mediterranean locations 300 km south of the site and from the Atlantic (Taborin 1993). The efforts dedicated to their production, the level of standardization as well as various quantitative assessments (well over 10,000 pierced ornaments are known from the Palaeolithic, P. Mellars personal communication) have also been subject to analysis (e.g. White 1993). An important point arising from these quantitative data is that while there may be many levels at which the use of beads was individually negotiated and their materiality responded to, they nonetheless were not merely the result of a spontaneous reaction to a situated material possibility such as 'I find a shell with a hole in and put it on a string around my neck'. Long-distance exchange may have other reasons than the objects gained, but the wide-ranging exchange, together with evidence of deliberate and meditated production, shows, nonetheless, beads as standardized items integrated in a material and cultural repertoire. There is, for instance, evidence that 'In general ivory and steatite boards were produced by a set of regionally specific highly standardised techniques' (White 1992: 554), that the use of material was based on 'choices' (ibid.: 549), and that basket beads were 'mass' produced (ibid.: 550–1). Such qualities show that beads within some communities had become part of the cultural universe; during the Upper Palaeolithic beads and perforated ornaments became things to think and act with. It is therefore appropriate that their communicative and symbolic roles are recognized as an important dimension of these societies (e.g. Mithen 1996), and it is obvious that the ways in which they may have been involved in the conception, creation and legitimization of group and personal identities should be subject to analysis (LaBouff 1997, White 1992).

It is worth emphasizing that these ornaments, while personal, were not individualistic, although regionally distinct forms exist (White

1993), and that their use probably was restricted to being worn as pendants or attached to clothing (LaBouff 1997: 5). In that sense they may be thought of as body ornament, which as 'personal adornment is one of the most powerful and pervasive forms in which humans construct and represent beliefs, values and social identity' (White 1992: 539). In this emphasis, there is a danger of seeing ornaments as a direct reflection of social identities, causing Palaeolithic beads to be interpreted in terms of social ranks and hierarchical differences as opposed to emphasizing how they are elements of a technology of self and body. The beads suggest awareness of the self and of differences and similarities between different selfs, and, furthermore, this is an awareness that is instrumentalized through material constructions and elaboration. Wearing beads one makes oneself into a cultural construct. For our understanding of the beads it is, however, important to recall that they were removable items, a quality discussed in chapter 7, which means that they had no permanent relationship to the body (Sørensen 1997). Their presence, rather than being a fixed marker of the person's identity, may therefore have involved temporal communication indicating time, events, roles or even mood. The fact that they were common means that they became integral to a commonly and communally understood and agreed behaviour, and it is in that sense that they were meaningful in a manner that we can trace.

The use of ornaments is not the same in all parts of Europe. First, there are obvious concentrations such as in France or Russia where individual sites may have several hundreds or even thousands of beads (White 1993), while many other areas had very little or apparently no use of ornaments. Second, while the use of ornaments at a certain level is similar throughout the Upper Palaeolithic, they are nonetheless also used in locally distinct manners. In the Eastern Gravettian sites quantitative differences in ornament use have, for example, been interpreted as being due to differentiation between individuals. This is, for instance, argued for some of the lavish Sungir burials mentioned earlier (Arnold 1996, White 1993, Soffer 1985). On the other hand, despite potentially different social organization between, for instance, the French Aurignacian and the Russian Eastern Gravettian, personal ornaments were used in a similar manner in both (LaBouff 1997). Such divergence gives us the potential for exploring whether and how the person is becoming a cultural subject in different manners within the various cultural contexts of the Upper Palaeolithic.

It is therefore useful briefly to introduce the ways in which these ornaments have been considered in terms of style and social identity (as reviewed by LaBouff 1997). In these arguments the concept of active style (Conkey 1983) or Wiessner's concept of assertive style

(1984) have frequently been used to present ornaments as either deliberate abstractions or as symbolic of concepts such as group identity (LaBouff 1997: 8). Interpreting the social communication of the ornaments according to such concepts implies, however, an intentionality that immediately assigns a specific form of social consciousness to Palaeolithic society. The notion of active or assertive style furthermore arbitrates between passive and active as if an item cannot be 'merely' decorative and nonetheless still affect its context. It also assumes that symbolic meaning is a deliberate aim that is embedded within the object when more often it results from practice, as discussed in chapter 5. Rather than assigning the production of Upper Palaeolithic ornaments such intentionality I suggest that their meaning and communicative impact arose as a result of practice and in particular through repetitive associations. Despite current emphasis upon the diversity of this material, and their low numbers in terms of the space and time involved, it is possible to see the ornaments in terms of repetition as they are not evenly distributed in either time or space but concentrated on certain locations where they were part of recurrent practices. This means that the important observation is not whether beads or perforated animal teeth or shell exist but rather that they at certain points in time become common, repetitive and routinely used by some communities. This removes the rather detached notion of active style, replacing it with an emphasis upon action. It also means that style is recognized as an outcome of practice, as the latter becomes involved with meaning as it produces codes of reference. It is in such terms that ornaments from the Upper Palaeolithic can be discussed with regard to the expression of self and personhood and be used to explore the associated constructions of gender identities.

Externalizing selves and others: figurines

Other striking cultural forms from the Upper Palaeolithic are the so-called figurines that are interpreted as representations of humans and predominantly females. Currently some 200 figurines are known, and a number of classification schemes have been developed (Conkey 1985, Delporte 1979, Gamble 1982, Gvozdover quoted in Conroy 1993, Leroi-Gourhan 1968). They are mainly found in settlements, and on some sites they appear in large numbers. These images are well known and they have been much debated by archaeologists, including feminist ones (e.g. Conkey 1997). Their inclusion in gender studies has focused primarily upon their role in contemporary debates and ideological formations as they provide popular images that are pliable in evolutionary discourses (e.g. Conkey 1997, Dorse 1997, Moser 1992, 1993, 1998), or upon questions about whom they portray or represent, and how they should be interpreted in terms of prehistoric meaning and significance as well as cognitive abilities. The appearance of these images at a time which has been interpreted as the boundary of the emergence of fully modern behaviour has inevitably meant that they have been entangled with notions about what it means to be human (Conkey 1997, Dorse 1997). While it is important to emphasize that their analysis is complicated and probably always biased in some manner, this by itself does not mean that we should refrain from analysing the figurines in terms of humanness and gender. It does, however, profoundly emphasize the need for self-reflection in such analysis.

As is often emphasized (Conkey 1997), the dating of the figurines is problematic and so is deciding which objects should be included, as some are fragmented and others so highly schematized that it is questionable whether they represent humans (Delporte 1979: 210–15, 221–6). These problems, however, only limit a study of figurines if they are analysed as specific phenomena with an essentialism that demands unambiguous definitions and boundedness.

As already mentioned, the internal differences amongst figurines has recently been stressed (Conkey 1997). Difference and similarity are not objective criteria, however, but depend on the value and emphasis of the comparison; things are similar or different in terms of something. One may, therefore, argue that figurines are similar in terms of providing a three-dimensional but miniature similarity to the human body and in that sense they are all the same, in contrast to, for instance, hand axes. They, as a category, are at the same time internally different in terms of many variables such as size, degree of naturalism, material or carving techniques. Despite such diversity the figurines have in common the fact that they represent naked or almost naked human bodies with some parts of the body enhanced or emphasized and others only sketched. The parts commonly emphasized (and at times probably even exaggerated) are the breasts, abdomen and thighs, and in this emphasis the figurines are made to appear as female bodies. Typically the feet and hands are merely suggested and facial features (in contrast to some of the engravings on slabs; see for instance Bahn and Vertut 1988: figure 93) are usually vague, although indication of hair and at times plaits or similar dressing are more common. In the limited cases where specific types of adornment or appearance are indicated, this seems be a matter of a loin-piece, string or beads across the chest and sometimes wrists, and lines around the waist. On a few figurines remains of pigment (ochre) have been found (Bahn and Vertut 1988: 84), suggesting that either they were coloured or were used in activities in which they became covered by ochre. Their apparent similarities have been used to argue for stylistic rules or conventions for figurines (e.g. Gamble 1982, Conkey 1985). As an example, analyses of the figurines from Kostenki, Russia, have been used to suggest that certain conventions were used in the presentations of the female body (Gvozdover quoted in Conroy 1993: 156), which, if correct, may indicate that women's bodies are being culturally mediated according to social norms. Incidentally, this convention is consistent with our own perception of what makes women's bodies distinct and female (ibid.: 156) – and that is why we 'read' many of these objects as female figurines! More broadly based analyses of data from Europe and Siberia have suggested that conventions at differing levels of complexity and spatial distribution existed (ibid.: 156). The important point to stress here is that convention is an outcome of routine practice; it is through repetitive performance and association that it comes into existence. The possibility of Palaeolithic figures being produced according to certain conventions does, therefore, not necessarily suggest that there existed a normative view of women, but rather that the reification and externalization of women as bodies locally became bound by certain ways of presenting them. It is in the production and reproduction of these images that they, within certain temporal and spatial contexts, are related to each other and to social norms. This means that they are neither insular pieces of individual art nor personal portraits but furthermore that they are not just incidentally produced objects.

The association between these figurines and fertility (and pregnancy) as well as sexuality has often been drawn (e.g. Russell 1993). Probably their nakedness alone easily makes them sexual objects to archaeologists, and added to this the obvious voluptuousness of the bodies, the curves and smoothness of many (but not all) of the figurines, for us augment their sensual character. Despite these reactions to such images it is clearly questionable both whether our concept of sexuality would be appropriate for the societies that made them and also whether what we see as sexual had the same connotation to them. It is therefore probably much more difficult to discuss the figurines in terms of what they mean than to consider what they did. What kind of cultural practices and responses to the experience of difference within communities may they inform us about?

Gender and the Palaeolithic: self-reflection and artifice

Although there may be a general underlying acceptance of early hominid life being affected by sexual dimorphism and that gender differences as such are part of the behavioural package of modern humans, this is rarely said. In fact, while critique of origin research has been clearly stressing some of the serious problems that affect this research few studies have commented particularly upon the emergence of gender. In current discussions sexual differences drift into gender some time around the Upper Palaeolithic but we have avoided the striking and challenging questions of how it emerged as a cultural construction and what happened because of this. Without such questioning, gender easily becomes part of evolutionary history and adaptation. Leibowitz (1983) and more recently Conroy (1993) are amongst the few to have focused explicitly upon the emergence of gender outside an evolutionary approach, that is, the existence of a division between sex and gender in the Pleistocene is not taken for granted. Leibowitz argues that gender as an extension of sexual division of labour began with *Homo erectus* some 300,000 years ago in connection with the inventions of fire and the projectile point, and that prior to this time sexual division of labour was less explicit as females combined productive activities (i.e. searching for food) with bearing and nursing children (Leibowitz 1983, Balme and Beck 1993, Russell 1993). Conroy places the emergence of gender much later, arguing that it postdates the advent of language and is linked to the use of symbols as part of its institutionalizing process (1993: 153). The origin of language and its relationship to other cognitive traits is, of course, in itself a complex question. Nonetheless her argument is interesting insofar as it emphasizes two central propositions that have been somewhat ignored by discussions of gender in this period. First, she stresses that it is by participating in language that we can construct concepts and ideas that generate gender, and that through language things can come to stand for the symbolic properties of gender (ibid.: 154). Second, socialization, of which gender is a part, is argued to be delivered through repetition and a form of social comparison (ibid.: 154).

The occurrence of ornaments and figurines suggests that when we approach the Palaeolithic with the aim of understanding how gender is becoming part of its cultural package, we may usefully try to focus more closely upon the individual and the articulation of individuals within the community. This may provide a constructive addition to current group-orientated studies of the period. The reason why this is relevant is that gender is an *individualized social identity that is culturally constructed*. This is because gender, in various complex manners, relates both to the construction of social norms and to self-perception *vis-à-vis* such norms, that is, social comparison.

It is important to recognize the significance of this ability of self-reflection and of being able to differentiate among different kinds of selfs, and even more so of being capable of expressing this comparison in various externalized forms. In particular, the emphasis upon external expression makes it possible to separate the discussion of the difference between primates and humans in terms of sameness in sexually based behaviour from the discussion of gender in early human societies. This is a useful separation since these discussions otherwise easily blur the concern with gender with that of sexual dimorphism as they continue to discuss the former in terms of sexually based behaviour rather than through a recognition of a difference constituted through cultural practice. Lack of evidence of self-reflection does not, of course, signify its absence prior to this time. It is, however, possible to identify a time horizon from when we begin to see humans expressing this awareness and reflections in material forms in ways not seen before; these forms and their associated activities, in turn, must have given these societies things to think with and communicate through. This must have affected them, and we see this in the expression of distinct attitudes and awareness of people, as seen, for example, by the use of formal burials (while this is a controversial issue there appear, with a few exceptions, to be no *ceremonial* burials prior to around 30,000–28,000 BP; Mellars 1996). Such reflection upon self and others is deeply embedded within the production of figurines and use of ornaments, phenomena which in each their own way may be understood as an externalization of the body – it is materialized. It becomes relevant also to consider the reasons and purposes of such reflections or at least to wonder whether these questions can be contemplated for such early communities. The differential treatment or attitudes towards male and female, old and young, may be hinted at by burials and more solidly documented by the female topic of many figurines. This differential emphasis upon various groups within the community must relate to the ways in which they are conceptualized, thought about and acted upon. One may argue, therefore, that the construction of gender that emerged in the Upper Palaeolithic was primarily about confirming and reflecting that difference exists and potentially less concerned with directing interpretation of what those differences are, or should be, about. Thus, while the archaeology suggests that gender, as a concern with socially and culturally constituted people (and their bodies), is clearly emerging as a distinct aspect within some communities during this period, we have little reason also to associate this with any evaluation or ranking of these differences. We may wonder, therefore, whether what we observe in these early societies is gender emerging as a structure but not yet as a coherent practice of performance with its citation to cultural codes.

The archaeological data cannot establish whether or not gender systems existed prior to the Upper Palaeolithic, but data demonstrates that around this time gender appears in a manner that separates it from biological behaviour. In particular, objects such as ornaments and figurines suggest that gender, as an aspect of self-awareness of difference, now began to be perpetuated not solely through behaviour but was also repeated and reified through cultural machination. There is an abstraction involved in this. Such cultural expressions move us beyond the individualism of the person and give weight to the normative world in which individuals learn about and express themselves. The importance of Palaeolithic gender research may therefore largely be this insight into gender systems' abstract and culturated character, and how this appears even at stages where the material culture and institutional structures are limited. Gender expressions already in the Palaeolithic take on forms that are cultural and that do not relate to necessary or agreed divisions of labour or differences in strengths and abilities – the concern with gender is already then about the internalized social experience and its externalized reflexive relationship to differences within the group. During this period societies and their individuals began to give form to, rather than just live out, the differences that society will always contain. This, probably, also had various consequences for how they lived their lives. Gender became external identity, an artifice; and material culture was used for its instrumentalization.

11
Reflections

'What is your book about?', Megan asks. I begin to explain about food,
and her and Kim Michael's clothes, about the different rooms in our
house and about meeting new people or getting new things. 'Am I in
it?', she interrupts. 'Yah, kind of', I say, 'but I can't write a book about
you, there is just too much of you!' . . . 'Hmm', she says, 'very interest-
ing', and she returns to her play.

In this book, I have tried to discuss gender not as an essential identity
but as the outcome of how individuals are made to understand their
differences and similarities from others and how this involves material
culture. Gender does not have a locus nor does it take a particular
form. We may find, however, that there are substantial similarities
between communities in terms of the forms and reasons they give to
this difference and the ways they attach this to people's bodies. Gender is not static. It is flexible, and in its elasticity it stretches and un-
folds in manifold ways so that depending upon its contexts, including
the life progress of individuals, we see it differently. The study of gender must embrace this diversity; but concomitant with the increased
sophistication of our definition of gender its study has become complex and unlimited. One response is to argue that, rather than study
gender as a totality of individual and social experience and constructions, only particular facets of its complex constituency can be explored in detail by any one discipline. This volume has therefore aimed
to understand and argue for how archaeology may at one and the
same time refine and enlarge its particular way of understanding and
studying gender in terms of its specific disciplinary abilities. This does
not imply that such different dimensions of gender are unrelated and
can be separated through a smooth academic dissection; in fact they
most often intersect and in various ways constitute each other. It is
possible, however, as part of an analytical discourse on gender, to let
particular characteristics come into focus and to explore them fore-
most. For archaeology, the aspect of gender that we can investigate
with the greatest expertise is the ways in which gender construction
and the living of gender involve and affect material things. This book
has therefore been about gender as experienced through objects and
physical arrangements and practices. It has also been about gender as

a social dialogue about membership and conventions and about normative behaviour that comments upon and constructs people in terms of difference. It has been about the use of material things in the creation of in- and exclusions. I have also, partly in reaction to the currently substantial emphasis upon the individual and embodiment, consistently stressed the importance of the social, the group. Furthermore, by focusing attention upon 'We' a dimension is emphasized and introduced that prevents cultural analysis from being couched in terms of a futile confrontation between the individual, the 'I', and 'Them'. I hope this will infuse our discussions with awareness of the intersection of the social and the individual. Throughout the volume it is maintained that although much of what constitutes (and gives meaning to) gender is lived through and experienced by the individual, it is also always deeply involved in social life – in fact the social dimension of gender is one of its most interesting and striking aspects.

The starting point of the volume was therefore not primarily that individuals experience themselves as gendered but more so why it is also the case that we can recognize other people's gender and make sense of the world and operate in it through such routine interpretations and assumptions about people. I aimed to incorporate in our analysis reflections upon such simple, daily-life occurrences as walking down the street and seeing on the other side people, whom I see as men and women. I did not talk with them, nor did I observe their naked bodies; triggered only by my watching I interpret the world in terms of gender. Another example: I walk into a shoe shop and go directly to the ladies' section. How do I recognize these shoes as 'matching' my gender? What fascinates me about such situations is how deeply conventions about male and female are embedded within the material culture with which we surround ourselves, and how expediently and competently we interpret, recognize and respond to these object-meanings within our own familiar worlds. This, I believe, is what we refer to when we speak about the concretization of meaning, the impact of convention and the importance of performance. The reference, in chapter 8, to the gender performance, which used to be enacted when a man and a women were entering or leaving through the same door, is another example that I have found useful – maybe because I was part of the generation who saw this particular behaviour challenged and changed. The doorway per se is not gendered, and neither are the other items, such as shoes, clothing, appearance and the way the body is made to move, that inform the examples I mention. But as a physical locale doors, as well as the other materialities that I have tried to introduce, have the potential for gender and discourse about its meaning being attached to them; they can become a place for the acting out and thus for the experience of gender. It should be stressed, therefore, that material things are not gendered separately from the practices that engender them; rather they have the potentiality for becoming involved with gender in a number of ways. It is some of these dimensions, and their impact upon social life in prehistory, that I try to argue for and outline in part II of the volume as a contribution towards developing archaeology as a gender-informed interpretative engagement with the past.

Gender archaeology, as it has evolved over the last two decades, has been substantially affected by its early roots in the women's movement and its various contemporary political aims. It has therefore largely focused upon identifying places for women and making them visible within various dimensions of the past as well as the discipline. I discuss this development in the first part of the volume. I outline its history; how it was needed, its benefits and some of the less useful expectations and research practices that we developed. I also argue, however, that gender archaeology has other potentials and that their further exploration are of importance for archaeology as a discipline and for its contribution to the understanding of gender generally.

Thus, acknowledging our dependence upon the social sciences but insisting nonetheless upon archaeology as a distinct type of intellectual discourse, I have tried to explore what a more literate interpretation of gender *archaeology* may imply. The basic question running through the various arguments and examples outlined is, therefore, how is gender materially constituted and what is the significance of the intersection of social and material concerns? Such an emphasis should not, however, be accepted without also appreciating how this implies inscribing gender within disciplinary constraints. This means it is being recognized in terms of and placed within a disciplinary code as well as subjected to attempts to limit the applicability of concepts and observation; the study of gender becomes anchored within a framework of references and meaning, which enables disciplined discussion and an agreed basis of analysis. In this sense closure is certainly produced through the attempts at developing an explicit gender archaeology. It is, however, a restraint upon our study of the phenomenon of gender which is simultaneously enabling; it is beneficial for the specificity of research and for its ability to reach informed and substantial conclusions. At another level, it may, however, dull our reasoning. Such closure also furthers – not by intent but through practice – the distinction between political action and academic research. In defence of the project of engendering archaeology through its own intellectual and analytical strengths, I argue that without this urge to 'discipline' these concerns they will – as practice – continue to underplay their most unique potentials and contribute little to our understanding of gender and its variability.

To locate and develop these potentials I suggest that we need to appreciate how archaeology claims knowledge, and that this involves understanding what insights arise from the study of material culture. This is why chapter 5 is so central to the arguments that I make. Here it is argued that material things have specific characteristics and accordingly participate in social discourse in distinct ways. The argument is about 'thingness' and how this quality affects how we experience the world. Basically, I hold that an effect of the physicality of material culture is that it brings a distinct dimension to gender: as gender is affected by and affects material condition it gains physical consequences and impact. I argue that gendered meaning acted out through material discourse affects people's lives in critical ways. I also suggest that there are two distinct aspects to material culture that are of importance for understanding gender construction; these are practice and communication, that is, doing it versus communicating it.

It is the combinations of materiality and practices that lend themselves to the repetitive performance of gender as a difference as well as providing locales for its negotiation. The materialization of gender means it is given physical form, and through this objects are used to visualize difference and to create a location in which its evaluation and discursive understanding can be embedded. This also provides the background for understanding how gender meaning is *performed*, and thus recognized and learned, through repetitive acts which follow rules or schema and where each performance may be interpreted as a range of citation to earlier performances. Gender-coding and gender citation may be elements used to frame and structure such performances. Objects, furthermore, are employed both for stage-setting the meaning of practice, as props for action and as visual memories of actions that have taken place.

I also emphasize gender negotiation as a cultural construct that is unstable and in need of maintenance and agreement. This means that understanding gender as a contract is helpful. This focuses our attention upon how agreements about or acceptance of rights and responsibilities are at the basis of the enactment of gender. It also means that understanding material objects as resources that are needed and desired, and which therefore become partner to such gender contracts and their material representations, is extremely useful for understanding how gender affects and is being acted out in a range of everyday situations. The second part of the volume discusses a number of such material locales.

Due to the impact of gender studies over the last decades we now, in general, accept that gender relations constitute a fundamental social structure in which both men and women participate as partners in the historical process. They react and function in relationship to their mutual similarities and differences, creating, manipulating and maintaining social institutions such as marriage, kinship, lines of obligations and alliances. They cohabit and collaborate. Thus, gender *cannot* be ignored in historical studies as it constitutes an essential mechanism of society and is embedded in its changes. This is why archaeology needs to incorporate gender in its discipline. Meanwhile, the concepts we have learned to use for our involvement with these critical issues are once again being questioned within the social sciences. Former stable, comfortable notions of sex and gender roles that we had begun to think with are being increasingly challenged, moving debates into realms outside the obvious reach of archaeology. The separation between sex and gender, between biology and culture, which originally provided to archaeology the *raison d'être* for gender as a legitimate and necessary research topic, has been under attack and, if it is not disappearing, new distinctions and meanings are being evoked. Variability is being emphasized, and former firm concepts, such as roles, are changing their meaning and implications. Experience, negotiation, manipulation and the strategic use of sex have come to the foreground, undermining assumed knowledge as our basic entities become slippery and escape easy classification. In this progress other issues have also been drawn into debates such as age and class structures and more particularly sexuality and embodiment.

These debates affect archaeology; but their practical and intellectual impact is still open for us to clarify and decide. Rather than abandoning the project of engendering the past because 'it is getting too difficult', these deconstructions, the volatile climate of debate and the shifting and vague form of former solid entities must be recognized as part of a challenging intellectual climate within which we must try to find our own voices and set distinct aims. Gender archaeology, due to its consistent and stubborn belief in and fight for its relevance to the study of the past, now has a role within archaeology. It has gained maturity, changed some of its practices, and expanded its reasons. This means that it should now also have the strength – both intellectual and in terms of position – to explore the wider implications of being both gender-sensitive and gender-critical in its practice and interpretation. Gender, we have increasingly recognized, does not just need to be found, identified and rescued; we need to think with gender, to investigate it as construction and to analyse its constituent parts and the ways it is maintained and reacted upon. These are the kinds of concerns that must inform the way we think about the past and communities. Engendering, one may argue, aims initially to unsettle certainty (Porter 1996: 106). This can be provoked by the framework we provide, by the questions we ask and the ways we analyse data. It is when we dare to foreground gender, challenge expectations and assumptions, and yet, at the same time, explore the past as a foreign country, where gender is part of its uniqueness, that we begin to think about that past in different ways.

References

Adelson, L. A. 1993. *Making Bodies, Making History: Feminism & German Identity*. London: University of Nebraska Press.

Allason-Jones, L. 1989. *Women in Roman Britain*. London: British Museum Publications.

Anderson, M. and A. Reeves 1994. Contested identities: museums and the nation in Australia. In F. E. S. Kaplan (ed.) *Museums and the Making of 'Ourselves'*. Leicester: Leicester University Press. 79–124.

ARC (Archaeological Review from Cambridge) 1988, vol. 7, 1.

ARC (Archaeological Review from Cambridge) 1992, vol. 11, 1.

Ardener, S. (ed.) 1975. *Perceiving Women*. London: J. M. Dent & Sons.

Arnold, Béat 1986. *Cortaillod-Est, un village du Bronze final 1. Fouille subaquatique et photographie aérienne*. Saint-Blaise: Du Ruau.

Arnold, Bettina 1991. The deposed princess of Vix: the need for an engendered European prehistory. In D. Walde and N. D. Willows (eds) *The Archaeology of Gender*. 366–74.

Arnold, Bettina 1996. 'Honorary males' or women of substance? Gender, status and power in Iron Age Europe. *Journal of European Archaeology*, 3, 2: 153–68.

Arnold, J. 1996. The archaeology of complex hunter-gatherers. *Journal of Archaeological Method and Theory*, 3: 77–125.

Arwill-Nordbladh, E. 1989. Oscar Montelius and the liberation of women: an example of archaeology, ideology and the early Swedish women's movement. In T. B. Larsson and H. Lundmark (eds) *Approaches to Swedish Prehistory*. B.A.R. International Series 500, Oxford: British Archaeological Reports.131–42.

Arwill-Nordbladh, E. 1994. Begriper vi begreppen? Om androcentrismen i några vanliga analytiska begrepp. *Meta. Medeltidsarkeologisk Tidskrift*, 94, 1: 35–47.

Arwill-Nordbladh, E. 1998. *Genuskonstruktioner i Nordisk Vikingatid. Förr och nu*. Gothenburg: Gothenburg University.

Ashelford, J. 1996. *The Art of Dress: Clothes and Society, 1500–1914*. London: National Trust.

Bahn, P. 1995/96. New developments in Pleistocene art. *Evolutionary An-*

thropology, 4, 6: 204–15.
Bahn, P. 1998. *The Cambridge Illustrated History of Prehistoric Art*. Cambridge: Cambridge University Press.
Bahn, P. and J. Vertut 1988. *Images of the Ice Age*. London: Windward.
Bailey, D. W. 1994. Reading prehistoric figurines as individuals. *World Archaeology*, 25: 321–31.
Balme, J. and W. Beck 1993. *Gendered Archaeology*. The Second Australian Women in Archaeology Conference. Research Papers in Archaeology and Natural History 26, Canberra: Australian National University.
Bapty, I. and T. Yates (eds) 1990. *Archaeology after Structuralism: Poststructuralism and the Practice of Archaeology*. London: Routledge.
Barber, E. W. 1994. *Women's Work: The First 20,000 Years. Women, Cloth, and Society in Early Times*. New York: W. W. Norton & Company.
Barnard, M. 1996. *Fashion as Communication*. London: Routledge.
Barnes, R. and J. B. Eicher (eds) 1992. *Dress and Gender: Making and Meaning in Cultural Contents*. London: Berg.
Barrett, J. 1988. Fields of discourse: reconstituting a social archaeology. *Critique of Anthropology*, 7, 3: 5–16.
Barrett, J. 1989. Food, gender and metal: questions of social reproduction. In M. L. S. Sørensen and R. Thomas (eds) *The Transition from Bronze Age to Iron Age in Europe*. B.A.R. International Series 483 (i–ii), Oxford: British Archaeological Reports. 304–20.
Barrett, J. 1994. *Fragments from Antiquity: An Archaeology of Social Life in Britain, 2900–1200 BC*. Oxford: Blackwell.
Barthes, R. 1967. *Elements of Semiology*. London: Jonathan Cape.
Barthes, R. 1977. *Image, Music, Text*. London: Fontana.
Beard, M. 1994. Women on the dig. *Times Literary Supplement*, 21 October 1994, 7–8.
Bender Jørgensen, L. 1991. *North European Textiles until AD 1000*. Århus: Århus University Press.
Bertelsen, R., A. Lillehammer and J. R. Næss (eds) 1987 (1979). *Were They All Men? An Examination of Sex Roles in Prehistoric Society*. Acts from a workshop held in Utstein Kloster, Rogaland, 2–4 November 1979, Stavanger: Arkeologisk Museum i Stavanger.
Bevan, L. 1997. Skin scrapers and pottery makers? 'Invisible' women in prehistory. In J. Moore and E. Scott (eds) *Invisible People and Processes*. 81–7.
Biel, P. 1985. Die Ausstattung des Toten. In D. Planck, J. Biel, G. Süsskind and A. Wais (eds) *Der Keltenfürst von Hochdorf: Methoden und Ergebnisse der Landesarchäologie*. Stuttgart: Konrad Theiss. 78–105.
Binford, L. R. 1992. Hard evidence. *Discover*, February 1992: 44–51.
Bogatyrev, P. 1971. *The Functions of Folk Costume in Moravian Slovakia*. The Hague: Mouton.
Bouloumié, B. 1988. Le symposium gréco-étrusque et l'aristocratie celtique. In *Les Princes celtes et la Méditerranée*. Paris: Rencontres de l'Ecole du Louvre. 343–83.
Bourdieu, P. 1977. *Outline of a Theory of Practice*. Cambridge: Cambridge

University Press.

Bourdieu, P. 1984. *Distinction: A Social Critique of the Judgement of Taste*. London: Routledge & Kegan Paul.

Bourdieu, P. 1990. *The Logic of Practice*. Cambridge: Polity Press.

Boye, L., B. Draiby, K. Hvenegård-Lassen and V. Ødegård 1984. Toward an archaeology of women. *Archaeological Review from Cambridge*, 3, 1: 82–5.

Brøndsted, J. 1966. *Danmarks Oldtid* II. Copenhagen: Gyldendal.

Brück, J. 1997. The early–middle Bronze Age transition in Wessex, Sussex and the Thames Valley. Unpublished Ph.D., Dept of Archaeology, Cambridge University.

Brumfield, E. 1991. Weaving and cooking: Women's production in Aztec Mexico. In J. W. Gero and M. W. Conkey (eds) *Engendering Archaeology: Women and Prehistory*. 224–54.

Brun, P. and C. Mordant 1988. *Le groupe Rhin-Suisse-France orientale et la notion de civilisation des Champs d'Urnes*. Nemours: Musée de Préhistoire d'Ile-de-France.

Brush, K. 1988. Gender and mortuary analysis in pagan Anglo-Saxon archaeology. *Archaeological Review from Cambridge*, 7, 1: 76–89.

Butler, B. 1996, Virginia Woolf, Madonna and me: searching for role-models and women's presence in museums and heritage. In A. Devonshire and B. Wood (eds) *Women in Industry and Technology*. 19–27.

Butler, J. 1990. *Gender Trouble: Feminism and the Subversion of Identity*. London: Routledge.

Butler, J. 1993. *Bodies that Matter: on the Discursive Limits of Sex*. London: Routledge.

Caplan, P. 1992. Engendering knowledge: the politics of ethnography. In S. Ardener (ed.) *Persons and Powers of Women in Diverse Cultures: Essays in Commemoration of Audrey I. Richards, Phyllis Kaberry and Barbara E. Ward*. Oxford: Berg. 65–88.

Casey, M., D. Donlon, J. Hope and S. Wellfare (eds) 1998. *Redefining Archaeology: Feminist Perspectives*. Canberra: ANH Publications.

Chabot, N. J. 1990. A man called Lucy: self reflection in a museum exhibition. In F. Baker and J. Thomas (eds) *Writing the Past in the Present*. Lampeter: St David's University College. 138–42.

Champion, T., C. Gamble, S. Shennan and A. Whittle 1984. *Prehistoric Europe*. London: Academic Press.

Chapman, R. 1990. *Emerging Complexity: The Later Prehistory of Southeast Spain, Iberia and the West Mediterranean*. Cambridge: Cambridge University Press.

Claassen, C. (ed.) 1992a. *Exploring Gender through Archaeology: Selected Papers from the Boon Conference*. Monographs in World Archaeology 11, Madison, Wis.: Prehistory Press.

Claassen, C. 1992b. Questioning gender: an introduction. In C. Claassen (ed.) 1992a. *Exploring Gender through Archaeology: Selected Papers from the Boon Conference*. 1–9.

Claassen, C. (ed.) 1994. *Women in Archaeology*. Philadelphia: University of

Pennsylvania Press.

Clarke, D. L. 1972. A provisional model of an Iron Age society. In D. L. Clarke (ed.) *Models in Archaeology*. London: Methuen. 801–70

Coles, J. and A. Harding 1979. *The Bronze Age in Europe*. London: Methuen.

Colomina, B. (ed.) 1992. *Sexuality & Space*. New York: Princeton Architectural Press.

Conkey, M. W. 1983. On the origins of Palaeolithic art: a review and some critical thoughts. In E. Trinkaus (ed.) *The Mousterian Legacy: Human Biocultural Change in the Upper Pleistocene*. B.A.R International Series 164, Oxford: British Archaeological Reports. 201–27.

Conkey, M. W. 1985. Ritual communication, social elaboration, and the variable trajectories of Palaeolithic material culture. In T. D. Price and J. A. Brown (eds) *Prehistoric Hunter-Gatherers: the Emergence of Cultural Complexity*. Orlando, Fla.: Academic Press. 299–323.

Conkey, M. W. 1989. A report from the year 2050. *Archaeology*, January/ February, 42, 1: 35–9, 81.

Conkey, M. W. 1991. Contexts of action, contexts for power: material culture and gender in the Magdalenian. In J. M. Gero and M. W. Conkey (eds) *Engendering Archaeology: Women and Prehistory*. 57–92.

Conkey, M. W. 1997. Mobilizing ideologies: Paleolithic 'art', gender trouble, and thinking about alternatives. In L. D. Hager (ed.) *Women in Human Evolution*. 172–207.

Conkey, M. W. and J. W. Gero 1991. Tensions, pluralities, and engendering archaeology: an introduction to women in prehistory. In J. W. Gero and M. W. Conkey (eds) *Engendering Archaeology*. 3–30.

Conkey, M. and J. Spector 1984. Archaeology and the study of gender. *Advances in Archaeological Method and Theory*, 7, 1–38.

Conroy, L. P. 1993. Female figurines of the Upper Palaeolithic and the emergence of gender. In H. du Cros and L. Smith (eds) *Women in Archaeology: A Feminist Critique*. 153–60.

Craik, J. 1994. *The Face of Fashion: Cultural History in Fashion*. London: Routledge.

Dahlberg, F. 1981. *Woman the Gatherer*. New Haven: Yale University Press.

Damm, C. 1991. From burials to gender roles: problems and potentials in post-processualist archaeology. In D. Walde and N. D. Willows (eds) *The Archaeology of Gender*. 130–5.

David, F. 1992. *Fashion, Culture and Identity*. Chicago: University of Chicago Press.

Delporte, H. 1979. *L'Image de la femme dans l'art préhistorique*. Paris: Picard.

Devens, C. 1991. Gender and colonization in native Canadian communities: examining the historical record. In D. Walde and N. D. Willows (eds) *The Archaeology of Gender*. 510–15.

Devonshire, A. and B. Wood (eds) 1996. *Women in Industry and Technology: from Prehistory to the Present. Current Research and the Museum Experience*. London: Museum of London.

Díaz-Andreu, M. and M. L. S. Sørensen (eds) 1998a. *Excavating Women: A History of Women in European Archaeology*. London: Routledge.

Díaz-Andreu, M. and M. L. S. Sørensen 1998b. Excavating women: towards an engendered history of archaeology. In M. Díaz-Andreu and M. L. S. Sørensen (eds) *Excavating Women: A History of Women in European Archaeology*. 1–28.

Dietler, M. 1995. The cup of Gyptis: rethinking the colonial encounter in Early Iron Age western Europe and the relevance of the world-systems models. *Journal of European Archaeology*, 3, 2: 89–111.

Dietler, M. 1996. Feasts and commensal politics in the political economy: food, power and status in prehistoric Europe. In P. Wiessner and W. Schiefenhövel (eds) *Food and the Status Quest: An Interdisciplinary Perspective*. Oxford: Berghahn Books. 87–125.

Dobres, M.-A. 1988. Feminist archaeology and inquiries into gender relations: some thoughts on universals, origins stories and alternating paradigms. *Archaeological Review from Cambridge*, 7, 1: 30–44.

Dommasnes, L. H. 1976. Yngre jernalder i Sogn – forsøk på sosial rekonstruksjon. Unpublished Magistergradsavhandling, Bergen University.

Dommasnes, L. H. 1982. Late Iron Age in western Norway: female roles and ranks as deduced from an analysis of burial customs. *Norwegian Archaeological Review*, 15, 1–2: 70–84.

Dommasnes, L. H. 1992. Two decades of women in prehistory and in archaeology in Norway: a review. *Norwegian Archaeological Review*, 25, 1: 1–14.

Dorse, A. 1997. Ritualising the Body: Early Upper Palaeolithic 'Art' & the Emergence of Social Identity. Unpublished M.Phil. dissertation, Dept of Archaeology, Cambridge University.

Douglas, M. 1975. *Implicit Meanings*. London: Routledge and Kegan Paul.

Douglas, M. 1980. *Purity and Danger: An Analysis of the Concepts of Pollution and Taboo*. London: Routledge and Kegan Paul.

Dransart, P. 1992. Pachamama: the Inka Earth Mother of the long sweeping garment. In R. Barnes and J. B. Eicher (eds) *Dress and Gender*. 145–63.

Du Cros, H. and L. Smith (eds) 1993. *Women in Archaeology: A Feminist Critique*. Occasional Papers in Prehistory 23, Canberra: Australian National University.

Eicher, J. B. (ed.) 1995. *Dress and Ethnicity*. London: Berg.

Eicher, J. B. and M. E. Roach-Higgins 1992. Definition and classification of dress: implications for analysis of gender roles. In R. Barnes and J. B. Eicher (eds) *Dress and Gender*. 8–28.

Ellison, A. 1981. Towards a socioeconomic model for the Middle Bronze Age in southern England. In I. Hodder, G. Issac and N. Hammond (eds) *Pattern of the Past*. Cambridge: Cambridge University Press. 413–38.

Engels, F. 1884. *The Origin of the Family, Private Property and the State.* 1970 edition, London: Lawrence & Wishart.

Engelstad, E. 1991a. Feminist theory and post-processual archaeology. In D. Walde and N. D. Willows (eds) *The Archaeology of Gender*. 116–20.

Engelstad, E. 1991b. Images of power and contradiction: feminist theory and post-processual archaeology. *Antiquity*, 65/248: 502–14.

Engelstad, E., G. Mandt and J.-R. Næss 1992. Equity issues in Norwegian archaeology. *K.A.N. (Kvinner i arkeologi i Norge)*, 13–14: 67–77.

Etienne, M. and E. Leacock (eds) 1980. *Women and Colonization: Anthropological Perspectives*. New York: Praeger.

Evans, C. J. 1988a. Acts of enclosure: a consideration of concentrically organised causewayed enclosures. In J. C. Barrett and I. A. Kinnes (eds) *The Archaeology of Context in the Neolithic and Bronze Age: Recent Trends*. Sheffield: Dept of Archaeology and Prehistory. 85–96.

Evans, C. J. 1988b. Monuments and analogy: the interpretation of causewayed enclosures. In C. Burgess, P. Topping, C. Mordant and M. Maddison (eds) *Enclosures and Defences in the Neolithic of Western Europe*. B.A.R. International Series 403, Oxford: British Archaelogical Reports. 47–74.

Falk, P. 1994. *The Consuming Body*. London: Sage.

Fischer, S. 1978. Body image. In T. Polhemus (ed.) *Social Aspects of the Human Body: A Reader of Key Texts*. 115–21.

Fletcher, R. 1995. *The Limits of Settlement Growth: A Theoretical Outline*. Cambridge: Cambridge Unversity Press.

Fonnesbeck-Sandberg, E., B. Pauly Hansen, K. Jespersen, L. Bender Jørgensen, K. Løkkegård, T. Matz, U. Fraes Rasmussen, L. Slumstrup, I. Stoumann, F. Waagebech, T. Wanning, S. Wiell, L. Wienecke and S. Ørnager 1972. Han, hun og arkæologien: 'Arkæologiske Studier'. *Kontaktstencil*, 4: 5–10. Copenhagen: Institute of Archaeology.

Foucault, M. 1978. *The History of Sexuality*. Harmondsworth: Penguin.

Freud, S. 1905. Three contributions to the sexual theory. In J. Strachey (ed.) *The Standard Edition of the Complete Psychological Works of Sigmund Freud*. vol. 7. London: Hogarth Press.

Fürst, E. L. 1995. *Mat – et annet språk: Rasjonalitet, kropp og kvinnelighet*. Oslo: Pax Forlag A/S.

Gaarder Losnedahl, K. 1994. Kvinne og museum. *Nytt om Kvinneforskning: Feministisk museumkritik*. Oslo: Norges Forskningsråd. 5–11.

Galan Domingo, E. 1993. *Estelas, Paisaje y Territorio en el Bronce Final del Suroeste de la Peninsula Iberica*. Madrid: Complutense.

Gamble, C. 1982. Interaction and alliance in Palaeolithic Europe. *Man*, 17: 92–107.

Gatens, M. 1996. *The Imaginary Body*. London: Routledge.

Gejvall, N.-G. 1970. The fisherman from Barum – mother of several children: Palaeo-anatomic finds in the skeleton from Bäckaskog. *Fornvännen*, 65: 281–9.

Gero, J. 1996. Archaeological practice and gendered encounters. In R. P. Wright (ed.) *Gender and Archaeology*. 251–80.

Gero, J. M. and M. W. Conkey (eds) 1991. *Engendering Archaeology: Women and Prehistory*. Oxford: Blackwell.

Gibbs, L. 1987. Identifying gender representation in the archaeological record: a contextual study. In I. Hodder (ed.) *The Archaeology of Contextual Meanings*. Cambridge: Cambridge University Press. 79–89.

Gibbs, L. 1990. Sex, gender and material culture patterning in later Neolithic and earlier Bronze Age England. Unpublished Ph.D., Dept of Archaeology, Cambridge University.

Giddens, A. 1979. *Central Problems in Social Theory.* London: Macmillan.

Giddens, A. 1984. *The Constitution of Society.* Cambridge: Polity Press.

Gilchrist, R. 1988. The spatial archaeology of gender domains: a case study of medieval English nunneries. *Archaeological Review from Cambridge*, 7, 1: 21–8.

Gilchrist, R. 1994. *Gender and Material Culture: The Archaeology of Religious Women.* London: Routledge.

Gilchrist, R. 1997. Gender and medieval women. In J. Moore and E. Scott (eds) *Invisible People and Processes.* 42–58.

Gimbutas, M. 1965. *Bronze Age Cultures in Central and Eastern Europe.* The Hague: Mouton.

Gimbutas, M. 1974. *Gods and Goddesses of Old Europe.* London: Thames and Hudson.

Goody, J. 1982. *Cooking, Cuisine, and Class.* Cambridge: Cambridge University Press.

Grab, T. 1991. Women's concern are men's concerns: gender roles in German museums. *Museum*, 171: 136–9.

Grøn, O. 1991. A method for reconstruction of social organization in prehistoric societies and examples of practical application. In O. Grøn, E. Engelstad and I. Lindblom (eds) *Social Space: Human Spatial Behaviour in Dwellings and Settlements. Proceedings of an Interdisciplinary Conference.* Odense: Odense University Press. 100–17.

Grosz, E. 1994. *Volatile Bodies: Towards a Corporeal Feminism.* Bloomington, Ind.: Indiana University Press.

Hager, L. D. 1997a. Sex and gender in palaeoanthropology. In L. D. Hager (ed.) *Women in Human Evolution.* 1–28.

Hager, L. D. (ed.) 1997b. *Women in Human Evolution.* London: Routledge.

Hägg, I. 1983. Viking women's dress at Birka: a reconstruction by archaeological methods. In N. B. Harte and K. P. Ponting (eds) *Cloth and Clothing in Medieval Europe: Essays in Memory of Professor E. M. Carus-Wilson.* London: Heinemann. 316–50.

Hallpike, C. R. 1978. Social hair. In T. Polhemus (ed.) *Social Aspects of the Human Body: A Reader of Key Texts.* 134–53.

Halstead, P. 1989. The economy as a normal surplus: economic stability and social change among early farming communities of Thessaly, Greece. In P. Halstead and J. O'Shea (eds) *Bad Year Economics: Cultural Responses to Risk and Uncertainty.* Cambridge: Cambridge University Press. 68–80.

Hänsel, A. 1997. Das metallene Tafelgeschirr im Opfer. In A. and B. Hänsel (eds) *Gaben an die Götter.* 83–6.

Hänsel, A. and B. (eds) 1997. *Gaben an die Götter: Schätze der Bronzezeit Europas.* Berlin: Staatliche Museen zu Berlin.

Harding, S. 1986. *The Science Question in Feminism.* New York: Cornell University Press.

Hastorf, C. A. 1991. Gender, space, and food in prehistory. In J. M. Gero and M. W. Conkey (eds) *Engendering Archaeology: Women and Prehistory.* 132–59.

Hastorf, C. A. 1998. The cultural life of early domestic plant use. *Antiquity*,

72, 278: 773–82.

Helbæk, H. 1958. Grauballe mandens sidste måltid. *Kuml*, 83–116.

Helms, M. W. 1988. *Ulysses' Sail: An Ethnographic Odyssey of Power, Knowledge, and Geographical Distance*. Princeton, N.J.: Princeton University Press.

Higgs, E.S. (ed.) 1972. *Papers in Economic Prehistory*. Cambridge: Cambridge University Press.

Hiler, H. 1929. *From Nudity to Raiment: An Introduction to the Study of Costume*. London: W. & G. Foyle.

Hill, E. forthcoming. The liminal body: mediating the social through sacrifice. *Cambridge Journal of Archaeology*.

Hill, J. D. 1997. 'The end of one kind of body and the beginning of another kind of body'? Toilet instruments and 'Romanization' in southern England during the first century AD. In C. Haselgrove and A. Gwilt (eds) *Reconstructing Iron Age Societies: New Approaches to the British Iron Age*. Oxford: Oxbow Books. 96–107.

Hingley, R. 1990. Domestic organisation and gender relations in Iron Age and Romano-British households. In R. Samson (ed.) *The Social Archaeology of Houses*. Edinburgh: Edinburgh University Press. 125–47.

Hjørungdal, T. 1994. Poles apart. Have there been any male and female graves? *Current Swedish Archaeology*, 2, 141–8.

Hodder, I. 1986. *Reading the Past*. Cambridge: Cambridge University Press.

Hodder, I. 1989. This is not an article about material culture as text. *Journal of Anthropological Archaeology*, 8: 250–69.

Hodder, I. 1990. *The Domestication of Europe*. Oxford: Blackwell.

Hodder, I. 1997. Commentary: the gender screen. In J. Moore and E. Scott (eds) *Invisible People and Processes*. 75–8.

Høgsbro, K.-E. 1994. Kvinder i musealt regi. In M. Alenius, N. Damsholt and B. Rosenbeck (eds) *Clios døtre gennem hundrede år*. Århus: Museum Tusculanums. 87–110.

Holm-Olsen, I. M. and G. Mandt-Larsen 1974. Kvinnens stilling i norsk arkeologi. *Kontaktstencil*, 6: 68–75.

Horne, D. 1984. *The Great Museum*. London: Pluto.

Hugh-Jones, C. 1979. *From the Milk River: Spatial and Temporal Processes in Northwest Amazonia*. Cambridge: Cambridge University Press.

Jesch, J. 1991. *Women in the Viking Age*. Woodbridge: Boydell Press.

Jones, S. 1991. Presenting the past: towards a feminist critique of museum practice. *The Field Archaeologist*, 14: 247–9.

Jones, S. and S. Pay 1990. The legacy of Eve. In P. Gathercole and D. Lowenthal (eds) *The Politics of the Past*. London: Unwin Hyman. 160–86.

Jonsson, I. 1993. En Kvinnohistoriker går på museum: en undersökning hur kvinnor och män, kön och makt presenteras i några svenska museiutställningar. In *Det Dolda Budskapet. Kön, makt och Kvinnor, män i museiutställingar*. Norrköping: Arbetets Museum. 11–27.

Joseph, N. 1986. *Uniforms and Nonuniform: Communication through Clothing*. New York: Greenwood Press.

Joyce, R. A. 1996. Performance and inscription: negotiating sex and gender in classic Maya society. Unpublished paper given at Dumbarton Oaks.

Kaiser, S. 1983–4. Towards a contextual social psychology of clothing: a synthesis of symbolic interactionist and cognitive theoretical perspectives. *Clothing and Textile Research Journal*, 2: 1–8.

Kehoe, A. 1992. Unshackling tradition. In C. Claassen (ed.) *Exploring Gender through Archaeology*. Madison, Wis.: Prehistoric Press. 23–32.

Kent, S. (ed.) 1998. *Gender in African Prehistory*. Walnut Creek, Calif.: AltaMira Press.

Kenyon, K. M. 1969. Women in academic life. The Galton Lecture 1969. *Journal of Biosoc. Science*, supplement 2: 107–18.

Killen, J. T. and J.-P. Olivier 1989. *The Knossos Tablets*. 5th edition, Salamanca: Ediciones Universidad de Salamanca.

Kinchin, J. 1996. Interiors: nineteenth-century essays on the 'masculine' and the 'feminine' room. In P. Kirkham (ed.) *The Gendered Object*. 12–29.

Kirkham, P. (ed.) 1996. *The Gendered Object*. Manchester: Manchester University Press.

Kirkham, P. and J. Attfield 1996. Introduction. In P. Kirkham (ed.) *The Gendered Object*. 1–11.

Kjærum, P. 1955. Tempelhus fra stenalder. *Kuml*, 7–35.

Knapp, B. and L. Meskell 1997. Bodies of evidence on prehistoric Cyprus. *Cambridge Archaeological Journal*, 7, 2: 183–204.

LaBouff, N. 1997. Personal ornamentation in the Upper Palaeolithic: Aurignacian ornaments of southwest France. Unpublished M.Phil. dissertation, Dept of Archaeology, Cambridge University.

Ladier, E. and A.-C. Welté 1995. *Bijoux de la préhistoire. La Parure Magdalénienne dans la vallée de l'Aveyron*. Montauban: Muséum d'histoire naturelle de Montauban.

Laqueur, T. 1990. *Making Sex: Body and Gender from the Greeks to Freud*. Cambridge, Mass.: Harvard University Press.

Last, J. 1998. Books of life: biography and memory in a Bronze Age barrow. *Oxford Journal of Archaeology*, 17: 43–53.

Leibowitz, L. 1983. Origins of the sexual division of labour. In M. Lowe and R. Hubbard (eds) *Women's Nature: Rationalization of Inequality*. New York: Pergamon. 123–47.

Leroi-Gourhan, A. 1968. *The Art of Prehistoric Man in Western Europe*. London: Thames and Hudson.

Lesick, K. S. 1997. Re-engendering gender: some theoretical and methodological concerns on a burgeoning archaeological pursuit. In J. Moore and E. Scott (eds) *Invisible People and Processes*. 31–41.

Lévi-Strauss, C. 1970. *The Raw and the Cooked*. London: Jonathan Cape.

Levy, J. and C. Claassen (eds) 1992. Workshop 1: engendering the contact period. In C. Claassen (ed.) *Exploring Gender through Archaeology*. 111–26.

Lewin, R. 1989. *Human Evolution*. 2nd edition, Cambridge, Mass.: Blackwell Scientific Publications.

Lind, M. 1993. En Brännande treklöver – museer, kvinnor och betydelses produktion. In *Det Dolda Budskapet. Kön, makt och Kvinnor, män i museiutställingar*. Norrköping: Arbetets Museum. 4–9.

Lindstrom, L. 1996. Cargo cult. In A. Barnard and J. Spencer (eds) *Encyclopedia of Social and Cultural Anthropology*. London: Routledge. 85–96.

Lohof, E. 1994. Tradition and change: the mortuary rituals during the late Neolithic and Bronze Age in the northeastern Netherlands. *Archaeological Dialogues*, 1, 2: 98–118.

Lorenz, H. 1978. Totenbrauchtum und Tracht: Untersuchungen zur regionalen gliederung in der frühen Latenezeit. *Bericht der Römisch-Germanischen Kommission*, 59: 3–378.

Lucy, S. 1997. Housewives, warriors and slaves? Sex and gender in Anglo-Saxon burials. In J. Moore and E. Scott (eds) *Invisible People and Processes*. 150–68.

Lupton, D. 1996. *Food, the Body and the Self*. London: Sage.

Macdonald, S. and G. Fyfe (eds) 1996. *Theorizing Museums: Representing Identity and Diversity in a Changing World*. Oxford: Blackwell.

McDowell, L. and J. Sharp (eds) 1997. *Space, Gender and Knowledge*. London: Arnold.

McGovern, T. H. 1985. The Arctic frontier of Norse Greenland. In S. Green and S. Pearlman (eds) *The Archaeology of Frontiers and Boundaries*. New York: Academic Press. 275–323.

Maher, V. A. (ed.) 1992. *The Anthropology of Breastfeeding*. London: Berg.

Mandt, G. 1994. Trenger vi en feministisk museumskritikk? *Nytt om Kvinneforskning: Feministisk museumkritik*. Oslo: Norges Forskningsråd. 11–20.

Marchant, L. F. 1991. Primate reproductive biology and models of human origins. In D. Walde and N. D. Willows (eds) *The Archaeology of Gender*. 50–4.

Maurer, B. 1990. Feminist challenges to archaeology: avoiding the epistemology of the 'Other'. In D. Walde and N. D. Willows (eds) *The Archaeology of Gender*. 414–19.

Mauss, M. 1954. *The Gift*. London: Cohen & West.

Meadows, K. 1994. You are what you eat: diet, identity and Romanisation. In S. Cottam, D. Dungworth, S. Scott and J. Taylor (eds) *TRAC 1994*. Proceedings of the Fourth Annual Theoretical Roman Archaeology Conference, Durham 1994, Oxford: Oxbow Books. 133–40.

Mellars, P. 1989. Major issues in the emergence of modern humans. *Current Anthropology*, 30, 3: 349–85.

Mellars, P. 1996. *The Neanderthal Legacy: An Archaeological Perspective from Western Europe*. Princeton, N.J.: Princeton University Press.

Meskell, L. 1996. The somatization of archaeology: institutions, discourses, corporeality. *Norwegian Archaeological Review*, 29, 1: 1–16.

Meskell, L. 1997. Egyptian social dynamics: the evidence of age, sex and class in domestic and mortuary contexts. Unpublished Ph.D., Dept of Archaeology, Cambridge University.

Mestorf, J. 1889. Dolche in Frauengräbern der Bronzezeit. Correspondenz-Blatt der Deutschen Gesselschaft für Anthropologie, Ethnologie und Urgeschichte. XX Jahrgang, Nr 10. 150–4.

Michelman, S. O. and T. V. Erekosima 1992. Kalabari dress in Nigeria: visual analysis and gender implications. In R. Barnes and J. B. Eicher (eds) *Dress and Gender*. 164–82.

Middleton, D. and D. Edwards (eds) 1990. *Collective Remembering*. London: Sage.

Miller, D. 1985. *Artefacts as Categories: A Study of Ceramic Variability in Central India*. Cambridge: Cambridge University Press.

Miller, D. 1987. *Material Culture and Mass Consumption*. Oxford: Blackwell.

Mithen, S. J. 1996. *The Prehistory of the Mind: A Search for the Origin of Art, Science and Religion*. London: Thames and Hudson.

Mizoguchi, K. 1992. A historiography of a linear barrow cemetery: a structuralist's point of view. *Archaeological Review from Cambridge*, 11, 1: 39–49.

Moore, H. L. 1986. *Space, Text and Gender*. Cambridge: Cambridge University Press.

Moore, H. L. 1987. Problems in the analysis of social change: an example from the Marakwet. In I. Hodder (ed.) *Archaeology as Long-term History*. Cambridge: Cambridge University Press. 85–104.

Moore, H. L. 1988. *Feminism and Anthropology*. Cambridge: Polity Press.

Moore, H. L. 1990. Paul Ricoeur: action, meaning and text. In C. Tilley (ed.) *Reading Material Culture*. Oxford: Basil Blackwell. 85–120.

Moore, H. L. 1994. *A Passion for Difference*. Cambridge: Polity Press.

Moore, J. and E. Scott (eds) 1997. *Invisible People and Processes: Writing Gender and Childhood into European Archaeology*. London: Leicester University Press.

Moser, S. 1992. The visual language of archaeology: a case study of the Neanderthals. *Antiquity*, 66: 831–44.

Moser, S. 1993. Gender stereotyping in pictoral reconstructions of human origins. In H. du Cros and L. Smith (eds) *Women in Archaeology*. 75–92.

Moser, S. 1998. *Ancestral Images: The Iconography of Human Origins*. Stroud: Sutton.

Müller, S. O. 1884. Mindre Bidrag til den forhistoriske Archaeologis methode. *Aarbøger for Nordisk Oldkyndighed og Historie*, 161–216.

Næss, J.R. 1974. Kvinner i vikingtid. *Fra Haug ok Heidni*, 2.

Nelson, S. M. 1997. *Gender in Archaeology: Analyzing Power and Prestige*. London: Altamira Press.

Nordbladh, J. and T. Yates 1990. This perfect body, this virgin text: between sex and gender in archaeology. In I. Bapty and T. Yates (eds) *Archaeology after Structuralism*. 222–37.

Oelmann, F. 1959. Pfahlhausurnen. *Germania*, 37: 205–23.

Olivier, L. 1992. The tomb of Hochdorf. *Archaeological Review from Cambridge*, 11, 1: 51–63.

Olsen, B. 1997. *Fra ting til tekst: teoretiske perspek i arkeologisk forskning*. Oslo: Universitetsforlaget.

Parker-Pearson, M. 1996. Food, fertility and front doors: houses in the first millennium BC. In T. Champion and J. Collis (eds) *The Iron Age in Britain and Ireland: Recent Trends*. Sheffield: Sheffield Academic Press. 117–32.

Parker-Pearson, M. and C. Richards (eds) 1994a. *Architecture and Order:*

Approaches to Social Space. London: Routledge.

Parker-Pearson, M. and C. Richards 1994b. Architecture and order: spatial representation and archaeology. In M. Parker-Pearson and C. Richards (eds) *Architecture and Order.* 38–72.

Parker-Pearson, M. and C. Richards 1994c. Ordering the world: perceptions of architecture, space and time. In M. Parker-Pearson and C. Richards (eds) *Architecture and Order.* 1–37.

Partington, A. 1996. Perfume: pleasure, packaging and postmodernity. In P. Kirkham (ed.) *The Gendered Object.* 204–18.

Picazo, M. 1997. Hearth and home: the timing of maintenance activities. In J. Moore and E. Scott (eds) *Invisible People and Processes.* 59–67.

Pirie, V. 1985. Women, heritage and museums. *Archaeological Review from Cambridge,* 4, 1: 117–18.

Polhemus, T. (ed.) 1978. *Social Aspects of the Human Body: A Reader of Key Texts.* Harmondsworth: Penguin.

Porter, G. 1988. Putting your house in order. In R. Lumley (ed.) *The Museum Time Machine.* London: Routledge. 102–27.

Porter, G. 1991. Partial truths. In G. Kavanagh (ed.) *Museum Languages: Objects and Texts.* Leicester: Leicester University Press. 103–17.

Porter, G. 1996. Seeing through solidity: a feminist perspective on museums. In S. Macdonald and G. Fyfe (eds) *Theorizing Museums.* Oxford: Blackwell. 105–26.

Radley, A. 1990. Artefacts, memory and a sense of the past. In D. Middleton and D. Edwards (eds) 1990. *Collective Remembering.* 46–59.

Rajewski, Z. 1959. *Biskupin: Polish Excavation.* Warsaw: Polonia Publishing House.

Randsborg, K. 1984. Women in prehistory: the Danish example. *Acta Archaeologica,* 142–54.

Rappaport, R. 1984. *Pigs for the Ancestors: Ritual in the Ecology of the New Guinea People.* New Haven: Yale University Press.

Rega, E. 1997. Age, gender and biological reality in the Early Bronze Age cemetery at Mokrin. In J. Moore and E. Scott (eds) *Invisible People and Processes.* 229–47.

Riegel, H. 1996. Into the heart of irony: ethnographic exhibitions and the politics of difference. In S. Macdonald and G. Fyfe (eds) *Theorizing Museums.* 83–104.

Roach, M. E. and J. B. Eicher 1979. The language of personal adornment. In J. M. Cordwell and R. A. Schwarz (eds) *The Fabrics of Culture.* New York: Mouton Publishers. 7–21.

Robb, J. 1994. Gender contradictions, moral coalitions and inequality in prehistoric Italy. *Journal of European Archaeology,* 2, 1: 20–49.

Rosaldo, M. Z. and L. Lamphere (eds) 1974. *Woman, Culture and Society.* Stanford, Calif.: Stanford University Press.

Rosman, A. and P. Rubel 1971. *Feasting with Mine Enemy: Rank and Exchange among Northwest Coast Indians.* New York: Columbia University Press.

Russell, P. 1993. The Palaeolithic mother-goddess: fact or fiction? In H. du

Cros and L. Smith (eds) *Women in Archaeology*. 93–7.

Sandahl, J. 1995. Proper objects among other things. *Nordisk Museologi*, 2: 97–106.

Sayers, J. 1982. *Biological Politics: Feminist and Anti-feminist Perspectives*. London: Tavistock.

Scarre, C. 1998. *Exploring Prehistoric Europe*. Oxford: Oxford University Press.

Schneider, J. and A. B. Weiner 1989. Introduction. In A. B. Weiner and J. Schneider (eds) *Cloth and Human Experience*. Smithsonian Institution Press: Washington. 4–29.

Schumacher-Matthäus, G. 1985. *Studien zu Bronzezeitlichen Schmucktrachten im Karpatenbecken*. Mainz am Rhein: Philipp von Zabern.

Schwarz, R. A. 1979. Uncovering the secret vice: towards an anthropology of clothing and adornment. In J. M. Cordwell and R. A. Schwarz (eds) *The Fabrics of Culture*. The Hague: Mouton. 23–46.

Scott, J. W. 1986. Gender: a useful category of historical analysis. *American Historical Review*, 91, 5: 1053–75.

Scott, J. W. 1990. Deconstructing equality-versus-difference: or, the use of poststructuralist theory for feminism. In M. Hirsch and E. F. Keller (eds) *Conflicts in Feminism*. London: Routledge.134–48.

Sharp, L. 1952. Steel axes for Stone Age Australians. In E. H. Spicer (ed.) *Human Problems in Technological Change*. New York: Russell Sage Foundation. 69–90.

Shennan, S. 1975. The social organization at Branc. *Antiquity*, 49: 279–88.

Shennan, S. J. 1993. Commodities, transactions and growth in the central-European Early Bronze Age. *Journal of European Archaeology*, 1, 2: 59–72.

Sherratt, A. 1997. *Economy and Society in Prehistoric Europe: Changing Perspectives*. Edinburgh: Edinburgh University Press.

Shilling, C. 1993. *The Body and Social Theory*. London: Sage.

Slocum, S. 1975. Woman the gatherer: male bias in anthropology. In R. Reiter (ed.) *Towards an Anthropology of Women*. New York: Monthly Review Press. 36–50.

Sofaer-Derevenski, J. 1997. Engendering children, engendering archaeology. In J. Moore and E. Scott (eds) *Invisible People and Processes*. 192–202.

Sofaer-Derevenski, J. 1998. Gender archaeology as contextual archaeology: a critical examination of the tensions between method and theory in the archaeology of gender. Unpublished Ph.D., Dept of Archaeology, Cambridge University.

Soffer, O. 1985. Patterns of intensification as seen from the Upper Palaeolithic of the central Russian plain. In T. D. Price and J. A. Brown (eds) *Prehistoric Hunter-Gatherers: The Emergence of Cultural Complexity*. Orlando, Fla.: Academic Press. 235–70.

Sørensen, M. L. S. 1988. Is there a feminist contribution to archaeology? *Archaeological Review from Cambridge*, 7, 1: 9–20.

Sørensen, M. L. S. 1991. Gender construction through appearance. In D. Walde and N. D. Willows (eds), *The Archaeology of Gender*. 121–9.

Sørensen, M. L. S. 1992. Gender archaeology and Scandinavian Bronze Age studies. *Norwegian Archaeological Review*, 25, 1: 31–49.

Sørensen, M. L. S. 1996. Women as/and metalworkers. In A. Devonshire and B. Wood (eds) *Women in Industry and Technology*. 45–52.

Sørensen, M. L. S. 1997. Reading dress: the construction of social categories and identities in Bronze Age Europe. *Journal of European Archaeology*, 5, 1: 93–114.

Sørensen, M. L. S. 1998. Rescue and recovery: on historiographies of female archaeologists. In Díaz-Andreu, M. and M. L. S. Sørensen (eds) *Excavating Women*. 31–60.

Sørensen, M. L. S. 1999. Archaeology, gender and the museum. In N. Merriman (ed.) *Making Early Histories in Museums*. Leicester: Leicester University Press. 136–50.

Spector, J. 1993. *What this Awl Means: Feminist Archaeology at a Wahpeton Dakota Village*. St Paul: Minnesota Historical Society Press.

Spindler, K. 1994. *The Man in the Ice: The Preserved Body of a Neolithic Man Reveals the Secrets of the Stone Age*. London: Weidenfeld and Nicolson.

Stalsberg, A. 1987. The interpretation of women's objects of Scandinavian origin from the Viking period found in Russia. In R. Bertelsen, A. Lillehammer and J.R. Næss (eds) *Were They All Men?* 89–100.

Stalsberg, A. 1991. Women as actors in north European Viking trade. In R. Samson (ed.) *Social Approaches to Viking Studies*. Glasgow: Cruithne Press. 75–83.

Strathern, M. 1984. Subject or object? Women and the circulation of valuables in highlands New Guinea. In R. Hirschon (ed.) *Women and Property – Women as Property*. London: Croom Helm. 158–75.

Strathern, M. 1987. An awkward relationship: the case of feminism and anthropology. *Signs*, 12, 2: 276–92.

Taborin, Y. 1993. Shells of the French Aurignacian and Perigordian. In H. Knecht, A. Pike-Tay and R. White (eds) *Before Lascaux: The Complex Record of the Early Upper Palaeolithic*. Boca Raton: CRC Press. 211–29.

Tarrant, N. E. A. 1994. *The Development of Costume*. Edinburgh: National Museums of Scotland and Routledge.

Tax, S. 1979. General editor's preface. In J. M. Cordwell and R. A. Schwarz (eds) *The Fabrics of Culture*. The Hague: Mouton. v–vii.

Texeira, M. B. 1991. From strength to strength. *Museum*, 171: 126–8.

Thålin-Bergman, L. (ed.) 1975. *O forna tiders kvinnor*. Stockholm: Statens Historiska Museum.

Thomas, J. 1993. The hermenutics of megalithic space. In C. Tilley (ed.) *Interpretative Archaeology*. London: Berg. 73–97.

Thomas, J. 1995. Where are we now? archaeological theory in the 1990s. In P. J. Ucko (ed.) *Theory in Archaeology: A World Perspective*. London: Routledge. 343–62.

Thomas, J. 1996. *Time, Culture and Identity*. London: Routledge.

Tilley, C. (ed.) 1990. *Reading Material Culture: Structuralism, Hermeneutics and Post-Structuralism*. Oxford: Basil Blackwell.

Tilley, C. 1991. *Material Culture and Text: The Art of Ambiguity*. London:

Routledge.

Tilley, C. 1993. Introduction: interpretation and a poetics of the past. In C. Tilley (ed.) *Interpretative Archaeology*. London: Berg. 1–30.

Tilley, C. 1994. *A Phenomonology of Landscape: Places, Paths and Monuments*. London: Berg.

Treherne, P. 1995. The warrior's beauty: the masculine body and self-identity in Bronze Age Europe. *Journal of European Archaeology*, 3, 1: 105–44.

Tringham, R. 1991. Households with faces: the challenge of gender in prehistoric architectural remains. In J. M. Gero and M. W. Conkey (eds) *Engendering Archaeology*. 93–131.

Trocolli, R. 1992. Colonization and women's production: the Timucua of Florida. In C. Claassen (ed.) *Exploring Gender through Archaeology*. 95–102.

Urry, J. 1996. How societies remember the past. In S. Macdonald and G. Fyfe (eds) *Theorizing Museums*. 45–68.

Van der Leeuw, S. 1993. Giving the potter a choice: conceptual aspects of pottery techniques. In P. Lemonnier (ed.) *Technological Choices: Transformation in Material Cultures since the Neolithic*. London: Routledge. 238–88.

Vencl, S. 1994. The archaeology of thirst. *Journal of European Prehistory*, 2, 2: 299–326.

Wadley, L. (ed.) 1997. *Our Gendered Past: Archaeological Studies of Gender in Southern Africa*. Johannesburg: Witwatersrand University Press.

Walde, D. and N. D. Willows (eds). 1991. *The Archaeology of Gender*. Proceedings of the Twenty-Second Annual Conference of the Archaeological Association of the University of Calgary, Calgary: The Archaeological Association of the University of Calgary.

Washburn, S. L. and I. DeVore 1961. Social behavior of baboons and early hominids. In S. L. Washburn (ed.) *Social Life of Early Man*. Chicago: Aldine. 91–105.

Washburn, S. L. and C. S. Lancaster 1968. The evolution of hunting. In R. Lee and I. DeVore (eds) *Man the Hunter*. Chicago: Aldine. 293–303.

Webb Mason, S. 1995. All flint and no females: gender perceptions in public presentations of prehistoric hunter gatherers. Unpublished M.Phil. dissertation, Dept of Archaeology, Cambridge University.

Wels-Weyrauch, U. 1989. *Dynamique du Bronze Moyen en Europe Occidentale*. Strasbourg: Actes du 113ᵉ Congres national des Sociétés savantes. 117–34.

White, R. 1982. Rethinking the Middle/Upper Palaeolithic transition. *Current Anthropology*, 23, 2: 169–92.

White, R. 1989. Production complexity and standardisation in early Aurignacian bead and pendant manufacturer: evolutionary implications. In P. Mellars (ed.) *The Human Revolution: Behavioural and Biological Perspectives on the Origins of Modern Humans*. Edinburgh: Edinburgh University Press. 366–90.

White, R. 1992. Beyond art: towards an understanding of the origins of material representation in Europe. *Annual Review of Anthropology*, 21: 537–

64.

White, R. 1993. Technological and social dimensions of 'Aurignacian-age' body ornaments across Europe. In H. Knecht, A. Pike-Tay and R. White (eds) *Before Lascaux: The Complex Record of the Early Upper Palaeolithic.* 277–299. Boca Raton: CRC Press. 277–99.

Whittle, A. 1996. *Europe in the Neolithic.* Cambridge: Cambridge University Press.

Wichman, H. (ed.) 1968. *Norrländskt arbetsliv under 1700-talet: Länsmännens berättelser 1764 om allmogens årliga arbeten i Medelpad, Ångermanland och Jämtland.* Nordiska museets handlingar 65, Stockholm: Nordiska museet.

Wiessner, P. 1984. Reconsidering the behavioral basis for style: a case study among the Kalahari San. *Journal of Anthropological Archaeology,* 3: 190–234.

Willoughby, P. R. 1991. Human origins and the sexual division of labour: an archaeological perspective. In D. Walde and N. D. Willows (eds) *The Archaeology of Gender.* 284–91.

Wood, B. 1996. Wot! No dinosaurs? Interpretation of prehistory and a new gallery at the Museum of London. In A. Devonshire and B. Wood (eds) *Women in Industry and Technology.* 53–63.

Wright, R. A. (ed.) 1996a. *Gender and Archaeology.* Philadelphia: University of Pennsylvania Press.

Wright, R. A. 1996b. Technology, gender, and class: worlds of difference in Ur III Mesopotamia. In R. A. Wright (ed.) *Gender and Archaeology.* 79–110.

Wylie, A. 1991a. Feminist critiques and archaeological challenges. In D. Walde and N. D. Willows (eds) *The Archaeology of Gender.* 17–23.

Wylie, A. 1991b. Gender theory and the archaeological record: why is there no archaeology of gender? In J. M. Gero and M. W. Conkey (eds) *Engendering Archaeology.* 31–54.

Wylie, A. 1992a. Feminist theories of social power: some implications for a processual archaeology. *Norwegian Archaeological Review,* 25, 1: 51–68.

Wylie, A. 1992b. The interplay of evidential constraints and political interests: recent archaeological research on gender. *American Antiquity,* 52: 15–35.

Wylie, A. 1993. Workplace issues for women in archaeology: the chilly climate. In H. du Cros and L. Smith (eds) *Women in Archaeology.* 245–60.

Wylie, A. 1997. Good science, bad science, or science as usual? Feminist critiques of science. In L. D. Hager (ed.) *Women in Human Evolution.* 29–55.

Wylie, A., K. Okruhlik, S. Norton and L. Thielen-Wilson 1989. Feminist critiques of science: the epistemological and methodological literature. *Women's Studies International Forum,* 12: 379–88.

Wyss, R. 1971. Technik, Wirtschaft und Handel. In H. Drack (ed.) *Ur- und Fruhgeschichtliche Archaologie der Schweiz III. Die Bronzezeit.* Basel: Verlag Schweizerische Gesellschaft für Ur- und Frühgeschichte.

Yates, T. 1991. The writing machine: rock art and the concept of the body in the Bronze Age of Göteborgs och Bohus län, Sweden. Unpublished Ph.D.,

Dept of Archaeology, Cambridge University.

Yates, T. 1993. Frameworks for an archaeology of the body. In C. Tilley (ed.) *Interpretative Archaeology*. 31–72.

Zihlman, A. 1991. Did the australopithecines have a division of labor? In D. Walde and N. D. Willows (eds) *The Archaeology of Gender*. 64–70.

Zihlman, A. 1997. The Palaeolithic glass ceiling: women in human evolution. In L. D. Hager (ed.) *Women in Human Evolution*. 91–113.

Zihlman, A. and N. Tanner 1978. Gathering and the hominid adaptation. In L. Tiger and H. Fowler (eds) *Female Hierarchies*. Chicago: Beresford Book Service. 163–94.

Index

NB   The term gender archaeology is rendered as GA throughout this index.

Aboriginals, Australia   176
Abri Pataud, France   162
academia, women in   29
activities, gender-categorized   8
adultery   169–70
affective space   62
age, relationships based on   178
agency   63–4
    contact and   181
    self and   65–6
    and social construction of gender
        60, 71
    space, meaning and   153
agriculture, temporal sequence
    (Sweden)   109–12
Andaman   135
Anglo-Saxon life stages and
    costume   141
animals, clothing and contrast
    with   137–8
anthropology, verbal nature of
    information   74–5
antler-working   186
appearance, bodily 133, 134, 140–3
    archaeological investigation   132
    dress and social role (prehistory)
        136
    and gender categories   142
    and identity   128–9, 130
    relevance to GA   130
appropriation policy   24
architecture

monastic   158
    spatial construction of meaning
        and   149, 150–2, 160, 166
Aristotle   50
arts, prehistoric 190–2
    reinterpretations   184
    see also figurines; objects;
        ornaments
Arwill-Nordbladh, E.
    on Montelius   26
    on women in production   39
Athos, *Mount*   146
axes, introduction of steel   170,
    171
Aztec empire
    cloth exchange   142
    colonization and 173

Bachofen, J. J. and social
    organization   26
Baden culture   119
Barthes, R. and clothing (*Elements
    of Semiology*)   128
Barum, Sweden   51–2
beads   192*ill.*, 192, 193, 195–6
Beaker culture
    Bell   119
    burials (Britain)   93
beer   116
Being   152, 154
bicycles, gender-coded design   130
binary opposition

and food classification 101
of gender roles 30, 67, 70, 200,
201
of sex and gender 46
space and difference 147
biological essentialism 54, 183
Biskupin, Poland 163*ill.*, 165
body, the
adornment (Palaeolithic) 138,
193–7
closed and open 103–4
clothing and 131
corporate 50–1, 53, 58, 67, 85
'enclosure' (Eicher and Roach-
Higgins) 133
extensions 105*n*
feminism and 55
figurines and 198–9
food and 100, 102–4
lived 55, 64, 66
materialization 76, 87
and meaning 154
and mind 44
mutilation 87
and practice of self 95, 193
projection onto space 147, 151,
152
razors and 177
sexed 58, 68–70, 72
bog bodies, Denmark 116
Bogatyrev, P. on semiotics of
costume 128
Bohuslän, Sweden 163
bone-working 186
bones, cremated 180*ill.*
Bourdieu P. 151
on habitus 63–4, 148–50
brain size 187
breastfeeding 68, 69, 103, 105
Britain, women in archaeology 30
Bronze Age 116–17
burial practices 93, 116–17,
156–7
Central Europe 119–20
costume 134, 139–40, 141
Denmark 87
food containers 112–15

gendered objects 91–2, 136
hearths 161–2
life stages 141
metallurgy 39, 117, 178–80
spatial organization 150
swords 91–2
urns 157*ill.*
women and work 39
Yugoslavia 116
Brück, J. on spatial organization
150
burial and mortuary practices
and construction of gender
54, 85
cremation 179–80
house 156–7, 158*ill.*
and perception of the individual
53
and performance 87
and renegotiation of identity
92–3
self-reflection and 201
weapons and gender 51–2
see also grave goods
Butler, J.
on materiality of sex 76
on performative gender 87, 88
on sex and gender 54–5
buttoning and fastening dress,
gender-coded 130

cargo cult 170
Carlyle, T., *Sartor Resartus* 127
chaîne opératoire 88
Chalcolithic culture 157
children
bodily appearance and identity
128–9
involvement in food production
111
life stages and food 105
Christianity and nakedness 127
chromosome composition 46, 51
church
sacristy 151
seating arrangements 145
citation analysis 88

classification
    dress   133
    figurines   197
closure   23, 29, 40, 205
cloth, symbolism and exchange
    142
clothes see dress
club ties   125
codes of appearance   128–9
cognitive abilities, human   190
colonization   170, 172–7, 181
combination tables
    (archaeology)   133
communication
    costume as   131
    gender as   82
    objects/texts   77–8
    see also language
Conkey, M. W.
    and contexts of action   39
    and gender as concept   18, 20
    and gender negotiation   60
    and origins of gender   185–7,
    189–90
    and symbolic behaviour   58
constructedness, socio-cultural
    gender: 7, 53, 71, 168, 182,
    201, 207; and bodies   55; and
    contact   172–3; food
    and   103, 117; and material
    objects   75, 202, 203; and
    negotiation   60, 61, 206; as
    opposed to biological given
    10, 18, 43
    sex   49–50, 52
    see also gender-coding
contact   168–81
contextualization   5, 13
    and archaeological theory   12,
    39, 65, 67, 71, 207
    and Being   154
    and binary division of gender   57
    construction and definition of
    gender   41–2, 43, 91, 168
    dress and   134
    ideology and negotiation   61
    meaning and agency   64

objects   81, 89, 91
    and sex   46, 51
    and space   156
continuum
    society and sex categories   47
    space   147
contractual relations   168–9, 206
    drinking and   118
    household   159
cooking   100, 112, 165
copper   179
Corded Ware culture   85
Cortaillod-Est, Switzerland   162
costume see dress
Cree Indians, Canada   174
cremation   179–80
creolism   174
cross-dressing   129
Cuerto de la Mina, Spain   185–7
culturation, food   100–1
culture, basic assumption in study
    of gender   183–4

death
    house and   156–7, 158ill.
    see also burial and mortuary
    practices
deconstruction (analysis), dress
    134
'defeat of the female sex'
    (Engels)   38
dental caries   116
dependencies, interpersonal, food
    and   106
Descartes, R.   44n.
Díaz-Andreu, M.   28
diet   116
difference   15, 53, 124
    binary structures   147
    bodily appearance and   128–30
    burial practices and   92–3
    cultural response to   183
    different kinds of   56
    dress and (prehistory)   136, 141
    as dualism   44
    evolutionary   188
    figurines and   198

food and 99, 102
gender-intellectual 36–7
and gender negotiation 60, 94,
123
and nature of gender 7–8, 14,
68, 122, 182, 202, 204, 206
objects and 79, 81–2, 86, 89, 95
reproductive 68
and rights 75
space and 144, 145, 151
universal generalizations and 70
see also binary opposition of
gender roles; dimorphism,
sexual
dimorphism, sexual 188, 189,
200, 201–2
discourse
dress as 133
food and 101, 102, 106–17
gender as 60, 75, 82, 94, 99
objects 78, 81, 82, 91, 94, 206
social relations 122
DNA 45, 46
domestic, the 158n
dominance
and difference as binary
opposition 70
economic (gendered) 171–2
and individual agency 64
and use of tools 171
Dommasnes, L. H. and scientific
criteria 18
doors, men opening for women
159–60
Douglas, M. on food
categories 101
dress 90ill., 124–43, 126ill., 191ill.
contact and 180
drinking 108, 116, 117–21
dualism of body and mind, and sex–
gender distinction 44

Eastern Gravettian culture 196
effect, gender as 74
Eicher, J. B. and classification of
dress 133
embodiment

and archaeological theory 207
food and 102–4
see also body emotion and objects
76
Endo 81, 149
Engels, F., The Origin of the Family,
Private Property and the State
38
presentism 38
and social organization 26–7
environment 151–3
epistemology see knowledge, theory
of
equity issues 4, 21, 32
ethnocentrism 27, 39, 44, 50, 185
evolution 187–9
exchange
Bronze Age systems 117
objects and 195
existential space 151–2
experience
in archaeological theory 65, 207
body, space and 152
nature of sex 46, 47–8
practice as 155

fairground stands, suspension of
real-life identity 125–6
Falk, P. on closed and open bodies
103
fashion 132
femininity, constructed notion of
94
feminism
and background of GA 4–5, 9,
10, 11, 21, 26, 71, 76–7
and the body 55
and the individual in society 64
and museum objects 76
and origins of gender 183–4,
189
and prehistoric arts 190
and sex–gender distinction 44,
54, 57
and sociology of food 101
and theory of knowledge 35, 36
and visibility 40

feminism *cont'd*
   see also women's movement
fertility, figurines and   199
fetishism   78
fieldwork   30
figurines   137*ill.*,   138, 193, 197–
   9, 200, 201, 202
fire–dogs   161–2
Florence Nightingale nurses   125*ill.*
folk costumes, Moravian
   Slovakia   128
food   99–123
   contact and   180
   food-cultures   176
   land and   153
   space and   165
fossil records   187
   sex and   46
Foucault, M.   47, 49
Freud, S. on food and
   sexuality   103
fur trade   175

Gatens, M. and the corporate
   body   50–1
gender, nature/definition of 7–8,
   41–2, 52–4, 70–1
   in relation to sex   47–8
gender-coding   88, 91, 94
   children   80*ill.*
   dress   129–30
   and gender as performance   206
   grave goods   25
   see also constructedness, socio-
      cultural: gender; meaning;
      objects: and gendered meaning
gender roles, study of   27
Gibbs, L. on sex and gender   58,
   59
Giddens, A. on agency   63–4
gift   79, 117
Gilchrist, R.   158
grave goods   25, 92, 191 *ill.*, 192,
   196
Grotte du Pape, France   193, 194*ill.*
group membership, dress
   and   124–5

gypsies   177

habitus   64, 148–50
Hadar, Ethiopia   183
hair   137*ill.*, 138–9, 194*ill.*
Halstatt B plates   113*ill.*
Harding, S.   36
Hastorf, C. A. on food and diet
   99, 116
hearths   161–5
Heidegger, M.   152
hermaphroditism   57
'High Table'   151
Hjørungdal, T.
   and gender coding   25
   on sex and gender   59
Hochdorf, Germany   157, 158*ill.*
Hodder, I. on material culture as
   metaphoric text   77–8
Homo erectus   187, 200
Homo habilis   187
homosexuality   46
house   156–65
human head   194*ill.*
hunter-gatherer society
   contact and   176
   gender roles   108, 188
   task differentiation   185

ice man, Italian Alps   116
identity, personal/social   124
   bodily appearance and   128–9
   dress and   125–7, 138
   drinking and   121
   material culture and   202
   meals and   101, 105, 115, 122
   ornaments and   195–6
   razors, the body and   177
   relationship to space and   150
ideology   9, 71, 89, 107
   basis for transformation of   187
   and change   179
   and difference   57, 58
   figurines and   86, 197
   and food   107, 112
   and the household   159
   and levels of construction   134

and negotiation 61, 168
and objects 86, 94–5
and politics 32
search for origins and 183
and symbolism 72, 75
see also feminism; Marxism;
    presentism
Inca empire 116
cloth exchange 142
colonization and 173
individual (vs. social) 13, 56,
    67–8, 200–1, 204
agency 63–7
experience and meaning 154
habitus and 149
material culture and gender
    203
materialization of bodies 76
and sexual identity 46, 48, 50
social perception of 53
inference in knowledge 185
initiation, objects and 193n
instability of gender 7, 10, 52, 60,
    203, 206
interior design 83–4, 84ill.
Inuit 175, 176
inventors, women as 188
iron, introduction of 179
Iron Age 113
burial practices 156–7, 158ill.
Denmark 6, 116
hearths 162ill.–165
life stages and costume 141
long house 164ill.
isotope analysis 92, 116

Joyce, R. A. 87, 88

Kalaban, Nigeria 126, 141
K.A.N. (Journal) 3
Kenyon, K. 21
Kirkham, P., The Gendered Object
    76, 84
knowledge, theory of 18–19,
    34–7, 48
Kostenki, Russia 192, 195, 199
Kristeva, J. 105n.

labour division 58
and food 102, 106, 109, 115,
    122
gender negotiation and 63
iron technology and 179
and origins of gender 184,
    185–7, 188, 200
universal generalizations 68
Lacan, J. 47, 76, 105n.
lace, gender symbolism 83
'lack', women as (Aristotle) 50
lactation 103
'ladies' rooms' 144
land and landscape 152, 153–4
language 37, 200
Lacqueur, T. 49
Les Eyzies, France 195
Lévi-Strauss, C. and food
    classifications 100–1
life stages
dress and 136, 141–2
food and 104–5
markers on the body 135
and women's sexual role 189
Linear B scripts, Aegean 142
long house, Late Iron Age 164ill.
Lubbock, J. 26
Lucy (human fossil) 183

Magdalenian culture 185–7
magic, ornaments and 193n.
maize 116
manufacture and maintenance,
    women in 186–7
marginalization of GA 5, 11, 23,
    36
markers on the body, permanent
    135
marriage 168–9, 190
Marxism 11, 27, 55, 61, 88–9,
    153
see also Engels
materiality 6, 57
beads 195
conventions of space and 145
dress and 127
dress objects and 136

materiality *cont'd*
  and existence   152
  food   107
  and gender negotiation   63, 72–3
  material culture   9, 14–15,
    74–95, 203–6
  self-reflection and   201–2
  of sex   76
  study of   27
  see also objects
matrilineal societies, colonization
  and   172
Maya   87, 88
mead   118
meaning   154
  bodily appearance and   134
  concretization of   204
  dispersal/reinscription   160
  dress and (prehistory)   136–7
  food and   101, 102, 107
  framework for GA   205
  gendered   52
  museums and   33
  negotiation and   62
  objects   77–8, 81, 83, 90–1, 206
  pre-meaning   154
  space and   147, 149, 151–4,
    160, 167
  symbolic   86
megaliths   151
Merleau–Ponty, M.   152
  critique of agency   65
Meskell, L.
  on agency   65
  on sex and gender   55–6
Mesolithic Age
  burial practices   51–2
  contact   176
  hearths   162
Mesopotamia, cloth exchange   142
metallurgy
  Bronze Age   39, 178
  technological change   179
metaphor   182
  food as   103
  sex as, for gender   59
milk   118

Miller, D and object information
  75
missionary activities   170–1, 175
monastic architecture   158
Montelius, O.   26, 38
monument-building, Neolithic, and
  food/drink   119
Moore, H. L.
  on gender and redistribution   63
  on the nature of the personal
    agent   66
  and object information   75, 81
  quoted on negotiation   62
  on sex and gender   55
  on spatial meaning   149–50
Morgan, L. H. and social
  organization   26
Moser, S. and background of GA
  25
mother–child relationship, food and
  104–5
movement of people, contact
  and   171
museums   5–6, 32–4, 76
mythology, Norse   121
myths
  of GA   12, 20–40
  of origins   127
  of women in academia   29

nakedness, consciousness of   127
narrative and museums   33
Neanderthal man   176
needs claims   62
negotiation/renegotiation
  of appearance and difference
    129
  and archaeological theory   207
  and beads   195
  definition   61
  and food production/circulation
    101, 113
  of gender and gender relations:
    52, 60–3; and
    constructedness   76, 206;
    contact and   173; food
    and   109, 122, 123; and

materiality 15, 82; objects
and 95; relations 168–70;
rights and obligations 5; and
social concerns 90; and social
systems 7; space and 144;
and stability 13; technological
change and 179
of identies 92
of meaning 86
and spatial organization 166
Neolithic Age 85, 93
Bohemia 119
drinking 118–19
hearths 161
life stages and costume 141
pedestal bowls and clay spoons
114ill.
Scandinavia 114, 115
New Archaeology, the 11
newness, contact and 177–81
nineteenth century, world-view and
archaeology 37–8
Nordbladh, J. 46–7, 55
Norse settlements 175
Norway, women in archaeology
31–2
Nuremburg, Germany, sumptuary
regulations 131
Nydam, Denmark 6

objects 15, 74–83, 194
and action, negotiation and
change 136
art 191–3
contact and 171
in costume analysis 134–6
emotive properties 76
and gendered meaning 14, 52,
72–3, 89–92, 93, 94, 124, 184,
192, 203
as identifiers of events 87–8
and material tradition 9, 14,
94–5
maternal 105
and practice 206
sex and 51
and social reproduction 95

technology and change 170
Ojibwa Indians, Canada 174
order, meals and 101
orifices, food and 100
origins
dress and 127
of gender 182–202
of humans 187–90
illustration of 8, 15
and social interaction 138
ornaments 191–7
contact and 177
and culture 202
dress (Bronze Age) 136, 139
gender and 86, 88, 91
and individual articulation 200
markers on the body 135

pair-bonding 185, 190
self-reflection and 201
Palaeolithic Age 138, 183–202
Austria 137ill.
France 162, 194ill.
peer-culture and dress codes 132
pendants 138, 195–6
perception 154
performance
and convention 199, 204
dimension of event 87
experience as 155
food and 107, 109
gender as 87, 123, 206
spatial structure as 166
phenomenology 152–5
pig feast, Papua New Guinea 107
political, the, definition
(Moore) 62
Portugal, women in
archaeology 31–2
positionality 13
positivism 10–11, 18
postmodernism 11, 27, 34, 50
potlatch (Northwest Coast
Indians) 107
pottery 119
function 112, 115
production 17

power
  discipline of archaeology and
    28, 35
  gender negotiation and   62
  in the household   159
  and individual agency   64
  objects and   89
  performance and the distribution
    of   87–8
  relations revealed through
    food   102
  and sexual categorization   49
  see also dominance
practice
  closure   205
  and convention   199
  gender as   68–9, 82, 86–9, 147,
    173, 183, 203
  objects and   206
  of self   95
  and space   148, 155
  and symbolism   197
praxis and objects   89
presentism   34, 37–8, 40, 45, 183,
  189–90
psychoanalysis   47
punks, dress   132

Raddusch, Germany   119–20,
  120ill.
razors   177
redistribution of resources, gender
  negotiation   61, 63
reflexivity   58
Rega, E., analyses of prehistoric
  diet   116–17
reinterpretation of origins of
  gender   184, 185–7
repetition
  of gender performance   199, 206
  and ornaments   197
  and socialization   200
representational images, prehistoric
  190–2
reproduction, social   7, 9, 62, 95,
  107
  space and   149

rites of passage   92–3, 142
  and dress   126
  food and   104, 117
  and hair   138
rituals
  drinking   119–21
  eating   103, 107
Roach-Higgins, M. E. and
  classification of dress   133
rock carvings   47
rock shelters   185–6
Rogaland, Norway   164ill.
roles, assumption of, costume
  and   131
Roman Empire
  and contact   176–7
  dress   140–1

Sandahl, J., characterization of
  objects   76
Sartor Resartus (Carlyle)   127
Sayers, J. on sex–gender
  distinction   54
Scandinavia
  and background of GA   21–2
  women in archaeology   30, 31–2
  see also names of places and
    periods; mythology; Norse
    settlements; Vikings
scarification   135
Schloss Gottorp (museum)   6
seating arrangements   145
selective memory in
  archaeology   28
self, the   65–7
  dress, bodily appearance and
    129, 141
  food and   102, 104
  ornaments and   197
  practice   95, 193
  reflection   201
  technology of   196
semiotics   77
  and dress   128
sex and sexuality   45–52
  and archaeological theory   11,
    207

figurines and   199
food and   103
and gender   12, 13, 125
hair and 138–9
markers   51
ontological status   44
roles   58
sex–gender distinction   18, 42–5,
   46, 54–9, 71, 207
'sexual revolution'   130
sexism and origins of gender   184
shell pendants   195
Sherratt, A. on the Bell Beaker
   culture   119
skeletons
   and diet (Inca)   116
   sex   46, 51–2, 116, 139
social organization and gender
   26–7, 43, 157–65
Sofaer-Derevenski, J.   x–xi, 58
space, gendered   144–67
Spanish Empire   173–4, 175–6
spectacles, gender-coded design
   130
Spector, J.
   and gender as concept   18, 20
   and gender negotiation   60
   and symbolic behaviour   58
   and task differentiation   185
spectrum of sexual identity   46–7
   individual life   55
steel, introduction of   170, 171
stelae   92
stereotyping   26, 69
structuralism   60
   Bourdieu and   148–9
   and food classification   100
   post-structuralism   66, 77
   and spatial archaeology   147–8
style, ornaments, and identity
   196–7
subjectivity   66
   and burial practices   53
   food and   101, 102–4
   and meaning   152
   and responses to power structures
   64

space and the embodiment of
   144
subsistence exploitation/
   production   153, 180
sumptuary laws, England,
   Germany   131
Sungir burials, Russia
   192ill., 192, 196
swords and gender construction
   91–2, 132, 136, 139
symbolism
   beads   195
   cloth   142
   food   99–100, 104–5
   gender politics   74
   gender in terms of behaviour
   58, 82–6
   origins of gender and   200
   ornaments and style   197
   and theory of cultures   128

task differentiation and origins of
   gender   185–7
taste and food   100
technological change and contact
   170, 178–9
temporal sequence, labour division
   in food production, Sweden
   109–11
terminology, disciplinary   37
texts, objects as   77–8, 82
theatre, costume   125
Theoretical Archaeology Group
   22
third/fourth genders   46, 57
Tilley, C. on space   152–3
time
   dimension   74
   time-space geography   147
Timucuan Indians, Florida, USA
   173–4
toiletries in the Roman Empire
   141, 177
tools   184, 186
Tószeg, Hungary   161
'tradition', food production
   sequences   111

transformation of substances, food
  100
Tustrup, Denmark   114*ill.*

Uniform dress   124–5
unisex dress   140
universal generalizations   67–70
  binary opposition and   147
urns   157*ill.*

verbal information, anthropology
  74–5
vessels, drinking   120
Victoria and Albert Museum,
  London, costume department
  127
Vikings
  contact   175, 176
  life stages and costume   141
Vinca culture   161
visibility of women   26, 31, 32,
  33–4, 39, 40, 71

Warnborough, UK   148*ill.*
warrior elite, drinking rituals and
  121
widowhood and hair   138–9
Willendorf, Austria   193
wine   118, 120
Women, Culture and Society
  (Rosaldo and Lamphere)   22
women, socio-economic status of

colonization, contact and
  171–2, 173–4, 176
hunter-gatherer society   189
technological change and
  178–9
women in archaeology   28–34
see also equity issues; visibility of
  women
Women in History and Museums
  32
women's costumes, differences in
  139–40
women's movement   67
  departures of gender studies from
  43
  and gender negotiation   60
  and the gendered individual in
  society   64
  and origins of GA   17, 21, 31,
  71, 205
Wylie, A. and background of GA
  17, 18, 20, 21
  and evaluation of knowledge
  claims   36

Yates, T.   46–7, 55
Yir Yoront, Cape York, Australia
  171

Zihlman, A. on origins of gender
  184